Understanding Digital Television

An Introduction to DVB Systems with Satellite, Cable, Broadband and Terrestrial TV

Lars-Ingemar Lundström

ELSEVIER

AMSTERDAM • BOSTON • HEIDLEBERG • LONDON
NEW YORK • OXFORD • PARIS • SAN DIEGO
SAN FRANCISCO • SINGAPORE • SYDNEY • TOKYO
Focal Press is an imprint of Elsevier

Focal Press

Acquisitions Editor: Angelina Ward
Production Manager: Paul Gotterher
Development Editor: Beth Millett
US Marketing Manager: Christine Degon Veroulis
UK Marketing Manager: Lucy Lomas-Walker
Assistant Editor: Doug Shults
Cover Designer: Eric Decicco
Book Production: Borrego Publishing (www.borregopublishing.com)

Focal Press is an imprint of Elsevier
30 Corporate Drive, Suite 400, Burlington, MA 01803, USA
Linacre House, Jordan Hill, Oxford OX2 8DP, UK

 Recognizing the importance of preserving what has been written, Elsevier prints its books on acid-free paper whenever possible.

Library of Congress Cataloging-in-Publication Data
(application submitted)

British Library Cataloguing-in-Publication Data
A catalogue record for this book is available from the British Library.

ISBN 13: 978-0-240-80906-9
ISBN 10: 0-240-80906-8

For information on all Focal Press publications visit our website at www.books.elsevier.com

05 06 07 08 09 10   10 9 8 7 6 5 4 3 2 1

Printed in the United States of America

Understanding Digital Television

An Introduction to DVB Systems with
Satellite, Cable, Broadband and Terrestrial TV

Contents

Contents

    Solving the Need for Analog Recorded Video   222
    Digital Video Recording   224
    Interconnecting Devices   230
    Twin Tuner Receivers   232

11 THE HOME CINEMA   235
    Home Cinema Display Components   236
    Aspect Ratios   242
    Connecting Home Cinema Components   248
    Home Cinema Sound   249
    Program Sources   261

12 HDTV AND THE FUTURE OF TELEVISION   263
    High Definition TV (HDTV)   264
    Practical Aspects of Receiving HDTV   269
    HDTV Connectors   269
    The High Definition Multimedia Interface, HDMI   272
    First Generation HDTV Transmissions in Europe   273
    HDTV Recording   277
    Television of the Future   277
    3D Television in Color   281
    Holographic Television   282

    Appendix A   Digital Television in North America   287
    Commercial Television Systems   288
    Stereo Sound   290
    Frequency Planning and the Transfer to Digital TV in North America 290
    Connectors Around the World   292

    Appendix B   North American Satellite Geography   293
    North American Satellite Systems   294
    Satellite Receiving Systems in the U.S.   295
    The Three LNB Multi-Focus Dish   296
    Coverage and Antenna Pointing Maps for North America   297
    Finding the Satellites and Aligning the Antenna   302

    Index   309

Preface

By the end of the 1960s, when I started to get interested in how the TV set at home really worked, color television and the second national TV channel was introduced in Sweden. The old medium-wave radio, with glowing electron tubes underneath its cover, made it possible to listen to voices from distant countries, but the TV programming choices were quite small at this time. I only had Swedish TV 1 and TV 2 and the one national Danish channel to watch during my childhood. But I was lucky to live on the south coast of Sweden, which gave me some special opportunities.

During the summer, and sometimes during winter high pressure weather conditions, we could receive TV channels from other countries. The proximity to the European continent meant we received two East German channels in black and white and three West German channels in color. In those days, Germany was divided, and these two parts used different color TV systems.

To my parents' consternation, I put large antenna constructions on the roof of our house. And after a while, I succeeded in bringing even more exotic channels in our house. In addition to more East European TV signals, we could also watch TV from Spain and Italy. A very special event occurred in June, 1978, when I succeeded in receiving an Icelandic test card.

The most challenging task for a DXer in Europe has always been to be able to receive a trans-Atlantic signal. After reading about this in one of the few books that existed at the time about TV DXing, receiving trans-Atlantic broadcasts became my quest. I believe that I did succeed for a short while, somewhere in the lower VHF bands. Using my (in those days) well-trained eyes, I saw what I think was a North American station identification sign. But to be honest, I'm not 100 percent sure that I really saw that sign deep down in the noise a quarter of a century ago. Sometime you just see what you want to see.

To sporadically be able to watch exotic TV and listen to exotic radio from distant countries became a compelling journey from the living room into the surrounding world. But being able to watch sporadic fragments of a TV show or a movie is not very amusing for people who expect to be able to watch a program from its beginning to end.

By the end of 1979, I got the opportunity to participate in a very interesting project while I finished my exam at the Lund Institute of Technology. The aim was to receive signals from the newly launched European test satellite OTS 2. The first European TV satellite, OTS 1 (Orbital Test Satellite) was destroyed when the launch failed. Now its replacement, OTS 2, was in orbit and had begun its test transmissions. Philips in Sweden wanted to receive the signals in a project for test and demonstration. Of course it was also a way to get PR. According to the experts a dish with a diameter of 7 to 8 meters (23 to 26 feet) would be required to get something moving on the screen. However the only dish that we could produce had a diameter of 3 meters (less than 10 feet).

But by the end of summer 1980, a picture showing a frogman was displayed on the test monitors in the Philips TV factory. This success excited me and my colleague, Lars Andersson, about the potential of satellite TV, so the next step was to construct our own satellite receivers to be able to watch satellite TV at home. While building these receivers, we developed two handbooks that, when published in 1983, described the basics for receiving satellite TV signals in your home for the first time in Scandinavia. These two handbooks were followed by several more during the 1980s and 1990s as technology evolved.

Throughout the 1980s and the 1990s, I have had the pleasure of participating in most of the projects that have revolutionized TV distribution in the Nordic countries, such as the first Nordic TV Satellite, the introduction of Cable TV and digital stereo TV sound and the construction of the commercial terrestrial TV4 distribution network in Sweden. Finally I was also involved in establishing the Nordic Sirius satellite system.

Much has happened in the world of TV broadcasting during the last 10 years. The most dramatic change has been the transition to digital TV, though it has not been easy. The advantage in using digital techniques is not easy for the everyday man to understand. And most certainly there have been lots of "digital fundamentalists" to whom the transition to digital is almost a religious way. But by the end of the day, the whole issue is what the viewer really wants. He or she does not really care if the signals are analog or digital. It is what is possible and what is useful that counts.

Throughout the years I have followed the development by writing articles in the Swedish magazine for home electronics "Elektronikvärlden" (The World of Electronics). In the past five years, almost every article has treated some aspect of the analog to digital transition of media devices in your home. As a result of all these articles, one day I realized I had a large gallery of illustrations for various aspects of the TV media. And looking at these illustrations made me realize that there was a need for a book that encompassed most aspects of digital TV. So, I collected all material in a structure covering four main ways of digital TV distribution. The result was a 12-chapter book for the Swedish market.

My next intention was to develop the book even further and to bring it to European readers outside my home country. This was quite simple since the same satellite systems and technical standards are used all over Europe, North Africa and the Middle East. Then I realized that adding appendices about broadcasting in North America makes the first 12 chapters interesting to the North American reader and makes an interesting technical comparison between European and North American broadcasting. The differences proved to be not as large as I thought they would be. In a world of globalization, this must be an interesting as well as an important task to try to fulfill.

I have had the advantage of working with the three traditional ways of distributing TV: satellite, cable and terrestrial transmitters. These distribution forms make up a large portion of the book. During recent years a fourth media has entered the scene -- the Internet. These four ways of distribution not only compete with each other but they also complement each other. Together they form our new world of media.

Also my ambition has been to give the historic aspects of the TV media as a part of the development of human storytelling and the fantastic technical developments in this field. The book may also give a hint about where we might be heading in the future. Digital TV and HDTV are most certainly not the end of the road. Instead it is the beginning of a new era that provides us with completely new ways to tell stories and to get stories told to us.

As I completed this book, I realized that it is actually three books in one. You can choose yourself how you want to read it. It can be read as an historical book describing the timeline of the TV media from the early days and its development into today's situation, with speculations about the future. Another way is to regard the book is as a textbook about digital TV that covers most of the basics facts in this subject. And finally, perhaps the most important way to read it is as a handbook for the everyday viewer who has problems in connecting all the electronic devices required in modern home media systems. Throughout the years, I have met hundreds of people who needed to have these practical questions answered. Many of these answers are, I hope, covered in this book.

One challenge that is difficult to overcome for topics such as digital TV is the constantly changing nature of the technology. I have tried to keep the content as "time resistant" as possible. My hope that the book will still provide interesting information in 10 years time, even if the material about the future of television will at that point represent the past.

When I was a child, before man set foot on the moon, it was technology that set the limits for human progress. But after the first moon landing, something strange happened. Suddenly, economy and politics set the limitations instead. Today, more than 30 years later, it seems as the digital technology has also provided the economical means to get advanced home entertainment that no one could have expected 20 years ago. In a world based on flat-panel TV sets, computers, satellites, optical fibers and many other digital communication systems, instead it must be the human fantasy that seems to set the limits.

Malmö, Sweden in the summer of 2006
Lars-Ingemar Lundström

The History of Television

Storytelling is really the foundation of our media society. Throughout the millions of years since the human beings learned to communicate with each other, the ways of expressing and storing information have changed. One of the latest additions to this is television—"a way to see in a distance."

FIGURE

1.1

During the Stone Age, people were active during the day using their weapons and tools. At night, they sat around the fire telling stories.

FIGURE

1.2

Modern man is active during the day. Weapons and stone tools have been exchanged for computers and mobile phones and at night, people sit around the television, watching stories.

THE EVOLUTION OF STORYTELLING

Ever since the human language became a reality, telling and listening to stories have been the most loved activities for humans. Since the dawn of culture, we have been sitting around the campfire every night listening to the stories that have been passed from one generation to the next. In the beginning, the stories and fairy tales had to be remembered and be told from generation to generation. After a while, humans began to document the stories in drawings on stones and walls in caves. Later, skin from animals and paper were used. The intellectual heritage did not have to rely on the human memory any more and the stories could live on, unchanged, for an extended period of time. This is essential since otherwise the human brain has a tendency to gradually change the meaning of the story.

The introduction of the printed word, thanks to Johannes Gutenberg, made it possible for the stories to be mass-produced and brought to a large number of people. Cultural mass production became a reality. No technical device was required to read a book, but the knowledge of reading was necessary. The family of the nineteenth century gathered around someone who was reading aloud from a book.

For a very long time, storytelling was limited to spoken words and text. However, by the end of the nineteenth century, Thomas Alva Edison began to change all that. He invented the phonograph, which made it possible to record sounds on a wax-coated roll. Another invention from that same era—the telephone—made it possible for one human being to talk to another human being at a very large distance, a drastic change in the ease and immediacy of communication. These inventions are both based on the observation that sound consists of small vibrations that propagate through air due to small local changes in air pressure. These air pressure changes can be transferred to a thin membrane. The movement of the membrane can be used to form a track in a spinning roll of wax or disc made of a similar material. For the first time, it became possible to store sounds. Another way of using the membrane is to get an electrical coil to move in a magnetic field. Then an electrical current is induced in the coil and this current can be connected to another coil in front of another magnet at a completely different location, making another membrane move to recreate the sounds. The alternating current in the copper wire between the early telephones was one of the first electrical signals. These discoveries paved the way for the fantastic telecom and media technology of today.

By the end of the nineteenth century, some scientists and inventors also became aware of the existence of electromagnetic waves. Radio waves are radiated from stars and other natural sources. As all radio waves, artificially created radio waves propagate through air as well as vacuum by the speed of light. Actually, radio waves are very much the same phenomenon as light but have a much longer wavelength than visible light.

Inventors began to use the electrical signal to control the appearance of radio waves. By doing this, the radio wave became a carrier for messages and even the copper wires became unnecessary, even when transferring voice messages. In the beginning of the twentieth century, almost explosive changes occurred in the technology of spreading and storing stories told by voice. A few decades into the new century, it became possible for millions of people to listen to one person simultaneously telling them all the same story. Radio broadcasting was born.

The ways to record music and other sounds also developed rapidly. Recorded voices from these years still act like the time machine that never before existed in human history.

The art of storytelling has evolved from one person sitting at the campfire telling a story directly from his memory to someone reading from a book in a radio studio with nations of people listening. Today, the TV is undoubtedly the largest storyteller. Hollywood and program providers all over the world have taken over a large portion of the storytelling at home. The basic principles are still the same. You gather every night and watch and listen to stories; some are fictional and some are real. Some people today even have the campfire in their living room in the form of the modern fireplace.

THE HISTORY OF THE TV SET

The invention of television and the technological advances that have occurred in the last 120 or more years have introduced a number of systems, solutions and methods of broadcasting sound and images into viewers' homes.

Mechanical Television (1880–1930)

As early as the end of the nineteenth century, some inventors were speculating about transferring pictures using electrical signals. Transferring sounds is quite easy, since a microphone provides an electrical signal that directly corresponds to the vibrations in the air that are caused by the sounds.

However, a picture is something much more complicated. Even a picture in black and white consists of a very large number of more or less luminous points that each provide a signal describing how light varies by time at that specific point. Transferring signals describing each point separately would mean a very large number of signals and would be practically impossible to implement. Some kind of compression of the information would be needed to decrease this large number of signals to just one signal describing the whole picture.

In 1884, German inventor Paul Nipkow got a patent for a mechanical device that could scan a picture. The device included a vertical rotating disc in which there were holes arranged in a spiral form. When a picture was projected against the disc, it was only possible for the light from one point at a time to penetrate the disc and to reach a photosensitive cell located on the other side of the disc. By spinning the disc, the light that penetrated the disc described the picture point by point. After one turn of the disc, the complete picture had been scanned. The electrical signal produced by the photosensitive cell is a primitive video signal. At the receiver end, a similar rotating disc with holes is used. This receiver disc rotates with the same speed as the transmitting disc. An electrical source of light that is controlled by the video signal is located behind the receiver disc. A picture can now be viewed in front of the receiver disc.

In those days, Nipkow was regarded as a very strange man with a very strange interest. However, his invention, the sequential scanning of a picture, is the basis for television, computer screens and digital photography. It is without doubt one of the largest inventions ever made when it comes to visualization.

You can also say that Nipkow laid the foundations for compression of electrical signals by simplifying the signals describing the picture to just one single signal with the scanning device. He did this to make the signal easier to transfer to the receiver. This simplified signal is still accurately perceived by the viewer because our brains process the signals from our eyes very slowly. Even though we only can see one point of the picture at a certain moment, we have an accurate experience of a complete picture, as long as the disc spins fast enough. In a corresponding way, the movement we think we see in a movie are really only a series of still pictures shown in a rapid flow.

Using the imperfections of our senses became one of the recurring methods during the further development of television.

Nipkow never succeeded in putting his TV system into practice. The electronic components required to do so were simply not available at the time of his invention. It was the Englishman John Logie Baird who implemented the first cameras and TV sets that really worked, in the 1920s. Baird started the first TV transmissions from England and produced kits for his mechanical TV set, called a televisor. Most of the kits were sold to radio amateurs all over Europe.

The picture on these televisors was very small and had very poor resolution. The Baird televisor was connected to the speaker output of an AM radio and the signal controlled the luminosity of a gleaming lamp located behind the perforated rotating disc. Audio was transmitted on a separate channel and received by another set. The transmissions from England were carried out in the medium wave band. The 25,000 kits that Baird succeeded in getting distributed were sold mostly to curious people, and the "technology" did not achieve widespread sales or use.

FIGURE

1.3

Mechanical television was a product of a mechanical era and produced the first electrical video signal. The worst problem was keeping the receiving and the transmitting discs synchronized with each other.

Electronic Television (1930s and 40s)

It was obvious from the beginning that mechanical television had to be replaced by something else before TV could become a commercial success for the general public and there were many experiments with different electronic solutions. A major invention was the iconoscope, a predecessor to camera tubes that was combined with new, improved TV systems. Using electronics made it possible to get TV systems with the picture divided into many more lines than before. As a result, the picture had considerably improved resolution.

> *Continued mechanical developments*
> *Baird was almost certainly aware that electronics sooner or later would beat mechanical television, but he continued to try to develop mechanical solutions to compete with the electronic ones. By increasing the number of holes in the discs and (at a later stage) combining mechanics and electronics, he fought on in an untiring way. Finally, he even produced equipment for mechanical color TV by using discs with different sets of holes that had filters for the basic red, green and blue colors.*

In the 1920s there was a great interest in developing electronic tubes to be used in radio sets.

The iconoscope was a kind of electronic tube. The electrons are accelerated towards an anode that consists of a light-sensitive material. The light-sensitive layer will increase its conductivity as it is illuminated and thus the current through the tube will increase compared to if the electron beam is hitting a non-illuminated area. The current through the tube will be proportional to the illumination of the specific point where the electron beam happens to hit (see Figure 1.4).

FIGURE 1.4 In the first electronic TV systems, the video signal was produced by an iconoscope where an electron beam swept across a projected picture of the subject.

Charged particles (such as electrons) are deflected when they pass through a magnetic field. Around the tube, coils control the beam both horizontally and vertically. In this way, it is possible to get the beam to scan the picture line by line. Electronic scanning can be made much faster than is possible in mechanical television making electronic television capable of handling a very large number of lines and a large number of pictures each second.

In the beginning, there were several television broadcast systems in use. North and South America decided to use a system with 525 lines and a picture rate of 30 pictures per second. The reason for the latter was the use of 60 periods AC. In those days, there was a large risk for picture disturbances if the picture rate was not an even multiple of the AC frequency. In Europe, 50 Hz AC is used and consequently the somewhat lower 25 Hz picture rate was selected.

In Europe, there were also different opinions about what number of lines should be used. Great Britain introduced an early 405 line system while France's first system had 819 lines (you could say that the French were ahead of time, using an almost HDTV system). Other parts of Europe introduced the current standard definition 625 line system right from the start. However not all lines are used for picture transmission. It takes some time for the electronic beam to jump from the lower to the upper part of the picture in order to start on the next picture frame. Therefore, in the European system, only 576 lines are active parts of the picture and 49 lines are in the vertical blanking interval. At a later stage, it was discovered that these lines could be used for teletext transmission.

The duration of each line is 64 micro seconds (64 millionths of a second). However, not even all of these micro seconds are used for picture transmission. The first 12 micro seconds are used for the electronic beam to jump from the end of a line to the beginning of the next one. This time interval is called the horizontal blanking interval.

When introducing electronic TV, synchronizing pulses were put in the horizontal blanking interval to tell the TV set when the beam should turn back and start to draw the next line. Another pulse was introduced in the vertical blanking interval to tell the set that the beam should start drawing a new frame. In this way, automatic synchronization was introduced and the viewer could relax in front of his TV instead of being occupied with manual synchronization of the transmitter and receiver, as in the days of mechanical television.

However, in the childhood days of television, there was yet another problem. On the receiving end, an inversed iconoscope, the cathode ray tube, was used. In the picture tube, the picture is produced by an electron beam that scans a surface of zinc sulfide which emits light when it is hit by the electrons (see Figure 1.5). In early cathode ray tubes, the light emitted by the zinc sulfide had time to go out before the whole picture was drawn. The result was a flickering picture. To prevent flickering, a technique called interlaced scanning was introduced, where only every other line is scanned. For example, 312.5 lines (of which 288 are active lines) are scanned before the beam starts on top again to draw the remaining lines. Each 312.5-line scan is a half picture and is called a picture frame. Thus the complete picture consists of two consecutive frames.

These frames are displayed at a frame rate of 50 Hz, double the picture rate of 25 pictures per second. As a result, a much more stable picture was achieved without flickering. Another interesting consequence is that movements are actually displayed at a rate of 50 Hz, instead of 24 pictures per second that is the case for ordinary film at the movies. That is the reason why television seems—to the small percentage of people sensitive to these kinds of effects—to present movements in a more realistic way than film

The other kind of scanning is progressive scanning, where the complete picture is drawn in one single scan line by line. Progressive scanning first came into use in computer screens, by which time cathode ray tubes had evolved so there was no real need for interlaced scanning anymore. However, interlaced scanning has continued to live on in the televisions systems until this day.

FIGURE

1.5

In cathode ray tube for black-and-white television, the picture is drawn on a zinc sulfide surface that will emit light as it is hit by the electrons.

In the early days of television, there was no other media for distributing TV besides terrestrial transmitters. However, unlike radio transmissions, television needed more bandwidth to house all the information contained in the analog TV signal. The higher resolution pictures made possible by electronic television created a need for about 250 times more bandwidth than radio required.

The technique for transmission that requires the least bandwidth is amplitude modulation (AM), where the strength (amplitude) of the radio wave varies according to the voltage level of the video signal. Since television in Europe did not make its breakthrough until the 1950s, frequency modulation (FM) was selected for the audio sub carrier. Radio based on FM transmission became the normal way for distributing radio channels. FM makes it possible to distribute the signals in a way that is much less sensitive to noise and disturbances than AM is. However there is a cost: bandwidth.

Inverted Video Signal

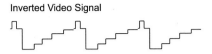

Unmodulated Carrier

Amplitude Modulation (Analog Terrestrial TV and Cable TV)

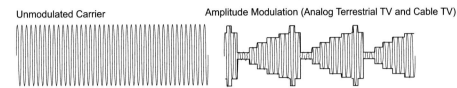

FIGURE

1.6

In analog terrestrial TV, amplitude modulation is used for the picture signal (the video). The audio is transmitted on a separate subcarrier that is frequency modulated.

COLOR TELEVISION (1950S AND 60S)

As we have seen already, Baird worked on a system for mechanical TV distribution in color. But it would take many years until color TV could be introduced to the general public.

A color picture is actually a combination of three pictures, each representing the color contents corresponding to each of the basic colors in the picture: red (R), green (G) and one blue (B).

In color television, the optical picture was divided into its three basic components using a prism or a set of mirrors and a number of color filters. Each picture component was focused on a separate camera tube (a more modern iconoscope). In today's cameras, the camera tubes have been replaced by solid state mosaics that produce the three electronic R, G and B signals.

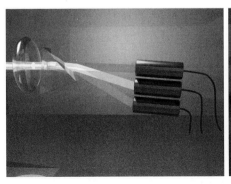

FIGURE

1.7

By using color filters or a prism, a picture can be separated into its three basic color components. (See color plate.)

In principle, it would require three parallel TV channels to distribute the R, G and B signals. However, this would result in a large waste of the scarce frequency ranges that are available for terrestrial transmission.

There is, however, a clever solution to all this. Our vision is only sensitive to sharpness when it comes to differentiating between dark and light. When it comes to colors, our vision does not require the same resolution it does for black and white, and we can do with a much more diffuse display of colors still believing that we are viewing a sharp picture.

Color TV Systems

The systems for color TV that were developed during the 1950s and 60s are based on a black-and-white picture that is transmitted at near full resolution. A European black-and-white picture requires approximately 5 MHz bandwidth. Of this, 1 MHz was removed in the upper frequency range of the video spectrum so that the black-and-white video signal occupies the spectrum between 0 and 4 MHz. In the spectral area between 4 and 5 MHz, a subcarrier is put around the frequency 4.43 MHz. The subcarrier contains information about which color (nuance) and how strong color (color saturation) that should be represented in each pixel. Since this color information will be held within only a fourth of what a black-and-white picture requires, the color signal has poor resolution. But this does not impact the final image transmitted, since the eye does not look for contours in color.

The color information is phase modulated, i.e., the phase angle of the subcarrier represents the color nuance while the amplitude of the subcarrier represents the saturation of color at that pixel.

The color subcarrier is compared with a reference signal that is updated on each line by being compared with a small portion of reference signal that is transmitted in the beginning of each line. This small portion of reference signal is called burst.

This system decreases the need of frequency space, making the color TV signal to fit within a common black-and-white TV channel, but it also provides full backward compatibility. This was important because it enabled the black-and-white TV device to receive the color TV transmissions though only in black and white. It would not have been very realistic, from an economical point of view, to have special transmissions to color TV devices in the 1960s.

The U.S. was the first to introduce commercial TV in color. The American system, National Television System Committee (NTSC), was introduced quite early and has been in use ever since. Unfortunately this system has a number of technical problems. One problem is keeping track of the color subcarrier phase when the signal is subject to reflections against buildings or mountains. These reflections cause the TV receiver to get one signal directly from the transmitter and one delayed, reflected signal. This can make the color tone in a human's skin change from bright red to green. An old joke is that NTSC really does not mean National Television System Committee but "Never The Same Color."

The Germans took a step ahead in the mid-60s by introducing the Phase Alternating Line (PAL) system. The PAL system is quite similar to the NTSC system, but the phase reference is shifted plus or minus 90 degrees from one line to the next. This converts the color tone errors (caused by reflected TV signals) into color saturation errors, which the human eye is not as sensitive to.

The French invented their own system, Sequential Couleur avec Mémoire (SECAM). In this system, the phase stability problem is completely avoided by using frequency modulation instead of phase modulation, making the transmissions insensitive to reflexes.

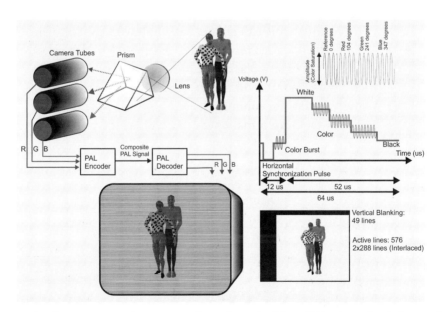

FIGURE

1.8

In the European analog system for color television, PAL, the color information is coded in a phase modulated subcarrier at 4.43 MHz. The phases of the carrier indicate the color tone and the amplitude symbolizes the saturation of the color. (See color plate.)

The color TV signal can be described in two different ways, as either a combination of the three basic color signals R (Red), G (Green) and B (Blue) or as a combination of the components Y, U and V. In the latter method, Y is the monochrome black-and-white signal while U and V are the two color difference signals that are contained in the color subcarrier. It is possible to get the R, G and B signals from the Y, U, V signals and vice versa by simply adding and subtracting the signals with each other according to certain algorithms.

Early Picture Tubes for Color TV

Unfortunately it was quite hard to manufacture a color TV picture tube in the early days of color television. The problem is that the tube must contain three electron cannons instead of one (as in the black-and-white tube). In addition to this, the inside of the tube must be covered with very small points of zinc sulphides that are doped with various types of pollutants in various ways so the three basic colors can be reproduced when the surface is bombarded with electrons.

The most difficult part is that the electron cannons can only illuminate their own respective points of sulfide. The solution to this problem is a plate containing hundreds of thousands of tiny holes. This plate is located between the electron guns and the sulfide dots, restricting the electrons from each gun to the dots that respectively represent the color of that gun.

If we have a group of three little dots—one red, one green and one blue—the total impression is black when none of the dots emit any light. If only one of the three dots is bright, we will see the color of that dot. If each of the

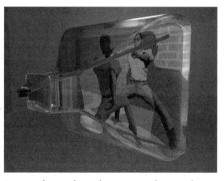 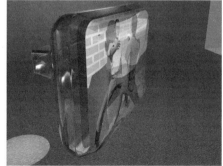

FIGURE

1.9

In a color tube, there are three electron guns instead of one as in a black and white tube (See color plate).

three dots emits an equal amount of light, we will see white or a shade of grey, depending on the intensity of light from the three dots.

By letting each of the three dots emit a certain combination of light, any hue of color can be produced.

A VIDEO RECORDER IN EACH HOME (1970S AND 80S)

Since a video signal contains a lot more information than an audio signal, it took until the end of the 1970s until it became possible for average consumers to have a videotape player in their homes. A sound tape recorder can handle frequencies up to approximately 15 kHz, providing acceptable sound quality. A videotape player must be able to handle frequencies up to several MHz.

By the end of the 1970s, a war between standards for the competing technical solutions for home video broke out. Among the early systems were Philips VCR (Video Cassette Recording), Betamax from Sony and VHS (Video Home System). VHS ended up the winner after a number years of struggle where, among other things, Philips had time to introduce yet another system, Video 2000, that was more technologically advanced and actually clearly better than VHS. But, perhaps due the wide range of pre-recorded films on VHS, that system won in spite of its lower quality and greater cost.

The home video recorder gave the TV viewers a lot more freedom. Now, it became possible to view programs that were transmitted at inconvenient times. Sometime, two good programs conflicted on the two only Swedish channels that I could watch at that time, and it was the same in most European countries. There were only one or two state-owned channels on the air. With the video recorder, it became possible to record a program on one channel while watching the other. Then it became possible to watch the recorded program at a time when the content of both channels was boring. In those years much of the content consisted of political debates and other less interesting stuff and the video recorder became a relief.

CABLE TELEVISION AND DTH SATELLITES (1980S AND 90S)

The next big step in the development of television in Europe—already in use in the U.S.—was the establishment of cable TV, which provided more program choice than ever before. However, the satellites that were used for TV distribution in the early 1980s were quite weak. In Europe a dish size of about 1.5 meters was required for reception of the signal. This was too big for ordinary viewers to handle by themselves, so cable TV became very popular. But by the end of the 1980s, new and stronger satellites were introduced that could be used by consumers, so Direct-to-Home broadcasting became the new way to increase the number of TV channels in your home.

At the same time, it began to become too costly to expand cable TV to more households. The rest of the population in most countries did not live in blocks of apartments and it was expensive to include individual homes in the larger cable networks. With stronger satellites and more sensitive receiving equipment, it was possible to use smaller parabolic dishes and the satellite receiver became each household's property.

In the beginning of the 1990s most satellite transmissions were made using the same technology as for terrestrial TV, i.e., by using composite PAL signals in Europe and NTSC signals in North America. However there was an important difference. Instead of using AM frequency modulation, FM was used. FM only requires about one-tenth of the transmission power that would have been required for AM. This is important since power in satellites is scarce. The power has to be picked up by the solar panels and it has to be stored in onboard batteries that could provide power when the satellite goes into the shadow of the Earth.

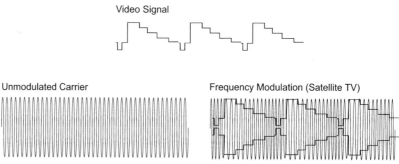

Video Signal

Unmodulated Carrier

Frequency Modulation (Satellite TV)

FIGURE

1.10

In analog satellite transmissions, frequency modulation is used.

MULTIPLEXED ANALOG COMPONENTS SYSTEM (EARLY 1990S)

Even if the PAL system has a better performance than the NTSC system, there are some technical problems. Both systems use composite signals including both the black-and-white (luminance) as well as the color (chrominance) signals. In other words, they contains all three color components in the same signal and a person wearing a shirt with a black-and-white check pattern could look like a person wearing a rainbow pattern shirt instead. This phenomenon is called cross color. On top of all this, the analog audio in TV transmissions was not that good since it was often spoiled by annoying interference from the video signal.

Large efforts were made in the 1980s to find a new, partly analog, TV system that would be better than the existing ones. The system chosen in Great Britain was the Multiplexed Analogue Components (MAC). The MAC system is based on the transmitting the black-and-white and chrominance components of the video signal in different time slots. The audio would be digital.

If we study a line in a MAC signal (which has duration of 64 microseconds), like the one in Figure 1.11, we can see that the first 10 microseconds are used to transmit the digital line synchronization word (a short, unique sequence of digital bits replacing the synchronization pulses of the old systems) and digital

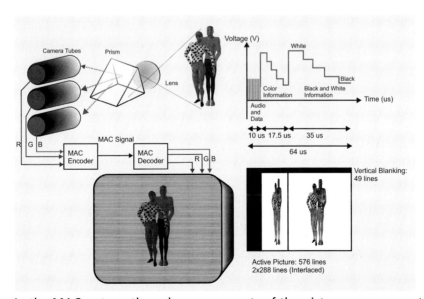

FIGURE

1.11

In the MAC system, the color components of the picture were separated by transmitting the black-and-white part of the picture in the beginning of each line and the color information was sent in the later part of each line. (See color plate.)

audio. Thus the line synchronization interval is used to transmit useful information, which is not the case in the analog PAL signal except from the PAL burst and the line synchronization pulse itself.

The next 17.5 microseconds are used to send the color information, where every other line is used for the U and V signals respectively. The remaining 35 micro seconds are used to send black-and-white (luminance) information. This means that the video signals are compressed and relocated in time as is shown in Figure 1.11. As a result, a MAC receiver was much more complicated than a PAL satellite receiver. All MAC signal processing was to be made digital and this was a step in preparation for the coming digital television systems.

Since the Y, U and V signals are kept completely apart during the transmission and these signals are easy to convert to the basic R, G and B components, the system is said to be a component encoded system. This also applies to digital television systems. All components are completely separated from each other throughout the complete transmission and reception chain.

The MAC system is also better than PAL because it also broadcasts digital audio and it enabled true wide screen format video transmissions. However the MAC system was introduced well before the 16:9 widescreen sets had become popular and by the time that happened, the pure digital TV systems were about to be introduced. Even more unrealistic were the plans to use MAC for distribution of HDTV.

HD-MAC: Obsolete Before It Was Even Introduced
During the 1992 Olympic Games in Barcelona, the last desperate effort to get the MAC system established in Europe was made, by doing HDTV test transmissions using the MAC system based on a 1250 line concept. Since the MAC system does not contain any subcarriers, it is possible to increase the bandwidth enough to house the additional information. However in 1992, HDTV was still something futuristic and the large flat display systems that are required for a successful launch of HDTV did not yet exist. HDTV based on conventional cathode ray tubes is not interesting enough to justify the cost of introducing HDTV. Even if it were, the TV stations would probably not have accepted the extremely high costs for distributing uncompressed analog HDTV signals.

In the end, it was only France and the Scandinavian countries that really got to use the MAC system commercially. The only real reason to introduce the system was the possibility to encrypt TV signals in a more efficient way than before. In that way, the MAC system became important for the introduction of pay TV in these countries.

The MAC system existed in four different versions: B-MAC, C-MAC, D-MAC and D2-MAC. The difference between the systems was the number of audio signals and some other parameters. D2-MAC became the most widespread system, with two digital stereo channels on top of the video.

The MAC system introduced digital audio for TV distributed primarily via satellite. However, as an alternative to MAC, it was also interesting to be able to add digital audio to improve the existing terrestrial PAL transmissions. For that reason, many European countries introduced the British NICAM (Near Instantaneously Companded Audio Multiplex) audio system which is based on a second sound subcarrier that is located at 5.85 MHz (PAL B/G) above the picture carrier in most countries except from Great Britain where it was located at 6.552 MHz due to different channel spacing (PAL I).

In Germany, an analog stereo TV system, the A2-system, was introduced in the 1980s. The A2 system became common in European TV sets at a very early stage. However the system does not have the same performance as NICAM. The NICAM subcarrier is not frequency modulated as is the case for the analog audio but uses QPSK (Quadrature Phase-Shift Keying).

The dream of being able to distribute video as a digital signal to home TV sets grew larger and larger throughout the 1990s and by the end of the decade it became a reality. However, it was quite a long route, as we shall see in the next chapter.

2 | What Is Digital TV?

CHAPTER

FIGURE

2.1

Digital TV opens up a world of new possibilities.

TV transmissions contain a lot more information than radio broadcasts. The analog 625 line video signal contains about 250 times more information as a pure audio signal. The fact that a video signal requires this large amount of information has always been a problem for TV distribution.

Unlike an audio signal, the video signal does contain a lot of repeated information, since two consecutive frames of a transmission contain very similar information. This repeated information may be used to decrease the amount of information that has to be transferred from the transmitter to the receiver. However, in order to be able to extract the essential parts of the information, we need computers to process the TV signal and carry out all the necessary calculations. Since computers work with digital signals, we have to first convert the analog signal into a stream of digital bits before computers can reduce the amount of information. This process is complex, but it makes it possible to transmit eight to ten TV channels using a satellite transponder that before only had the capacity for one single analog signal. Using the same kind of techniques, it is also possible to fit a two-hour movie on a comparatively small DVD disc.

SHANNON'S INFORMATION THEOREM

There are certain natural laws that put limitations on how information may be transferred. Shannon's information theorem is such a natural law, saying that all transfer of information is limited by two factors: the received amount of signal power and the bandwidth of the channel used for the transmission. This is a phenomenon that should be regarded as a law of nature and therefore is impossible to circumvent. The amount of received power is decided by the strength of the transmitter and the efficiency of the antenna used for reception. The bandwidth is the amount of frequency space that is occupied by the transmitted signal.

Actual radio signals are always limited in bandwidth as well as signal power. This applies to radio signals distributed by satellites, terrestrial transmitters and cable TV networks. If we want to increase the amount of information in the signal, we either have to increase the power of transmission, the amount of bandwidth or both. The alternative is to decrease the quality of the signal—something we probably wish to avoid.

When using satellite for distribution, there are several transmitters (called transponders) in each satellite. A transponder is limited in bandwidth and output power. A traditional satellite transponder has a bandwidth of about 30 MHz and may be used to transmit one TV channel. To transmit more than one TV channel through such a transponder, we must find a way to decrease the amount of information that is required for each TV channel.

The principles for reduction of unnecessary information have been known for long. The unnecessary parts containing repeated information has to be removed and a reduced compressed version of the signal has to be created. In the receiver the original signal has to be re-created from the compressed signal.

DIGITIZING A VIDEO SIGNAL

In order to be able to let a computer handle a TV signal we first have to get it digitized. When we have a digital signal it is quite simple to manipulate it as we wish. Getting the signal digitized means that the audio and video signals are represented by a series of digits, rather than any physical media. The digits are then sent to a receiver which has the ability to recreate the physical analog audio and video signals from this information. A digital signal contains a representation of the signal rather than the actual signal itself.

In the beginning of the twentieth century, tests using telegraphy to transmit pictures were made that are quite similar to our modern way of digital thinking. A transparent grid representing a coordinate system was put on top of a photographic image. Then the black and white squares representing the picture were read manually and converted into a series of dots and dashes that were telegraphed to the receiver. At the receiving end, the tedious process of filling the correct squares on a paper with a similar grid took place.

Today, we do not have to do this by ourselves. Modern analog-to-digital and digital-to-analog converters do this job in a quick and convenient way. Now, we are going to take a look at how this conversion between analog and digital and vice versa is done.

The name digital comes out of the word digit—digital transmission is the transfer of digits describing the signal. The receiver has the ability to retranslate these figures into the physical analog signal.

Analog-to-Digital Conversion

An electrical signal is electrical voltage that varies in time. By measuring the voltage at certain intervals, it is possible to get a series of measured values that approximately describe the signal. The device that performs the measurements is called an analog-to-digital (A/D) converter. The measured values can be transferred as digital numbers, bits, or a series of the digits 0 and 1. At the receiving end, these values are used to re-create the analog version of the voltage by means of a digital-to-analog (D/A) converter.

How Does the D/A Converter Work?
Re-constructing the digital signal to analog is done by translating each of the values included in the digital signal into an output voltage corresponding to each value. This creates a signal with a step-like shape rather than the soft waveform of the original signal. By passing the output signal through a low pass filter (a capacitor and a resistor), the quick transitions are filtered and the original signal is recreated as is shown in Figure 2.2.

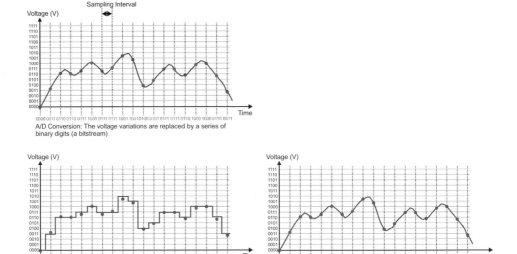

FIGURE

2.2

Digitizing converts the signal into a series of 0 and 1 that describes the appearance of the signal. In this example, the signal is described by four bit samples that allow for the signal to be represented in 16 levels since four bits may be combined in 16 different ways.

MEASURING AND COMPRESSING DIGITAL VIDEO SIGNALS

When performing the A/D conversion, there are two things to keep in mind: The first parameter is the number of levels used to represent the signal to enable the correct reconstruction of the signal. Second, it has to be decided how often the signal must be measured and the values sent to the receiver. Every measured value can be regarded as a sample of the signal and is therefore called just "sample." Really, we are just taking samples of the analog signal to create the digital signal.

Four digits describe every measured value. Four digits may be combined in 16 different ways: 0000, 0001, 0010, 0011, 0100, 0101, 0110, 0111, 1000, 1001, 1010, 1011, 1100, 1101, 1110 and 1111. In this case, it is said that the A/D converter has a resolution of four bits. However, 16 levels are not enough to describe a full quality video signal. Most A/D converters use seven- or eight-bit resolution. For reference, eight bits corresponds to 256 levels, and ordinary bitmap image software provides an excellent grayscale picture if the pixels are described by 8 bits. Audio requires much better dynamic than could be achieved by 8 bits and 256 levels. The audio of a CD record is stored in 16-bit samples. This corresponds to 65,536 levels.

When it comes to the question about how often to measure, or sample the signal, there is a special theorem, the Sampling Theorem. According to the Sampling Theorem, it is necessary to sample the signal twice as many times as the highest frequency of the signal being digitized. For example, an audio signal must be sampled (or measured) at least 40,000 times per second if the bandwidth is 20 kHz.

In a video signal with a bandwidth of 5 MHz, at least 10 million samples have to be taken every second in order to get a stream of bits containing enough information for the receiver to reconstruct the signal. Of course, the result is an immense amount of bits every second. The following calculations show what this means when digitizing a video signal.

A standard European 625-line signal consists of 576 active lines that form the picture. Every line is considered to consist of 720 pixels (pixel, short for "picture element"). The total number of pixels in a picture is 414,720 (576 x 720).

As we discussed earlier, 8 bits are required to describe each pixel by 256 different levels between black and white. This means 8 x 414,720 bits = 3,317,760 bits required to describe each picture. The picture rate is 25 pictures per second; that results in 25 x 3,317,760 = 82,944,000 bits per second or 82,944 Mbit/s.

As we discussed in the previous chapter and as shown in Figure 2.3, a color picture really consists of three parallel pictures (red, green and blue). The final conclusion is that 3 x 82,944 Mbit/s = 248,832 Mbit/s.

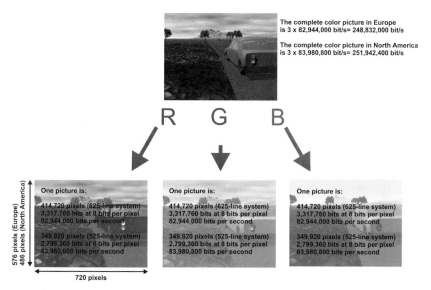

FIGURE

2.3

A color pictue really consists of three pictures (red, green and blue). Alternatively, the picture may be represented by the black-and-white Y signal along with the U and V color difference signals. (See color plate.)

A similar calculation can be made on a North American TV signal comprising 486 x 720 pixels at 30 pictures per second. The resulting number of bits will be 486 x 720 x 8 x 30 = 83,980,800 bits per second (83,981 Mbit/s) for each of the three basic color components. As a total we get 251,942 Mbit/s.

In professional digital television, the analog signal is digitized using Y, U and V signals instead (see Chapter 1, "The History of Television"). The Y signal (black-and-white content) is sampled using 10 bits at a rate of 13.5 million samples per second. The color difference signals (U and V) are both sampled also using 10 bits but at half the sampling rate—6.75 million samples per second. In that way we can take advantage of the fact that the eye is less sensitive to resolution when it comes to the color content in the picture compared to the sensitivity to resolution in the luminance signal. The formula to find resulting bitrate will be the same as in the example above; 10 x (13.5 + 6.75 + 6.75) million bits per second equaling 270 Mbit/s.

However, 270 Mbit/s is much too much data to be transmitted in a practical way. A signal of this kind can be distributed inside a TV production company or stored on professional digital video recorders. But a satellite transponder (that previously could be used to distribute one TV channel) can only house between 38 and 44 Mbit/s, if QPSK modulation is to be used. The same problem exists in a cable TV channel, and the lack of bandwidth is even worse when it comes to terrestrial television where 22 Mbit/s in a conventional transmission channel is quite common.

The conclusion will be that uncompressed digital TV channels requires much more bandwidth than is the case for analog TV channels. Therefore we must find a way to compress the digital TV signal in a way that it requires less bandwidth. The uncompressed signal becomes more or less unusable when we leave the building of the TV station.

Note
There are, however, ways to distribute uncompressed video in optical fibers. These possibilities, however, are only used for professional purposes.

Compressing Digital Signals

In order to be able to handle the digital video signal, we have to go further in trying to minimize the amount of information in the signal. To solve this, a number of experts got the task to find new and smart methods to eliminate unnecessary information in digital images and digital video sequences. For this purpose, the expert groups JPEG and MPEG were formed.

Compressing Still Images

The Joint Photographic Experts Group (JPEG) got the task to develop a standard to compress digital still images. This was very important in order to be able to store images in computers as well as transferring pictures in between computers in an efficient way. Today the JPEG standard is used everywhere. The most common applications are in digital cameras and when distributing pictures over the Internet.

A picture consists of a number of pixels. The two pictures in Figure 2.4 each have a resolution of 540 x 405 pixels, giving a total of 218,700 pixels for each. You may choose different numbers of bits to describe each pixel. A common choice is to use 8 bits to describe the luminance level of a pixel. The choice of 8 bits makes it possible to describe one of 256 possible grayscale levels in between black and white.

A picture with 540 x 405 pixels in resolution will require 218,700 x 8 bits resulting in 1,749,600 bits or 218,700 bytes. (One byte is 8 bits.) Since a color picture consists of three pictures (RGB), three times as many bits are required to represent the color picture, i.e., 5,248,800 bits or 656,100 bytes. When I checked the sizes of the pictures in Figure 2.4, I found that both were about 640 kbytes when saved in the uncompressed bmp file format.

This matches up to our calculations quite well. An uncompressed picture with a certain number of pixels will always require the same number of bits and bytes, in this case 640 kbytes independent of the content of the picture. This is why the two images—though they show the subject in different perspectives—have the same uncompressed size.

Compressing a picture means that the picture file is recalculated using a certain algorithm (calculation rule) that takes several things into account. As an example, it may be possible to use the fact that a number of pixels that are located close to each other look a like and have the same value. In that case, it may be overkill to use 24 bits to describe each pixel and instead it may be enough to use 24 bits for the value of several pixels along with a less consuming description of where these pixels are located. In some cases this may result in a smaller image than one that describes each pixel separately.

It is possible to choose the compression level you want for the compressed JPEG file. As a general rule, it is possible to go down to about one-sixth of the original file size without affecting the quality of the picture in a noticeable way. On top of this, the compressed picture files will vary in size depending on the content in the picture (as is illustrated by Figure 2.4). For example, a large area of the same color, like the ball in Figure 2.4, would be considered one chunk of data that can be stored as a much smaller piece of data. Thus it is possible to use the fact that some pictures really contain less information than others and to reduce the need for bits and bytes in this way.

If the picture is completely black, there is only one level for all pixels in the picture. Then it would have been enough to tell that all pixels in the picture only have one value. I tried a completely black picture with the same resolution as the pictures in Figure 2.4 and ended up with a compressed file of just 4.06 kbytes.

On the other end of the spectrum, the worst picture to compress would be one where all pixels have different color and luminance levels. Such file would probably be just as big as an uncompressed file, at least if we had chosen a high-quality level for the compression process.

Fortunately, the world doesn't usually work this way and most pictures contain large areas where the pixels are more or less alike. For this reason, JPEG files are usually only one-tenth to one-fifth of the original file size. Otherwise the digital cameras would require five to ten times as large flash memories and it would take five to ten times as long to download pictures over the Internet.

Uncompressed size: 640 kbyte
Compressed size: 128 kbyte

Uncompressed size: 640 kbyte
Compressed size: 97.2 kbyte

FIGURE

2.4

The most common file format on the Internet and in digital cameras for image compression is JPEG.

Compressing Moving Pictures

The JPEG format is developed for compression of digital stills. When this task was done, another group of experts, the Moving Pictures Experts Group (MPEG), got a similar task to do the corresponding work for standardizing compression formats for moving pictures. The aim was to make it easier to handle movie clips in computers and to transfer these files between computers in a less bitrate-consuming way.

The first part of the standard got ready in the beginning of the 1990s and is called MPEG-1. The compression algorithm is optimized for video files with a small bandwidth below approximately 2 Mbit/s.

The compression is based on the principle of analyzing each picture in the video signal and to find the differences in between the pictures. On the Internet, you often watch TV in small windows which use fewer lines than conventional TV, which reduces the bitrate demand even more. This made it possible to transmit low bitrate TV through telephone lines using ordinary modems. And of course, broadband connections provided even better results.

MPEG-1 has been very popular for distributing video clips on the Internet but the standard can not achieve the performance that is required to replace analog television.

The next step was to establish a standard that could be used for standard television, thus completing the dream about distribution of digital TV via satellite, cable and terrestrial transmitters and even to store video on DVD records. The second standard, MPEG-2 is optimized for higher bitrates from 2 Mbit/s and up. You could say that MPEG-2 picks up where MPEG-1 ends. In MPEG-1 there are quite some problems in describing movements in the video content. Therefore apart from providing higher bitrates, MPEG-2 is also supporting motion compensation resulting in soft and natural movements in the picture.

MPEG algorithms are based on using groups of pictures (GOP) as is shown in Figure 2.5. In this example a GOP makes up half a second of video. Each GOP contains 12 pictures. However it is possible to select different numbers of

FIGURE 2.5

MPEG algorithms are based on using only the difference in information between the original pictures in the video file. In this example only one of every 12 pictures is saved or transmitted (marked in red). (See color plate.)

pictures and this example is only to explain the basic concepts of video encoding. In reality the process is more complicated.

In this example there are two GOPs per second. In each GOP, only the first picture is a complete picture. Then the remaining 11 pictures are calculated from the first picture and only the difference between the original pictures is stored with the file. All other pictures are recalculated at the receiving end. If there is a change of scenes in between two GOPs, a new GOP is started immediately and an "extra" full picture is transmitted.

To make it all even more economical, the first picture in each GOP is JPEG-compressed. The original 270 Mbit/s signal is reduced to a compressed bitrate of 3 to 4 Mbit/s and still it remains at an acceptable quality level.

Figure 2.6 shows the difference between two consecutive pictures in two different scenes. Black parts of the pictures do not contain any different information, while brighter areas show information that is different in the two consecutive frames. Thus the need for capacity (bitrate) varies all the time when using MPEG compression.

Quite obviously, the digital receiver will be much more complex than earlier analog receivers working with real time signals only. Signal processing at this level must, for practical reasons, be done using a computer. It is a software issue to be able to restore the original signal at the receiving end and most of the decoder is software that is housed in an integrated circuit. At the transmission end the compression equipment—the encoder—is a very complex device.

Difference between pictures 1-2   Difference between pictures 24-25

FIGURE

2.6

The difference between two consecutive pictures depends on the amount of movement in the picture. These two pictures show the differences between some of the pictures in Figure 2.5.

Encapsulating Into Transport Stream Packets

We have now achieved a compressed video signal at a bitrate of about 4 Mbit/s. However we also need to transmit audio and possibly teletext signals. The audio is compressed in an audio compression format called Musicam. The audio encoding can be chosen at different bitrates just as the video compression. A common bitrate for a stereo pair is 256 kbit/s, however also 192 kbit/s or 128 kbit/s may be chosen. A digital TV signal consists of at least two or three signals—one video, one audio and perhaps also a teletext signal at 200 kbit/s.

Fortunately it is quite easy to combine several digital signals into one single signal. This process of combining the signals is called multiplexing. However, in order to multiplex the signals, each signal first has to be divided into packages. By transmitting the packages at different intensities, it is possible to mix fast signals (video) with a high bitrate with those having a low bitrate (audio and teletext), as in Figure 2.7.

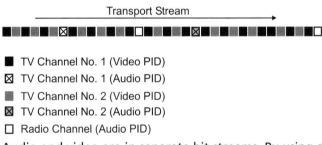

■ TV Channel No. 1 (Video PID)
⊠ TV Channel No. 1 (Audio PID)
▓ TV Channel No. 2 (Video PID)
⊠ TV Channel No. 2 (Audio PID)
☐ Radio Channel (Audio PID)

FIGURE

2.7

Audio and video are in separate bit streams. By using different intensity for the packets belonging to different signals it is possible to mix more capacity demanding signals as the video with less demanding content as audio or teletext channels.

The packages into which the signals are divided are called transport stream packets (see Figure 2.8). The length of each packet is 188 byte. The first four bytes in each packet is called the header. The first byte in the header contains a synchronization word that is unique and that indicate the start of a new packet.

This byte is followed by the Package Identification Data (PID), two bytes with the identity of the signal to which the packet belongs. This is the label that makes it possible to separate the signals again (called demultiplexing) at the receiving end. The fourth byte contains a counter that indicates the order between the packets that belong to a specific signal. This counter is also a way to determine if any packet has been lost on the way to the receiver. The remaining 184 bytes contain useful information, the payload. Together, these packets form the transport stream.

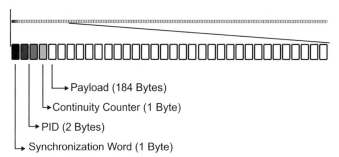

Payload (184 Bytes)

Continuity Counter (1 Byte)

PID (2 Bytes)

Synchronization Word (1 Byte)

FIGURE

2.8

The bit streams are divided into smaller packets each consisting of 188 bytes. The first 4 bytes are the header which is a tag identifying to which bit stream the packet belongs.

Splitting the information into packets achieves several advantages, in addition providing the ability to combine signals with different bitrates. The signal also becomes less sensitive to noise and other disturbances. Radio disturbances are actually short spikes of power and often have a very short duration. If one packet is disturbed, the receiver can reject that specific packet and then continue to unpack the rest of the packets.

IP traffic across the Internet is two-way communication. If a packet is lost, the sender is notified and can retransmit that specific package. Broadcasting signals are fed through a one-way distribution chain and no retransmission of lost packages can be done. To compensate for this, we have to use error protection. Error protection means adding extra bits according to clever algorithms. These extra bits make it possible for the receiver to repair the content of broken packages. Therefore to secure the signal even further, an additional 16 bytes are added to each individual packet. The information in these bytes is calculated based on the information in the 184 bytes of payload. The calculation is conducted using the Reed-Solomon encoding algorithm that, in this case, is configured to be able to correct up to eight errors in the 184 bytes of payload. If there are more than eight errors the complete packet will be rejected.

System Information

It is not enough to deliver packets containing audio and video. The receiver also must be able to know which packets contain what data. This is solved by including system information in the transmitted signal. The system information is a number of tables that are distributed in separate bit streams. The most important table is the Program Association Table (PAT), and this signal always has the packet address PID=0. The first thing the receiver has to do is to find the PAT and read the content of the table. In the PAT, there are references to which PID addresses contain the second-most important kind of table, the Program Map Table (PMT). Each radio or TV channel that is distributed in the transport stream is called a "service" and each service has its own PMT. In the PMT of each service, the receiver can find the PID for each component of that service. For a TV channel, that would be the PIDs that are associated with the video, the audio and the teletext information bit streams.

DIGITAL VIDEO BROADCASTING

Digital Video Broadcasting (DVB) is the standard for digital broadcasting that was first adopted in Europe. The original standard was based on MPEG-2 encoding of the video and Musicam encoding of the audio. In addition to referring to these standards, the DVB standard also tells how to combine several services as radio and TV channels in a multiplex. This is important if you wish to distribute the signal using satellite, cable or terrestrial transmitters. The DVB standard also contains rules for how the signals are to be distributed through three kinds of distribution media; DVB-S (Satellite), DVB-C (Cable) and DVB-T (Terrestrial)

In the United States there are some other digital TV systems, but DVB has proved to work very well and is now adopted in the U.S. and other parts of the world. The DVB standard also includes other kinds of tables containing information to the viewer about what programs are on right now and what comes up next.

Statistical Multiplexing

DVB is very much about how to putting several radio and TV services together to form a program bouquet contained in a transport stream.

We have already seen that the need for a large capacity in a video signal that varies all the time depending on the video content. In a multiplex of six to eight channels not all of the channels will need maximum capacity all the time. Sharing the capacity of a multiplex among the channels—giving the most bandwidth at any given moment to the most demanding channel at that moment—optimizes the use of the available capacity.

This is called statistical multiplexing and increases the usable capability by approximately 20 percent. In this way, a satellite transponder (having a capacity of 44 Mbit/s) that normally houses eight channels will instead be capable of handling 10 channels. A terrestrial DVB multiplex with a capacity of 22 Mbit/s will be able to handle five instead of four TV channels.

An optimum way of using statistical multiplexing is to combine channels containing lots of motion (such as sports channels and music video channels) with less demanding channels (such as news channels and channels which contain a lot of studio content) as in Figure 2.9.

FIGURE

2.9

Statistical multiplexing takes advantages of the variations in motion and capacity demands across the channels in a multiplex. (See color plate.)

Receiving the DVB Signal

Figure 2.10 illustrates the basic principles for treating the digital signal inside a digital set-top box. This is a visualization of how the signals are routed through the receiver, but of course, in reality, you can't follow the signals in this way. Large portions of the device are based on a computer, some memory and rather complex software.

All receivers have some kind of a front end. This front end, or tuner, is used to choose the transmission channel that is to be received from the radio spectrum. The transmission channel may be a signal from a satellite transponder, a cable TV channel or a terrestrial channel that contains a multiplex of digital radio or TV channels. The tuner is designed according to whether it is to receive signals from satellite, cable or terrestrial transmitters.

This design also applies to the demodulator that follows the tuner. The demodulator is different depending on what transmission media is to be used but its general purpose is to restore the transport stream.

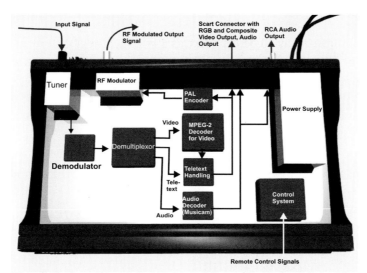

FIGURE

2.10

The digital receiver contains a number of basic functions. The tuner selects the desired transmission channel. The demodulator restores the transport stream. Then the demultiplexor sorts out the signal into its original components.

At the output of the demodulator, we obtain the transport stream. After this point, the signal is treated exactly the same regardless of what media has been used for transmission (satellite, cable or terrestrial).

The heart of the digital receiver is the demultiplexor. In the demultiplexor, the different tables in the transport stream are read and the receiver learns how the received signal is arranged. At the output of the demultiplexor, the different bit streams of the service that has been selected by the viewer are sent to the appropriate decoder. The information contained in the video packets is sent to the MPEG-2 decoder. The content of the audio packets are sent to the Musicam decoder and the teletext information is sent to the teletext system. In digital receivers, the teletext pages (which only exist in Europe) are stored in memory so the viewer can instantly select the desired page. Another alternative is to reinsert the teletext pages into the analog composite video signal and to use the teletext system that is integrated in the TV set. Sometimes both these methods are used simultaneously.

If the transmissions are encrypted, the decryption process also takes place in the demultiplexor system. Then the demultiplexor is connected to a CA (conditional access system) and the card reader that is associated with that part of the device.

There are at least three different methods for connecting the digital receiver to one or more TV sets. The simplest and giving the best results is to use the RGB-signals that may be obtained from the scart output. The scart connector, covered in more detail in Chapter 9, is a 21-pin connector with separate connections for the three color components of the color video signal. A scart cable has to be used to connect the digital receiver to the TV set to keep the three color signal components, R, G and B, separated all the way from the TV station to the set. This ensures optimum performance. Even the stereo audio channels are included in the 21-pin scart connector in a convenient way. The scart connector is a typical European device.

However, a video recorder can not handle RGB signals. The digital receiver must also have a composite video output containing a PAL signal. For this reason there is a composite video encoder in the device. The composite video signal is also available on one of the pins in the scart connector. Composite video can be used in most video devices as well as in all DVD recorders. European digital receivers always have the composite video integrated in the scart connection. However there are Asian and American receivers that also have a composite video output on an RCA connector.

Other interface options for connecting HDTV digital receivers
The introduction of plasma and LCD TV sets has introduced some new interfaces for the video signals. In the flat-panel TV sets as well as video projectors, there are also connections for component video. This interface consists of three RCA outputs carrying the luminance, Y signal and the two color difference signals. The component interface has been in use for video projectors for a long time and is also quite common in more expensive DVD players and recorders. Component outputs allow for progressive scanning, which is discussed further in Chapter 11, "The Home Cinema."

There are also other important digital interfaces, such as DVI and HDMI, that allow for digital connection between the receiver and the TV set. These interfaces are available in expensive DVD players but only HDTV receivers carry these interfaces so far. The same applies to the component video interface. We will take a closer look at this in Chapter 12.

High definition signals require either component, DVI or HDMI connections between the digital receiver and the display system.

Scart cables are quite thick and tough to handle if they are not quite short, so the signals may only be distributed to devices that are located quite close to the receiver. For this reason, the receiver usually has an integrated modulator (a small TV transmitter). Using the RF output of digital receiver makes it possible to connect the receiver through the aerial input of the TV set. Then ordinary coaxial cables may be used to distribute the signal to one or more TV sets in other rooms. A disadvantage of doing this is that the picture quality is lower and the audio will be restricted to mono.

PICTURE AND SOUND QUALITY

Bad analog signals result in noisy pictures and noisy sound. There is a big difference between analog and digital signals when it comes to distortions. Analog terrestrial TV is subject to reflections and white Gaussian noise. Analog frequency modulated signals are subject to spike noise but there are no reflections.

In digital TV, the audio and video is always the same, as long as the signal is strong enough to allow for reception. If reception is bad audio and video disappears completely, leaving a black screen and no audio at all.

However there is a thin window between useful reception and loss of signal. In this range you will get errors, called pixilation, in the picture. Pixilation is not really the right word. What you actually see on screen are the so-called "macro blocks" of the picture. When the picture is compressed for transmission, the encoder divides the picture into small squares, macro blocks. If the signal contains too many errors, the MPEG-2 decoder has problems in restoring some of the macro blocks in the right way, such as in Figure 2.11. You may also see freezing effects in the picture.

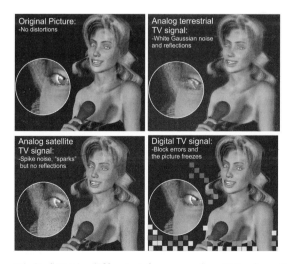

FIGURE

2.11

Digital TV is different from analog TV when it comes to distortions. Either you have a perfect picture or no picture at all. However there is a very narrow range between acceptable reception and loss of signal where you will see blocking effects in the picture. (See color plate.)

The DVB standard is used for satellite, cable and terrestrial distribution (see Figure 2.12). When watching TV over the Internet, MPEG-1 is still very much in use. In the last two years, IP-based TV (IPTV) through broadband connections has started to become the fourth way of distributing TV. In this case, the old copper wiring that once was used for telephony is used for media. Since higher bitrates may be used, MPEG-2 signals are encapsulated in IP packets instead of DVB packets. We will return to this in Chapter 7, "Digital TV by Broadband."

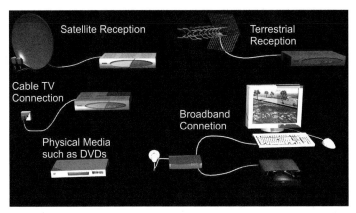

FIGURE

2.12

The digital TV signals may be transported and stored using any kind of distribution media. The MPEG standards are in use everywhere, even on physical media, such as DVDs.

MPEG-4: HDTV COMPRESSION

MPEG-2 is the compression standard that is used for DVB standard definition TV distribution. MPEG-2 is also used for high definition terrestrial broadcasting in North America and for some satellite based channels. However there is a new compression standard that will change everything.

MPEG-4 is the successor of MPEG-1 and MPEG-2 and may be used at all bitrates from 10 kbit/s to several Mbit/s. The new standard could be said to combine the best of performance in MPEG-1 and MPEG-2 and the same format can be used for signals having very low as very high bitrates. Therefore MPEG-4 is suitable for low bitrate Internet TV as well as standard definition and high definition TV. On top of this, MPEG-4 is much more efficient that MPEG-2. With MPEG-2, a bitrate between 3 to 5 Mbit/s is required for standard TV while MPEG-4 can produce an acceptable quality at bitrates down to 1.5 Mbit/s, if cutting-edge technology is used. MPEG-4 is also easier than previous formats to combine with computer graphics.

MPEG-4 is definitely a better way to compress video signals than the earlier standards. However, it seems that we are already stuck with MPEG-2. For standard definition TV, an immense number of MPEG-2 DVB compliant devices have already been sold.

Using MPEG-4 over the Internet is much easier since you only have to download a new codec for your software media player. Changing the standard in set top boxes is much more difficult.

But when it comes to HDTV, the bandwidth savings of MPEG-4 is very large. Today's European HDTV transmissions are carried out using the MPEG-2 format via satellite. It takes about 16 Mbit/s per TV channel to be able to handle HDTV in this way. Changing to MPEG-4 will require only 6 to 8 Mbit/s per channel. No doubt HDTV will be the most important use of MPEG-4 during the years to come. MPEG-4 can be carried inside DVB packets just as MPEG-2 is.

Another example of MPEG-4 is the DivX-format, which is based on this technology.

There are also some flash memory video cameras that use MPEG-4 to provide increased recording time, like the one in Figure 2.13. These video cameras provide video recording with devices that do not have any moving parts, so the power consumption is less and they are very small. And all this is really only due to the fact that they are using efficient compression algorithms. In the long run these smaller MPEG-4 cameras will replace cameras with cartridges and records.

FIGURE
2.13

This tiny, flash-memory-based video camera from Mustek is an example of an MPEG-4 device.

WHY CHANGE TO DIGITAL TV?

Of course people who have been satisfied with analog television might wonder why they should invest in digital receivers to view ordinary TV programs. Really, they might argue, there are analog systems providing acceptable picture and sound.

However this is not the complete truth. Those who try digital TV quite soon experience the increased performance. This could be compared with the introduction of the DVD. Having tried a DVD recorder, there is no way back to the VHS machine. People getting used to the superior performance from DVD recordings also want to be able to watch TV without noisy pictures and with a clear noiseless sound. This is also the reason why people are prepared to pay extra for the DVD version of a movie rather than the VHS edition. The same thing happened when the CD was introduced. People soon bought CDs for twice the price as an old LP.

Digital video always provide a guaranteed level of performance in the picture as well as in the sound.

3 | Satellite TV

FIGURE

3.1

Satellite TV is based on space technology.

Since the dawn of man, the horizon has been the limit of visual observation. At the end of the nineteenth century, humans started to get interested in radio waves, and quite soon it became evident that the horizon was still an obstacle for the propagation of this new means of communication.

In the early days of radio, only low frequency and long wavelength signals were used. These signals are reflected into the atmosphere and can reach beyond the horizon. That's why it is possible to receive radio from distant stations in the long-, medium- and shortwave frequency bands. Unfortunately, the reception is not very reliable, since the atmospheric conditions vary with time of day and weather. As an example, it is easy to listen to radio station from all of Europe in the medium waves at night while reception tends to be more local during the day. The same applies to short- and medium-wave reception all over the world.

In the 1950s, television was introduced in most European countries. Since a TV signal contains about 250 times as much information as a radio channel, more frequency space was required. To get access to more bandwidth, it is necessary to move to higher frequency ranges. However, radio waves at higher frequencies have the disadvantage of not being reflected in the atmosphere and propagate into space instead. The only solution is to locate transmitters close enough to each other that reception from beyond the horizon is never necessary.

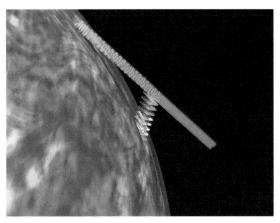

FIGURE

3.2
Radio waves at lower frequencies are reflected in the atmosphere in a random way. Radio waves at higher frequencies are not to a larger extent reflected in the atmosphere. In order to allow for broadband services, such as television, higher frequency bands must be used in order to get bandwidth that is large enough.

The higher the transmission towers are, the further the distance to the horizon will be, and the larger the area with a free line of sight from the transmitter will become. There are practical limitations for the maximum height of a transmission tower. In Europe there are many towers with a height of about 300 m (1,000 feet). This corresponds to the height of the Eiffel Tower in Paris. A 300 m transmission tower will cover a circular area with a radius of about 50 km (30 miles).

Constructing even higher transmission towers increases the coverage, but it is difficult. The tallest transmission tower ever built was in Poland and reached a height of 646 meters (2,120 feet). Twenty-five years after it was constructed, the tower collapsed during repair work. The tallest transmission tower today is in North Dakota and reaches a height of 628 meters (2,063 feet). TV transmission towers are the tallest buildings that have been constructed by the human being so far.

It is quite obvious that there are practical limitations for the height of transmission towers, but it would be desirable to get access to a much higher tower than the highest that has ever existed. There were early ideas about putting radio transmitters into aircraft and balloons. But keeping an aircraft or a balloon on location for years would have been impossible from a practical point of view.

In the October, 1945, issue of the radio amateur magazine "Wireless World," Arthur C. Clarke, who later became one of the most well-known science fiction writers, described something completely new. He claimed to have found a way to put a satellite in orbit around the Earth. The satellite would seem to be located at a stationary point in the sky relative to a specific location on the surface of the Earth. This would be the equivalent of an immensely high transmission tower.

The word satellite means "follower." A body of matter that is in orbit around the Earth also follows the Earth in its orbit around the sun. The moon is such a follower and orbits the Earth in slightly less than one month (perhaps the source of the name "moon"). The distance to the moon varies depending on its position in the Earth's orbit, but is at an average of about 384,400 km (238,855 miles). The time required to orbit the Earth at this distance is 27.3 days. An object in orbit around the Earth at a smaller distance will also make one turn in less time. An example of this is the space shuttle, which is in orbit at a height of about 300 km (186 miles) and circles the Earth in about 90 minutes.

Sir Arthur Clarke's ingenious idea is based on the assumption that there must be a distance from Earth where the satellite will orbit the planet in 24 hours. The distance is approximately 36,000 km (22,370 miles), which is about one-tenth the distance to the moon. Since the diameter of the Earth is about 1,200 km (746 miles), it would be possible to fit three globes in between the satellite and the Earth, as shown in Figure 3.3.

In order to get the satellite to move in an orbit that is synchronous with the rotation of the Earth, the orbit has to be parallel to the Earth's equator. The satellite must also move eastward and be at the distance of the geostationary orbit, 36,000 km (22,370 miles). If these conditions are all fulfilled, the satellite will appear to be in a fixed position in the sky in relation to any point of the Earth's surface.

Note

During the decades that followed, the world witnessed several more examples of Arthur C. Clarke's imagination and genius. In "Year 2001 – A Space Odyssey," he described a future spaceflight to Jupiter. This story was filmed at the end of the 1960s by Stanley Kubrik who was also ahead of his time. Clarke was finally raised to nobility for his feats.

FIGURE

3.3

The geostationary orbit is at a distance of 36,000 km (22,370 miles) from the Earth.

The big advantage of a radio transmitter in a geostationary orbit is that about 40 percent of the Earth's surface will have a free line of sight for the satellite. This is a significant difference to what may be achieved from a transmission tower located at the surface of the Earth. Since there is an optical free line of sight between the satellite and the receiver, much higher frequencies can be used. When transmitting from satellites, the microwave frequency bands, which have much more bandwidth than terrestrial frequency bands, are used. By the end of this chapter, we will take a closer look at how many channels may be transmitted simultaneously from each orbital position of the geostationary orbit.

However, there is no use in having a satellite that cannot be controlled from Earth. There also has to be a feed with programs that are transmitted from a ground station. This feed is called the uplink and the signal returning to Earth is the downlink (see Figure 3.4). In the satellite, there is a frequency conversion of the incoming signal. It is not possible to use the same frequency in the downlink as in the uplink.

But one satellite is not enough to cover the entire surface of the Earth. In his first article on geostationary satellites, Arthur C. Clarke suggested a system of three satellites that could communicate with each other, as in Figure 3.5. The three satellites together cover all of the Earth, except a limited area around the poles (where there are almost no humans at all). By communicating between the satellites, it will be possible to communicate between almost any points on Earth. These "intersatellite links" are not today used for TV distribution but they are of great importance for other professional and military purposes.

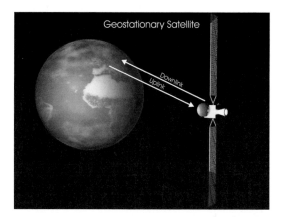

FIGURE

3.4
The signal from Earth toward the satellite is the uplink and the signal route back down again is the downlink.

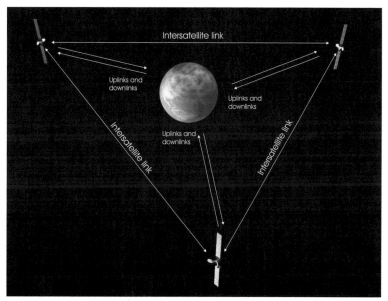

FIGURE

3.5
Already in his first article in Wireless World, Arthur C. Clarke anticipated the future use of "intersatellite" links.

One use is the communication between space stations and space shuttles and ground control. Manned spacecraft usually cruise above the Earth's surface at an altitude between 300 km (186 miles) and 600 km (372 miles), which permits communication with at least one of the three satellites. In Houston, at NASA Mission Control, only one antenna is needed to be in contact with one of these satellites and maintain constant contact with the astronauts. Previously, communications stations were needed all over the world in order to ensure continuous communication. Of course, this kind of satellite systems has a great military importance in order to be able to communicate with low-orbit spy satellites.

THE ROUTE TO ORBIT

Launching a satellite into orbit around the Earth is not that easy. The Germans developed the first long distance rockets during the World War II. The man in charge of all this was Werner von Braun, who, after the war, got to manage the development of American rockets in the space race against the Russians. Ultimately, he was in charge of the Saturn rocket of the Apollo project that led to getting the first man on the Moon.

Almost 19 years after Arthur C. Clarke's article about placing a satellite in geosynchronous orbit, this feat became a reality. In August, 1964, the first geostationary satellite, Syncom 3 was launched.

To use a minimum amount of fuel at launch, it is necessary to choose a location as close to the equator as possible. The French space consortium Arianespace uses a base in Korou in French Guyana, in northeastern South America. The location is just some 5.3 degrees north of the equator, making it a very suitable place for launching geostationary satellites.

If an orbit is not in the same plane as the equator, it is said to be inclined. If a satellite is launched from a location directly on the equator, it is possible to send it directly into a non-inclined orbit by launching it either straight to the east or west. It is also possible to launch the satellite into any inclined orbit by choosing another direction.

If the satellite is launched from a non-equatorial location, the satellite cannot be launched into a less inclined orbit than the latitude of the launching site because the center of the orbit must coincide with Earth's gravitational center.

When launching from the pad in French Guyana, the primary orbit will be inclined by at least 5.3 degrees. To compensate for the inclination and get the satellite into a non-inclined orbit it is necessary to use an upper rocket stage. The larger inclination, the more fuel will have to be used and the larger the launcher has to be. For this reason, the closer the launch site is to the equator, the smaller and cheaper the rockets can be.

In the U.S., the geostationary satellites are normally launched from Cape Canaveral in Florida. The latitude is at about 28.5 degrees and the orbits will be much more inclined than is the case from the French base at Korou. Somewhat larger launchers are used to compensate for the greater incline.

The Russians had big problems in getting their first geostationary satellite launched. It was not until 1976 that the Soviet Union launched its first geostationary satellite for distribution of TV, EKRAN-M. The location of their base in Baikonur in Kazakhstan, at a northern latitude of 45.6 degrees, was one of the challenges.

Putting a Satellite in Orbit

We will now take a closer look at how a satellite launch can be done. For this example, I have selected a launch using the now retired Ariane IV rocket that was used at Korou. This was a rocket especially popular to launch geostationary satellites.

The rocket had a height of 60 m (197 feet) and included three stages. The first and second stages used fluid oxygen and other fuels, while the third stage used a combination of liquid oxygen and hydrogen. This is an extremely explosive combination.

Ariane IV was capable of launching two satellites simultaneously, if one of the satellites was smaller. In these pictures, the launch of two medium size satellites is shown. A large thunder breaks loose as the giant rocket start to move upward. It is now T + 10 seconds, right at the start of the spaceflight. The giant first stage is assisted by four solid fuel rocket boosters to clear the tower. Solid fuel boosters are very good at providing a large thrust for a short time.

Quickly after clearing the tower, the rocket turns to the east as it passes over the Atlantic. Since the rocket is above water, it is easier to handle the falling

FIGURE

3.6

T + 10 seconds: An Ariane IV rocket has just cleared the tower.

rocket stages and boosters. And if anything should go wrong, it is also possible to let the rocket explode without causing too much damage.

At T + 1 minute and 7 seconds, the four solid rocket boosters are jettisoned and fall into the Atlantic. They have now done their job, providing that extra thrust necessary in the first stage of the launch. The first stage continues to add more speed to the equipage until it reaches an altitude of 85 km (53 miles), when it shuts down and the second stage takes over. We are now at T + 3 minutes and 35 seconds. The idea of using several stages is that it is possible to get rid of used parts as the rocket reaches higher altitudes and speed. This reduces the weight and makes it easier to continue acceleration of remaining parts using less fuel.

FIGURE 3.7 T + 1 minute and 7 seconds: The solid rocket boosters are dropped.

FIGURE 3.8 T + 3 minutes and 35 seconds: The first stage is separated.

At T + 4 minutes and 45 seconds, the rocket is at an altitude of 118 km (73 miles). For comparison, the ordinary cruise altitude of a commercial airliner is at about 10 km (6 miles) and the Concorde cruised about twice as high. At an altitude of 118 km (73 miles), the atmosphere is very thin and the faring that covers the satellites can be jettisoned. The air resistance protection provided by the faring is now less than the cost of its weight.

FIGURE

3.9

T + 4 minutes and 45 seconds: The protective faring is jettisoned to save weight.

At T + 5 minutes and 58 seconds, the second stage is shut down start to fall back into the atmosphere. The third stage will burn for about 12 minutes and is now in charge of getting the two satellites into their orbits. The altitude

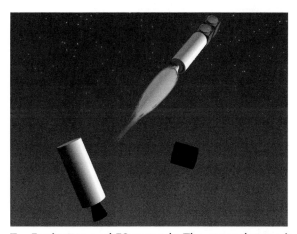

FIGURE

3.10

T + 5 minutes and 58 seconds: The second stage is separated.

is now about 150 km (93 miles) and the primary task of the third stage is to increase the speed rather than to further increase the altitude.

At about T + 18 minutes, the third stage has finished its burn at an altitude of about 250 km (155 miles). The remaining parts of the rocket and its cargo are now in geostationary transfer orbit (GTO). The final actions are now to separate the two satellites from the rocket.

FIGURE

3.11

T + 17 minutes and 46 seconds: The satellite and rocket reaches geostationary transfer orbit and the third stage shuts down.

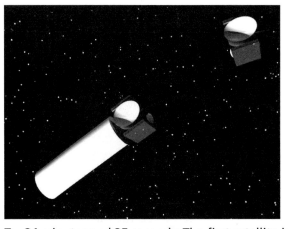

FIGURE

3.12

T + 24 minutes and 25 seconds: The first satellite is separated.

The second satellite is separated. The launch is a success.

Both satellites are now in a geostationary transfer orbit. They will remain in this orbit for a few days while all systems are checked and until the satellites are in an appropriate position for the next phase, the injection to geostationary orbit (GSO).

Both satellites safely in their own geostationary transfer orbit.

In the satellite itself we can find the forth stage, the apogee engine. The apogee is the uppermost point of an elliptical orbit. The lowest point in an elliptical orbit is called perigee. In order to obtain optimum result, the apogee engine is burned when the satellite is at its apogee. A lot of fuel will be consumed during this operation. A large satellite weighs about 4,000 kilograms

(8,800 pounds) at launch. Almost half of this weight consists of fuel that is used to circularize the geostationary orbit into a pure geostationary orbit and to get rid of the inclination.

In addition to this, there is fuel for station keeping of the satellite throughout its lifetime. Since the equatorial plane of the Earth is leaning in relation to the orbital plane of the solar system, the other planets and the moon will make a pull on the satellite. All these gravitational powers slowly pull the satellites into inclined orbits if no station keeping maneuvers are done.

An average satellite lifespan is 10 to 15 years. The consumption of fuel used for station keeping varies but may be in the range of 25 kilograms (55 pounds) per year.

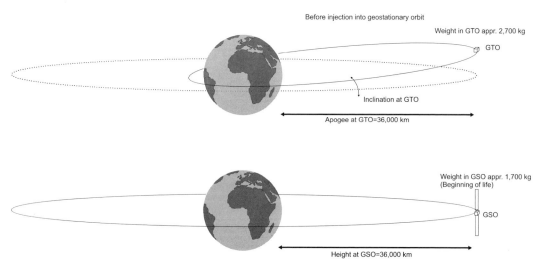

FIGURE

3.15

The satellite must gain more speed to get from geostationary transfer orbit, GTO, into geostationary orbit, GSO. The orbit also has to be adjusted to get rid of the inclination.

FIGURE

3.16

The apogee engine is fired to adjust the satellite into geostationary orbit.

Ariane V: the latest rocket technology
During the last years, efforts have been made to develop more powerful rockets. The most efficient choice of fuel is the combination of liquid oxygen and liquid hydrogen. The space shuttle is a good example of this technique. The shuttle has an external fuel tank containing liquid oxygen and hydrogen that is transferred to the main engines of the spacecraft. In addition to this, there are two solid rocket boosters with solid fuel. The successor of Ariane IV, Ariane V, also is based on similar principles.

FIGURE

3.17

The new generation of launchers, such as Ariane V, uses liquid oxygen and liquid hydrogen as fuel.

> *Initially, the goal of the Ariane V project was to make a rocket that could make European manned missions a reality. However, the budget has not been big enough to allow for these projects. Instead European astronauts have to go with American or Russian spacecraft.*

LAUNCH VEHICLES FROM ALL OVER THE WORLD

Apart from the space shuttle, the Americans have based their launchers on old designs that have been in use for decades when launching from Cape Canaveral. Both the Atlas and Delta rockets have been used for many years but the designs have been continuously updated in new models and versions. In space industry, relying on old designs is not considered wrong—proven designs are regarded as more reliable than new and untested technology.

In the beginning, the intention was to use the space shuttle to launch satellites, but this plan proved not to be very economical. There is no real use to bring along astronauts to do "simple" missions like launching a communications satellite.

Since the breakdown of the Soviet Union, the Russians have been struggling to commercialize their space industry. Russia has an agreement with Kazakhstan to continue to use their Baikonur base to launch satellites (using

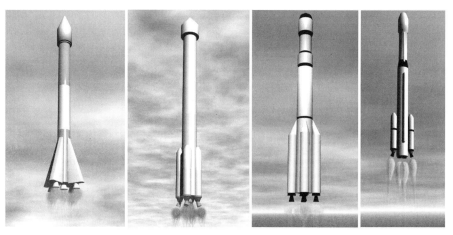

FIGURE

3.18

From left to right, the American Atlas IIA and Delta II, the Russian Proton K rocket, and the Chinese "Long March."

reliable Proton-type rockets) and manned spacecraft. On top of this, Russian rockets are used in the new Sea Launch system that will be described later on.

Today, the Chinese have their own launcher, the "Long March." They have also started their own manned missions. The Chinese astronauts are called "taikonauts." The Russian astronauts are called cosmonauts. Thus far, there is no special name for Europeans in space.

Sea Launch

A very exciting new initiative is Sea Launch—a very unconventional way of launching a satellite. The basic idea is to launch the rockets at sea in an area that is right on the equator and in a region with stable weather conditions. Combining Norwegian oil rig technology with Russian rockets and other space technology from Boeing, this seems to be a winning concept.

This concept is very favorable when it comes to aspects of security. It is possible to choose an area where there is quite little ship traffic and the launching company does not have to pay any government because the launch takes place in international waters.

FIGURE

3.19

Sea Launch has made it possible to launch geostationary satellites from a spot right on the equator.

STABILIZING SATELLITES

Once a satellite is in orbit around the Earth, it must become a stable platform for radio equipment. To get it all to work, the satellite must be in a stable orbit and the antennas must always be perfectly aligned with Earth, providing the right coverage areas.

Spin Stabilized Satellite

A simple way of avoiding uncontrolled tumbling of the satellite in space is making it spin. Anything spinning becomes stable around its spinning axis. A good example is a toy top spinning on the table. As soon as the top is spinning, it balances on the sharp point that is in contact with the table or the floor. Another example is a bicycle, where the large wheels spin and form two spinning axes that won't lean. This is why it's easy to ride a bike without focusing on the balance once you have reached a certain speed. A spinning axis does not want to change direction.

A spinning satellite consists of a cylinder that spins around its own axis. On top is an antenna that spins in the opposite direction. This is necessary since the antenna always has to point towards Earth. Spin stabilized satellites have always been regarded as being very reliable and still today this kind of satellites are still manufactured. A spin stabilized satellite is rotating around its axis about once a second.

One limitation of spin stabilized satellites is the number of transponders (the equipment required to distribute one analog channel or a multiplex of eight to 10 digital channels) it can carry. Since about two-thirds of the surface of the satellite's solar panels is not exposed to sunlight, it is not possible to obtain as much energy as a three-axis stabilized satellites (covered in the next section). Therefore the number of transponders that can be fitted into a spin stabilized satellite is limited to about 15.

The designers of the spin stabilized satellites have tried to compensate for the power problem by adding an outside skirt with additional solar cells. This skirt can be pulled out as soon as the satellite is in orbit. However, the limitations are so great that other designs are preferred in order to get a higher output of power.

Figure 3.20 shows the Hughes HS 376. The total height of the satellite in orbit is about 8 m (26.25 feet).

Three-Axis Stabilized Satellites

Using the three-axis stabilized satellite technology makes it possible to build much more powerful satellites. The attitude of a three-axis stabilized satellite is computer controlled. This computer controls momentum wheels that can be accelerated or slowed down to control the attitude by means of inertial forces.

FIGURE

3.20

Hughes HS 376 is the most common spin stabilized satellite platform.

In weightlessness, only inertial forces and the use of thrusters will make anything move in a certain direction. We have to completely rely on the mechanical laws of inertia.

The three-axis satellite always turns its Earth panel towards Earth. On the Earth panel, the antennas are mounted and point towards the desired coverage areas on the Earth's surface. In order to make this possible, the satellite platform has to make one turn around its own axis every 24 hours.

The main idea of using three-axis stabilized satellites is that the solar panels, mounted on two giant wings extending north to south, can be turned by servo motors to keep their broadsides pointed toward the sun. This maximizes the possibilities to obtain and store solar energy, enabling the satellite to contain more than twice the number of transponders of a spin stabilized satellite. The average three-axis stabilized satellite has a wing span of about 25 m (80 feet) and can hold more than 30 transponders (carrying 30 multiplexes).

There are even larger satellites. The Hughes 702, with a wing span of almost 46 m (150 feet), can house up to 72 transponders. However, some companies believe it is better to split up their transponders on several platforms as protection if anything should go wrong. In addition, technology continues to develop and a large number of digital TV channels may be contained even in smaller satellites. So there might not really be a need for those really large satellites, at least not at present.

Hughes is not the sole manufacturer of satellites in the world. There are other manufacturers in the U.S. and Europe, though the number of companies that have been able to survive in the increased competition is not that many.

The rapid technical development in the industry has forced them to form larger consortiums.

FIGURE

3.21

A three-axis stabilized satellite as the Hughes HS 601 is much more advanced and complicated than a spin stabilized satellite.

Satellite Life Expectancy

The largest problem with satellites is keeping them in the correct orbit, which requires thrusters to maintain the geostationary orbit. As mentioned earlier, satellites are placed in order with a supply of fuel for these adjustments; that fuel is generally expected to last for 12 to 15 years. There are techniques to reduce the fuel consumption, such as using an ion propulsion system. This system accelerates ionized fuel using electricity from the solar panels. In this way, the impulse created by the fuel is much larger than using conventional thrusters.

But the satellite manufacturers are not interested in developing satellites that have more than 20 years of life. The satellite manufacturers do not want to destroy their markets for the future. Therefore, the fuel reduction is used to decrease the weight of the satellite instead.

And there are also other things that would limit the lifetime of the satellite when the fuel problem is solved, such as the transmission equipment. The TWTs (traveling wave tubes) that are used for generating the transmission power have a limited lifespan, though there are some spare ones aboard the satellite. Another problem is the number of times that the onboard batteries may be recharged and the decreasing power of the aging solar panels.

SATELLITE PAYLOAD: THE TRANSPONDERS

All signals that are to be transmitted by the satellites have to originate somewhere. The satellite signals are transmitted from uplink stations that often use quite large antennas. In the antenna, the uplink power is concentrated into a narrow beam that is directed towards the satellite.

The uplink signals are generally transmitted at very high frequencies. Frequency bands that are used in Europe are 14 and 18 GHz.

FIGURE

3.22 The signals are transmitted towards the satellite using an uplink station. The uplink antenna is quite large and concentrates the uplink power into a narrow beam directed straight to the satellite.

Digital TV channels each have a very low bitrate, so they have to be collected into multiplexes to fill a complete transponder. The satellite transponder is a radio channel with a bandwidth of about 30 MHz. In the analog era, an FM-modulated TV channel would fill an entire transponder. Today 8 to 10 channels (or more) fit into a DVB multiplex that results in a total bitrate between 38 and 44 Mbit/s, which is suitable to fill the transponder bandwidth. One single TV channel uses about 4–5 Mbit/s.

Figure 3.23 shows the principal design of a satellite transponder.

The uplink signal is received by a parabolic antenna directed towards Earth. The first thing that happens inside the satellite is that the received signal is amplified. However it is not possible to retransmit the signal in the same frequency band as the uplink, so the signal is down-converted into the downlink frequency band. In Europe normally frequencies in the range 10.70–12.75 GHz is used. Finally, the downlink signal is amplified to an output level between

Conventional transponder with in AGC mode
(One analog TV channel or a multiplex of digital TV channels)

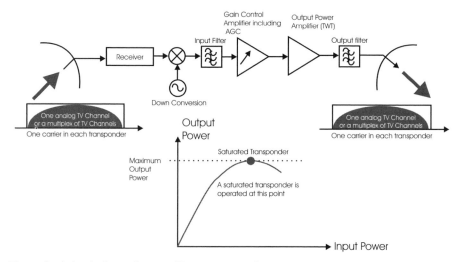

FIGURE

3.23

The principle design of a satellite transponder.

50 and 100 watts before the signal is beamed back to Earth using a downlink parabolic antenna on the satellite. In today's satellites, it is possible to use the same antenna for reception as well as for transmission in the satellite.

The performance of the satellite transponders are, to a large extent, decided by the transmission tubes. In most satellites traveling wave tubes, TWTs are used. These tubes work very much like other kinds of amplifiers. If the input power is increased so is the output power.

If the output power is quite low, the tube operates in its linear mode. If the output power is increased and we get closer to the maximum output power (the curve showing the output power versus the input power), the tube will bend and we get into the non-linear region of the tube's operational curve. The tube is said to be saturated when it is at maximum output power. Since this is the maximum output power of the tube, it is desired that the tube operate at this point when making transmissions to the general public so they can use the smallest antennas possible.

However, there is a problem in using saturated amplifiers. As can be seen in Figure 3.23, the output power as a function of the input power is not a straight line at the top of the curve. As a result we can only have one carrier in the transponder in order to get this to work. If we had several carriers in the transponder in non-linear mode, the carriers would mix with each other, causing intermodulation problems. Then new, unwanted signals would have appeared in the transponder. The effect is similar to what happens if you turn up the volume of your audio amplifier to its maximum—it doesn't sound very good. This is due to the occurrence of intermodulation products that are created inside the audio spectrum.

So it is necessary to have only one signal in the transponder. In the analog days, this was no problem since there was only bandwidth enough to house one TV channel in each transponder. But now, digital TV requires the multiplexing of several channels into one carrier to fill the entire transponder. Multiplexing means combining the bit streams of several digital TV channels into one single bit stream and is covered in Chapter 4.

Another transponder feature is the gain control amplifier that has an AGC (Automatic Gain Control) facility. The AGC keeps the output signal of the transponder at a saturated level, even if the incoming signal on the uplink is attenuated due to rain or other problems at the uplink station site.

Satellite Frequencies and Capacity

The satellites that distribute TV in Europe operate within the downlink frequency range of 10.70–12.75, a frequency range that is 2050 MHz wide. Each transponder occupies about 30 MHz of bandwidth. A very common bandwidth is 33 MHz.

Terrestrial broadcasting transmissions are limited to the frequency range below 1 GHz (1000 MHz). This means that each satellite orbital position gets more than twice the bandwidth than terrestrial systems.

The frequency range between 950 and 2150 MHz is called the L-Band. This frequency range is used to transport the signals from the parabolic dish into the satellite set-top box that is located close to the TV set. We will dig deeper into this in Chapter 4, "Digital TV by Satellite." We will also take a look at the terrestrial frequencies in more detail in Chapter 5 "Digital TV by Cable," and Chapter 6, "Digital TV by Terrestrial Transmissions."

Satellites have a giant frequency range. Not only is the frequency range twice that of terrestrial systems, it is actually (in the European case) four times larger than the terrestrial frequency ranges because of the polarization isolation of antennas that can be used for transmission and reception in the microwave bands is very high.

Therefore, satellites can use the same bandwidth twice. The satellites transmit both horizontal and vertically polarized signals and the available frequency range is doubled to a total of 4100 MHz. (More on polarization in Chapter 4).

Due to this, it is possible to fit 160 transponders in each orbital position over Europe. Of course, this means you need more than one satellite, because most satellites cannot house more than 30 or 40 transponders. While 160 transponders could have been used to transmit 160 analog channels, with digital technology they can easily carry between 1,200 and 1,600 channels. In the years to come, the numbers will be increased even more due to new and better compression techniques.

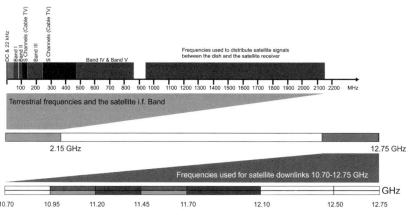

FIGURE

3.24

Frequency bands that are used for satellite transmission in Europe. (Appendix B covers the North American frequency bands.)

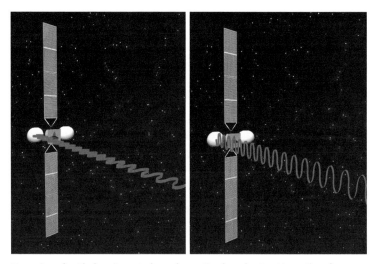

FIGURE

3.25

By using both horizontal and vertical polarization the frequency range may be used twice.

Every orbital position can contain a vast number of TV channels. But in addition, to this there are lots of orbital positions. The satellites are located like a string of pearls around the Earth's equator. One way to tell the position of a geostationary satellite is by the longitude of the site on ground that is right below the satellite on the equator.

The longitude divides the Earth into 360 degrees around the equator of the Earth. Zero degrees longitude is at the longitudinal line that passes through the observatory at Greenwich just outside London, called the Greenwich meridian.

If you move south from Greenwich until you end up at the equator, you will be right below the orbital position of 0 degrees. At this special orbital position, you will find a very special satellite, the Meteosat Atlantic satellite. Meteosat is a satellite-based weather surveillance system and you have probably seen weather pictures from this satellite. Then you have also gotten a glimpse of what the Earth looks like as seen from a geostationary satellite.

The orbital positions are calculated in degrees east and west of the Greenwich meridian, as the longitude of the point at the equator that is straight below the satellite.

FIGURE

3.26
The geostationary orbital positions are based on the longitude of the location that is straight below the satellite on the equator. The vertical lines mark longitude and the horizontal ones mark latitude.

Distance Between Satellites

A very common question is if there is any risk of collision between the satellites if there are in the same orbital position. An orbital position is not a small area, but rather a very large cube in space. The orbital position is really a "controlling box" approximately 100 km (60 miles) on each side, within which the satellite is allowed to move. Since station-keeping maneuvers are done only once every two weeks, the satellite is allowed to move within this quite extensive area.

With this large controlling box, it would have to be a coincidence (and really bad luck) for two satellites to get dangerously close to one another. But still, some security rules have been installed. For two or more satellites share the same orbital slot, they must be built by the same manufacturer and have the same ground control system. If two satellites of different kinds are to be co-located, they will have 0.2 degrees of separation. The satellites really are not in the same orbital slot, but would seem to be when using quite small antennas.

The next problem is what distance is required between two orbital slots in order to be able to use the same frequencies. The answer depends on the antenna size used for reception on ground. Large antennas have more narrow beams than small antennas. For professional satellite traffic, an orbital separation of three degrees has been chosen. This will work fine down to an antenna diameter of about 90 centimeters (3 feet). If even smaller antennas are used, there is a risk for inter-satellite interference. Smaller antennas will require a larger separation angle.

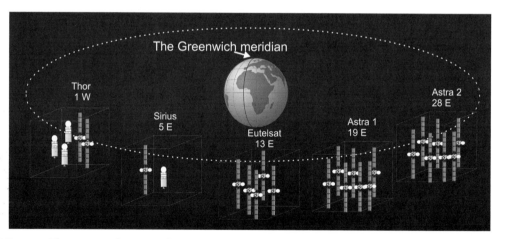

FIGURE 3.27   The geostationary orbit, as seen from space, along with its control boxes.

Satellite Antennas

The satellite illuminates the Earth's surface as a spot light would, and it is possible to direct the beams towards the desired countries and regions. The larger the antenna, the more narrow the beams and the smaller areas may be selected to be covered.

In the early days of geostationary satellites, it was not possible to launch and control large antennas in space. The coverage areas were very large and the power was spread over a big area. In combination with low output power from the satellites, it became necessary to use extremely big antennas on ground.

Today the transmission antennas in the satellites are parabolic dishes with a diameter of one and two meters and smaller areas on the Earth's surface can be covered with the larger antennas. An antenna of about 1 m (3.2 feet) in diameter will cover the whole of Europe if transmission is in the Ku-Band (12 GHz). Smaller areas, such as individual countries, are covered by antennas about two meters in diameter (6.6 feet).

During the 1990s, it became possible to shape the beams to follow the contours of the continents. This is now achieved by deforming the circular reflector in a way that deforms the beam from the antenna in a controlled way. The most fascinating thing is that the manufacturers today have computerized simulators that are able to predict what the beams will look like as soon as the satellite is in orbit if the reflector is deformed in a certain way.

Satellite Coverage Areas

The two main competing satellite systems in Europe are SES Astra and Eutelsat. Astra has two orbital slots, 19 degrees east and 28 degrees east. The 19 degrees east slot contains a mix of European channels, with the German channels most prominent. The second slot contains a wide representation of English-language channels.

Eutelsat's main position, the HOT BIRD position, is 13 degrees east. Here you will find a lot of Italian channels but also channels from other South European countries. Eutelsat has a giant fleet of satellites and has also bought some regional satellite systems.

There are still some smaller regional satellite systems. Some of them are partly owned by the larger satellite operators.

Figure 3.28 through 30 show some typical coverage areas for some important European satellites. In these maps, the signal strength is indicated by curves representing different signal levels. Chapter 4 provides a closer look at how to read these maps and decide what dish diameter is required to receive signals from the satellites. The weaker the signal, the larger dish is required.

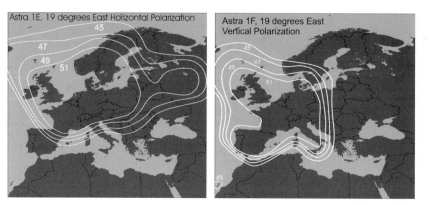

FIGURE

3.28

Examples of coverage areas for Astra's main orbital position, 19 degrees east.

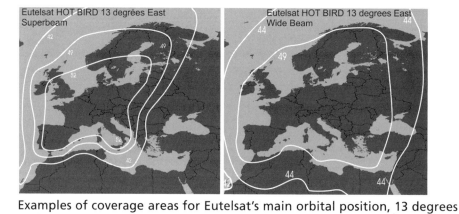

FIGURE

3.29

Examples of coverage areas for Eutelsat's main orbital position, 13 degrees east.

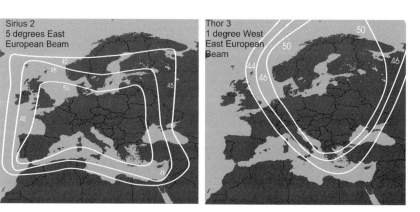

FIGURE

3.30

Examples of European coverage areas for two of the more regional satellite systems: Sirius at 5 degrees east and Thor at 1 degree west.

WHAT IS THE EQUIVALENT ISOTROPIC RADIATED POWER?

In the coverage diagrams, the curves indicate the signal strength from the satellite at different locations (comparable to height curves on a map). The signal strength is expressed in a unit called Equivalent Isotropic Radiated Power (EIRP). An isotropic source of radiation is a radiation source that radiates the same amount of power in all directions. The sun is an example of an isotropic source of radiation (see Figure 3.31).

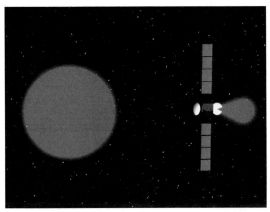

FIGURE

3.31

The satellite only has to produce a narrow cone of power. This is the reason why the TWTs of the satellite still can produce high EIRP levels.

If we are standing at a location on the Earths surface experiencing a certain radiation level from the satellite, the EIRP is the output power of a radiating source that would radiate the same power as we are experiencing but in all directions simultaneously. But a satellite is not an isotropic radiator. It uses an antenna to focus the transmitted power towards a limited area on the Earth's surface. This means that the EIRP can be much stronger than the actual output power of the satellite.

The reason why we are making a comparison with an isotropic radiation source is because such a source is well defined (a reference that simply radiates in all directions). The unit used for the EIRP in the coverage maps is called dBW. Watt (W) is a way to express power. Decibel (dB) is a figure representing a relationship. In this case, it is the relationship to the power of 1 Watt.

A relationship in linear scale may be recalculated to the decibel scale according to the formula in Table 3.1.

TABLE

3.1

The relationship in dB scale = 10 * Log, The relationship in linear scale, where Log stands for the 10-logarithm.

Watts	Decibels
1 W	0 dBW
2 W	3 dBW
4 W	6 dBW
10 W	10 dBW
100 W	20 dBW
1,000 W	30 dBW
10,000 W	40 dBW
100,000 W	50 dBW
1,000,000 W	60 dBW

The measurements you find in the coverage areas are around 50 dBW, which would correspond to 100,000 W. But it is obvious that a satellite transponder having an output power of about 100 W (the power consumption of an ordinary light bulb) cannot produce an output power of 100,000 W.

As discussed above a satellite is able to transmit this large amount of power towards a certain location because 100 Watts of output power is concentrated within a narrow beam using the transmitting antenna, rather than being sent off in all directions. With an output power of 100 W it is possible to achieve a high EIRP within a limited area using a directional antenna as is the case in a satellite.

Chapter 4 describes what diameter is required at different EIRP levels. A simple rule is that 51 dBW corresponds to a diameter of 60 cm (2 feet) and 45 dBW corresponds to a diameter twice as large, 1.2 meters (4 feet). Chapter 4 also includes more coverage diagrams and tables showing the relationships between EIRP and dish diameters.

4 | Digital TV by Satellite

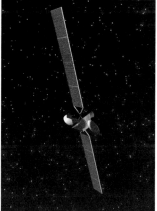

FIGURE

4.1

Satellite TV opens up window to the world outside.

The previous chapter described how the geostationary satellites distribute TV and radio channels using beams of microwave radio waves covering extensive areas on the Earth's surface. We will now move down to Earth and see how we can make use of the satellite signals.

SATELLITE POSITIONS AND POWER

Seen from ground, the geostationary orbit looks like a curve in the southern sky that extends from east to west (see Figure 4.2). From a location at the equator the orbit looks like a line straight across the sky. The orbital position that corresponds to the longitude of the location is straight up. The part of the geostationary orbit that is visible from the central parts of Europe is approximately between 60 degrees west and 90 degrees east, depending on location. This is 150 degrees of the 360 degree geostationary orbit. Orbital positions further to the west or further to the east are closer to the horizon and harder to receive. Positions even further away fall below the horizon. Orbital positions can be placed at a distance of three degrees apart, so about 50 orbital positions may be located within the visible part of the orbit.

The maximum angular height, elevation angle, of the geostationary satellites varies between 45 degrees in the southern parts of Europe and 10 degrees in the most northern parts.

FIGURE

4.2

The geostationary orbit extends from east to west in the southern sky. Here some of the more important European orbital positions are shown.

FINDING THE SATELLITE

We will soon return to the parabolic dish and what happens after that the signal has been concentrated at the focus. But first we will take a closer look at what it takes to point the antenna right towards the desired satellite.

When I first started working with satellite TV, more than 20 years ago, it was more or less a mystery to find a satellite. It was hard to calculate where in the sky the satellite really was. Today nobody has to care about that, because there are maps showing where in the sky to find a specific satellite wherever you are. As soon as you know the angles toward the satellite, the next step is to apply them in practice to the antenna.

Elevation Angle

The first angle is the angle of elevation to the satellite. This angle is the height of the satellite in degrees (see Figure 4.3). In the old days, it was easy to decide the angle of elevation for the center-feed parabolic dish most common then. The boresight direction of center-feed antenna is at right angles relative to the edge of the aperture of the dish (see Figures 4.2 and 4.36).

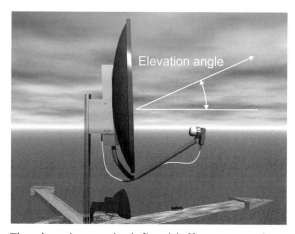

FIGURE 4.3   The elevation angle defined (offset antenna).

Today, most parabolic antennas are of the offset kind. These antennas are created by a segment being cut out from a deep parabolic surface, as in Figure 4.4.

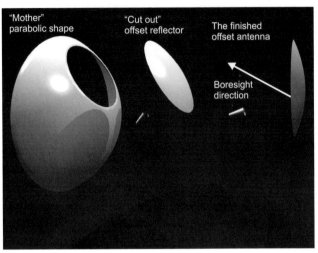

"Mother" parabolic shape

"Cut out" offset reflector

The finished offset antenna

Boresight direction

FIGURE

4.4

The offset antenna is created by a section being cut out from a deep parabolic surface.

The result is an antenna that does not have a symmetrical profile, making it hard to know the boresight direction of the antenna. The boresight direction of the antenna is the view direction of the antenna, the direction in which the antenna is most sensitive. The manufacturer might have put a scale or some kind of reference plane on the antenna identifying the elevation angle. The mount of the antenna has to be mounted absolutely vertically to ensure a correct angle based on the scale provided. (This is easily done with a water level or a weighted string.)

Azimuth Angle

The other angle that we need to know is the azimuth angle of the antenna. The azimuth angle is the angle between north and the location of the satellite. This is always counted clockwise. Figure 4.5 shows that a satellite located straight to north has an azimuth angle of 0 degrees, to the east has an azimuth angle of 90 degrees, to the south is 180 degrees and west is 270 degrees.

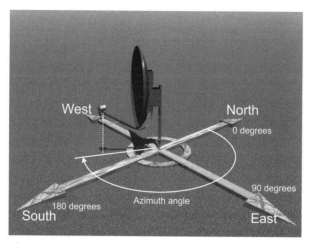

FIGURE

4.5

The azimuth angle defined.

A satellite positioned at a longitude that is more to the east than the longitude of the receiving site has an azimuth angle that is less than 180 degrees. A satellite positioned to the west of the reception site has an azimuth angle that is greater than 180 degrees.

Note

A common error is caused by people using compasses that have 400 degrees instead of 360 degrees when searching for satellites. In the satellite business, all angles are based on 360 degrees.

Even if you know the elevation and azimuth angles, it is not really that easy to find the satellites. It is also quite hard to transfer the azimuth angle to an antenna in practice. It is quite hard to know the point of the compass with any accuracy. Compasses only provide an approximate direction towards the north and are disturbed by metal objects that are close by.

Figures 4.6 through 4.17 are elevation and azimuth maps for some important European orbital positions. Elevations angles are read to the right and azimuth angles are on top. First is SES Astra, a part of SES Global, that operate satellites at three major orbital positions; 19 degrees east, 28.5 degrees east and 23.5 degrees east.

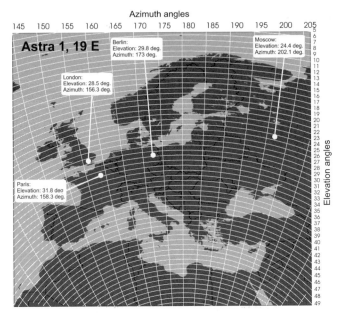

FIGURE

4.6

The main position of Astra at 19 degrees east, elevation and azimuth angles.

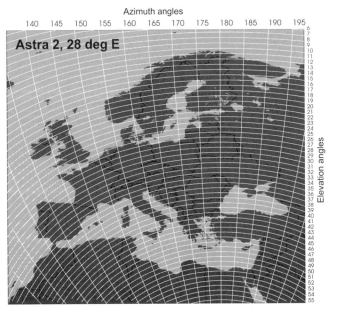

FIGURE

4.7

SES Astra's second orbital position is at 28 degrees east.

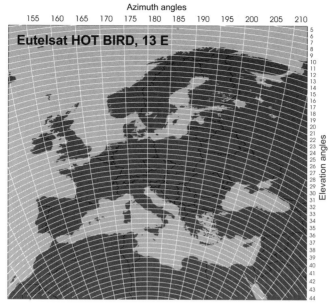

Azimuth angles

Eutelsat HOT BIRD, 13 E

Elevation angles

FIGURE

4.8

FIGURE

4.8

The most Eutelsat's most important orbital position is the HOT BIRD position at 13 degrees east.

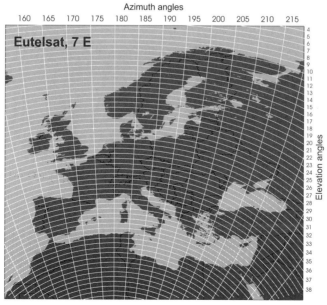

Azimuth angles

Eutelsat, 7 E

Elevation angles

FIGURE

4.9

Eutelsat's orbital position at 7 degrees east.

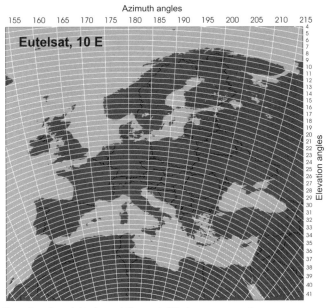

FIGURE 4.10

Eutelsat's orbital position at 10 degrees east.

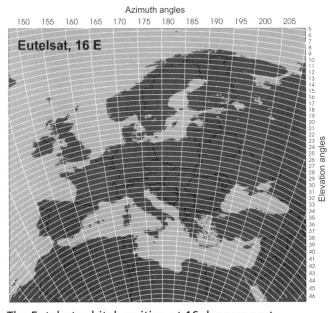

FIGURE 4.11

The Eutelsat orbital position at 16 degrees east.

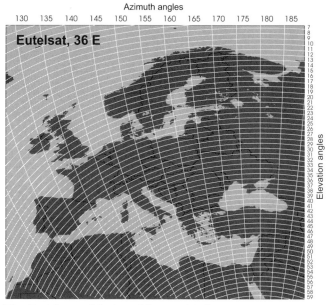

FIGURE

4.12

The Eutelsat orbital position at 36 degrees east.

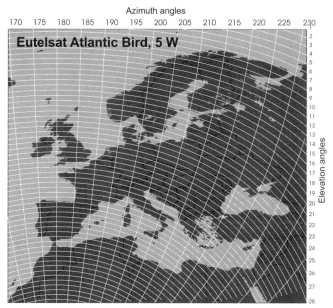

FIG

4.13

The Eutelsat Atlantic Bird orbital position at 5 degrees west.

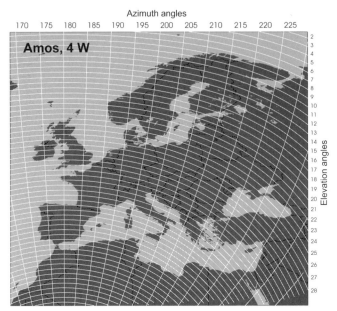

FIG   The Amos orbital position at 4 degrees west.

4.14

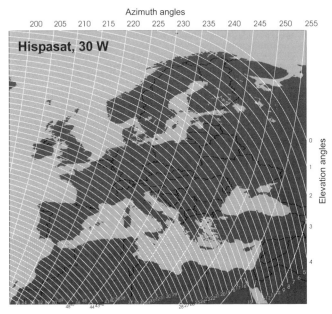

FIGURE   Farther west, we find the Spanish Hispasat system.

4.15

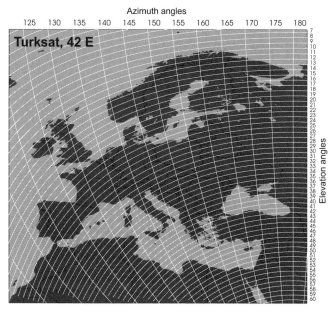

Farther east, we have one of the Turkish Turksat orbital positions.

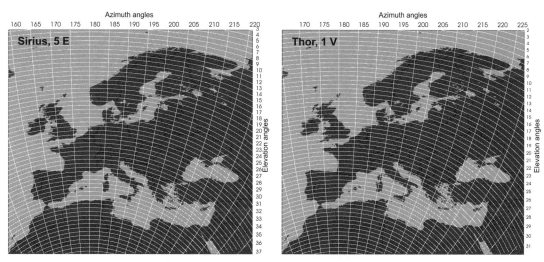

The "Sirius" and the "Thor" satellite systems are Scandinavian regional satellite systems that also have European coverage areas.

POSITIONING THE DISH

When installing a parabolic dish, a free line of sight to the satellite is a necessity. Sometimes there might be obstacles such as trees or buildings, and it may be hard to know if there is a free line of sight towards the satellite. But with the elevation and azimuth angles, it is possible to check the visibility to the satellite. The main problem is determining the antenna location without having the actual antenna in place for testing.

There are special aiming compasses which are a great help for testing the visibility. The Suunto compass is primarily intended for the lumbering industry in order to be able to measure the height of a tree without first having to cut it down but is a handy tool for determining the proper placement of satellite dishes.

FIGURE

4.18

There are professional instruments for finding the satellites, but you can also build your own.

Another cheaper alternative is using a protractor and a weighted string. If you look along the protractor, as in Figure 4.18, you can check the visibility at a certain elevation angle.

The trick of quickly finding the right satellite when pointing the dish is starting with the elevation angle. This angle is easier than the azimuth angle to determine, since a weighted string or a water level easily determines an exact vertical line. From this line, the exact angle of elevation can be measured. This measurement is easier if there is an integrated scale for the elevation angle in the antenna design. If there is no such scale, there might be a plane of reference in relation to which the true elevation angle is known. Check for that in the installation manual for the antenna.

Since the angle within which a satellite dish is sensitive is very narrow, it is hard to find the correct angle towards the satellite. You should first point the antenna in approximately the right direction to give yourself a better chance to actually look for the signal.

When you believe the antenna is pretty close to the right elevation angle, the next step is to search for the satellite by adjusting the azimuth angle and hopefully the satellite signals will show up.

By starting with the elevation angle, you avoid the tough task of establishing a true north-to-south line, which is necessary for deciding the azimuth angle prior to installation. And even if this direction is accurately known, it is almost impossible to use this knowledge to accurately point the antenna, because it is hard to transfer the direction to the antenna itself. Since you can attach a weighted string directly to the antenna, it is much easier to get to know the true elevation angle and to read the actual azimuth angle.

Satellite signals are really very weak. A typical satellite transponder has an output power of less than 100 Watts. This is comparable to the power consumption of an ordinary light bulb. The power is spread across an area that might be as large as Europe. Still, it is possible to receive the signals using a relatively small antenna. A parabolic dish with a diameter of 90 centimeters has an area of barely 0.65 square meters. Compared to the surface of Europe, the signal power collected by the dish is almost nothing; in technical terms, it is in the range of pikowatts, i.e., 0.000000000001 watt (12 decimals).

To handle the extremely low signal levels, we first have to collect all power that gets into the antenna. The easiest way of doing so is by using a parabolic reflector that optically concentrates the signal towards its focal point (see Figure 4.19). A lot of the power that hit the antenna could be found in the

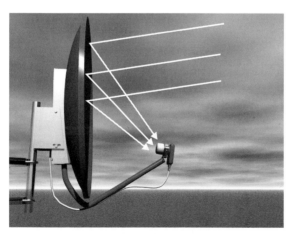

FIGURE

4.19

The parabolic dish concentrates the incoming power to one point, the focus.

focus. However there are losses that reduce the amount of useable power to about 55 to 75 percent.

LOW NOISE BLOCK CONVERTERS (LNBS)

When the received signal power has been concentrated in the focal point of the reflector, it has to be collected and treated further. The dish focus contains a Low Noise Block converter (LNB). There are three tasks for the block converter: amplify the weak signal, down-convert it into a lower frequency range, and choose polarization and what part of the frequency range that is to be received. The reason the signals have to be down converted is because microwave high frequency signals are attenuated too much to be transported to the receiver.

Inside the LNB, there are two small antennas about a quarter of a wavelength long. This would mean about 6 millimeters (in the 12 GHz band the wavelength is about 2.5 centimeters). The antennas are oriented at right angles to each other so that one receives the horizontal signals while the other receives the vertical. The antennas are followed by a low noise amplifier that usually consists of two low noise transistors.

The low noise transistors amplify the signal to about 20 dB, corresponding increasing the signal power level by 100 times. Now the signal goes to a mixer where it is mixed with a locally generated oscillator signal. After the mixer, a new signal is obtained that has the frequency which corresponds to the difference between the incoming signal and the local oscillator signal.

The LNB takes care of a complete "block" of frequencies that are amplified and converted to a lower frequency range. In the childhood days of satellite TV, there were low noise converters that could receive signals from just one transponder. Being able to receive a larger frequency range was a real sensation in those days and there was a demand for a "block" converter.

The down-converted signals coming from the mixer are amplified by an additional 30 dB (1,000 times) by two or three other transistors before the signal is fed to the indoor satellite receiver.

The Amazing Noise Reduction
These low-noise transistors are truly the miraculous part of the complete satellite reception system. Throughout the years, the noise figure (the noise level created by the transistors themselves) has decreased to between 0.3 and 0.6 dB. This might

not sound impressive, but about 20 years ago the noise figure was at about 2.5 dB. The decrease in noise level has also meant a decrease in dish size—a 1.5 meter dish only needs an antenna of about 88 centimeters in diameter. It is this decrease in dish size that has made the antennas small and opened up for cheap satellite TV for everyone.

Universal LNB

SES Astra saw the need for an LNB with a large input frequency range and suggested an LNB covering the whole range from 10.70 to 12.75 GHz. This is called the Universal LNB. To use the whole range, the frequency range has to be divided into two parts. The lower part is 10.70 to 11.70 GHz and the upper part is 11.70 to 12.75 GHz. As described above, a signal can be down-converted to a lower frequency by being mixed with a locally generated signal, the local oscillator signal. The down-converted signal is found at a frequency that is the difference between the frequency of the incoming signal and the local oscillator frequency.

If the frequencies in the lower frequency band are mixed with a local oscillator of 9.75 GHz, the difference with the signals of the incoming signals in the 10.70 to 11.70 GHz band will be signals in the frequency range of 0.95–1.95 GHz. Just the same, when the incoming signals are in the upper frequency band, 11.70-12.75 GHz, and the local oscillator frequency is 10.60 GHz, the difference between the signals will be between 1.10 and 2.15 GHz. Therefore, the LNB has to be able to switch between two local oscillator frequencies: 9.75 and 10.60 GHz.

Another result is that, a universal LNB will generate output signals in the range of 950 to 2150 MHz. This frequency range is called the satellite intermediate frequency band, or the L-Band, and is used to transport the signals from the LNB to the satellite receiver that is placed close to the TV set.

When a 22 kHz tone is sent from the receiver on the cable, the upper frequency range should be received and the LNB is switched to the 10.60 GHz local oscillator. With no tone on the cable, the lower frequency range should be received and the 9.75 GHz local oscillator should be in operation.

On top of this, the receiver must also be able to switch between vertical and horizontal polarization by switching between the two small antennas in the feed horn of the LNB. A way of doing this is by changing the supply voltage to the LNB between 14 volts for the vertical polarization and 18 volts for the horizontal polarization.

In order to be called a universal LNB, there is still one more requirement to fulfill. The LNB also must be able to receive digital, phase-modulated signals.

Finally the distance between the parabolic dish and the receiver should not exceed more than between 20 and 30 meters (70 to 100 feet). If this distance is exceeded, thicker cables or line extending amplifiers (line extenders) might be needed.

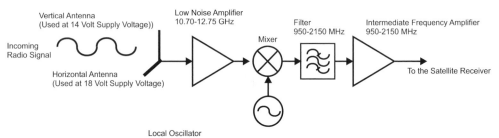

FIGURE 4.20   The principal design of a universal LNB.

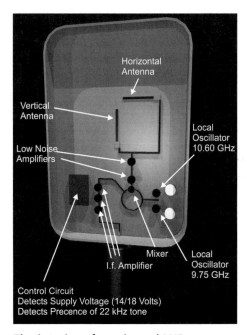

FIG 4.21   The interior of a universal LNB.

THE SATELLITE RECEIVER

The satellite receiver is an indoor device that receives signals in the frequency range of 950 to 2150 MHz (also called the L-Band). Since satellite TV is a truly multi-channel media, the receiver must be equipped with a processor and software that is capable of handling all the channels. This processor also controls the supply voltage to the LNB as well as the presence or absence of the 22 kHz tone. This controls the frequency range of the LNB to receive the TV channel requested by the viewer.

When the signal from the LNB enters the satellite receiver, it is first handled by the input stage, the tuner. The main purpose of the tuner is to select which transponder is to be received. To be able to do this, the tuner also has to send the right supply voltage to obtain signals of the right polarization, as well as supply the 22 kHz tone if the requested transponder is located in the upper part of the frequency band (11.70–12.75) GHz. The most important thing, however, is that the tuner chooses a more limited frequency range around the selected transponder and down-converts the signal further to a second intermediate frequency around 480 MHz. At this frequency, there is a filter that has a bandwidth of about 30 MHz (approximately corresponding to the bandwidth of a transponder).

Now the desired carrier containing the content in the requested transponder is sent on to the demodulator. The demodulator's job is to recover the digital bit stream of the digital DVB-S multiplex. In digital satellite TV, the most common kind of modulation is Quadrature Phase Shift Keying (QPSK). In this modulation scheme, the radio wave alternates between four different phase angles.

When the signal is demodulated and the original transport stream has been recovered, the next step is to demultiplex the transport stream to find the audio, video and teletext packets that belong to the selected TV channel. Last, these packets are sent to the audio and video decoder respectively. The rest of the process has already been described in Chapter 2.

Differences in Analog and Digital Satellite Receivers
The things that differentiate the digital satellite receiver from other kinds of digital receivers (cable and terrestrial) are the input frequency range of 950 to 2150 MHz and the QPSK demodulator. In addition, we have the signals that control the universal LNB, including the variable (14/18 volt) supply voltage and the 22 kHz signal injection.

Since phase modulation is used when transmitting digital signals via satellite and it is essential that the local oscillators in the LNB are very stable and produce a very stable phase angle (not produce any phase noise). If the phase angle of the local oscillators is unstable, the satellite receiver cannot decide whether this is due to the modulation signal or something else.

Analog satellite receivers were not sensitive to phase errors in the local oscillators so the designers of analog LNBs did not care about this. The introduction of digital satellite TV has meant that lots of old LNBs have had to be exchanged. Many digital satellite receivers also require that there is a universal LNB connected because the software is more or less adapted for the control signals to switch frequency range and polarization.

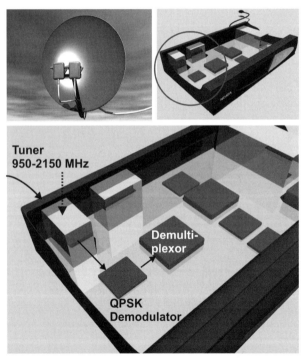

FIGURE

4.22

In the satellite receiver there is an input stage, the tuner, covering the frequency range 950–2150 MHz. This is followed by a demodulator capable of handling Quadrature Phase Shift Keying, QPSK.

MODULATING DIGITAL SIGNALS

Radio waves are electromagnetic waves that are created when electrons are moving forth and back in an electrical conductor. All radio waves originate in electrical oscillator circuits. If you wish to build an electrical oscillator, you can take the output signal of an amplifier and connect it to the input of the same amplifier, which will make the amplifier oscillate. If the oscillating amplifier is connected to an electric conductor, the electrons inside the conductor start to oscillate as well. But when electrical charges (as the electrons are) begin to move forth and back, electromagnetic waves start to propagate from the conductor.

When this radio wave hits another electrical conductor, the electrons in this conductor also start to move forth and back following the same pattern as in the "transmitting" conductor.

We have succeed in transferring the movement of electrons in the transmitting conductor (antenna) to the electrons in the receiving (conductor) in a completely wireless way.

However there is no reason to transfer this movement of electrons if there is no message carried by the radio wave. What we want to do is to use the radio wave as a carrier of information, a carrier wave.

Amplitude Modulation

The first technology for getting the wave to carry information was amplitude modulation, AM. AM is based on letting the strength or the amplitude of the radio wave vary in line with the signal containing the information that we want to transfer.

AM has been in use since the beginning of the twentieth century but has some critical drawbacks.

Amplitude modulation does not require that much bandwidth but on the other hand is quite sensitive to disturbances. Therefore AM requires quite a lot of transmission power in order to suppress noise and interference. AM has been used for transmission of the video in the analogue terrestrial TV networks.

Frequency Modulation

A better analog way of modulation is frequency modulation, FM. Frequency modulation is based on varying the frequency of the carrier wave in line with the message signal that is to be transferred. FM has a better resistance to noise and interference but also occupies more bandwidth than AM. In analog satellite transmissions of TV, frequency modulation has been used, because bandwidth is less expensive than transmission power.

Phase Modulation

When carrying digital signals, we only have to carry two messages, the digits "0" and "1." Therefore there are other more efficient ways to modulate a carrier wave than using AM or FM. The third way of modulation is phase modulation, PM. Phase modulation is achieved by letting the wave make a phase jump, as in Figure 4.23. In the simplest phase modulation scheme, the wave jumps in between two phase angles. This is called Binary Phase Shift Keying (BPSK). Each of the two phase positions symbolize the digits "0" and "1" respectively.

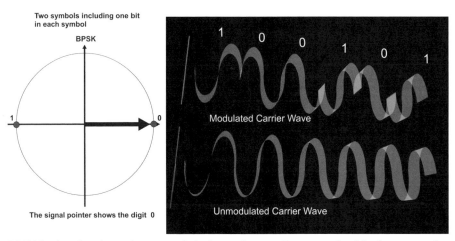

FIGURE 4.23

BPSK is the simplest phase modulation scheme. Compared with the unmodulated wave, the modulated wave has phase jumps that do not exist in nature.

Quadrature Phase Shift Keying (QPSK)

When it comes to distribution of digital TV via satellite, a higher modulation scheme that is used, Quadrature Phase Shift Keying (QPSK).

In QPSK, there are four phase angles instead of two so each phase angle represents a combination of two digits or bits: 00, 01, 10 and 11. As a result, the radio wave may carry twice as many bits as a BPSK modulated carrier jumping around at the same speed. This means the bandwidth of a QPSK modulated carrier will only be half the bandwidth of a BPSK signal. In other words, we get twice the bitrate through a transponder when using QPSK instead of BPSK. However this benefit comes with a cost. The phase angles in a QPSK signal are closer to each other so twice the amount of transmission power or twice the size of receiving antenna will be required when moving to QPSK.

Note
  The satellites of today have enough output power to make QPSK the best choice.

There are even higher modulation schemes that we will take a closer look at in the next chapter. In these modulation schemes, there are more phase angles and even several amplitude levels. Using higher modulation schemes makes it possible to get a higher bitrate throughput in the transponders but at the cost of signal quality and therefore requiring larger antennas. For this reason these schemes are only used for professional purposes when distributing via satellite.

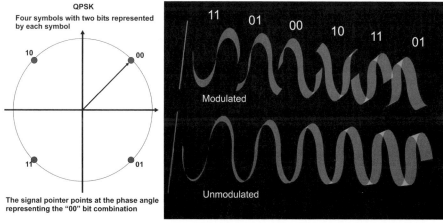

FIGURE

4.24

Satellite distribution to the general public is based on QPSK. The modulated carrier wave has small, 90-degree jumps in phase that do not exist in the unmodulated wave.

ERROR PROTECTION AND TRANSMITTED BITRATE

In digital transmission, there are different ways of protecting the signals from disturbances. In Chapter 2, the Reed Solomon encoding technique, where 16 additional bytes were added to each packet, was described. This technique could correct up to eight errors in a packet.

This kind of error protection is used in satellite transmissions. But there is another way of securing the quality of the signal.

Forward Error Correction

By adding yet more bits to the complete signal—not on a packet-level but on a bit stream-level—the transmission quality can be secured even more. This method is called Forward Error Correction (FEC).

There are different levels of FEC. In the least ambitious level, FEC=7/8 is used. FEC=7/8 means that the extra error-protecting bits will occupy one-eighth of the total number of bits in the bit stream.

The other levels of FEC are 5/6, ¾, 2/3 or 1/2, and they require even more capacity. In the most ambitious level, FEC=1/2, half of the bits in the bit stream are required for error correction. The most common level of FEC is ¾, which is regarded as a suitable compromise between quality and use of capacity for error protections.

The bitrate calculation for a conventional 33 MHz satellite transponder may look as follows:

The useful bitrate is 38 Mbit/s. Adding 16 bytes for Reed-Solomon protection on the 188 byte packets will increase the bitrate to ((188 + 16) / 188) * 38 Mbit/s = 41.2 Mbit/s. A further use of FEC=3/4 will increase the bitrate to 41.23 * 4 / 3 = 55.0 Mbit/s. If QPSK is used to transfer this signal, the symbol rate (the speed at which the signal jumps between different phase angles) will be 27.5 MS/s (mega symbols per second).

Note
   The symbol rate is one of the parameters that you will find when navigating the installation menus of a digital consumer satellite receiver trying to make a manual channel search.

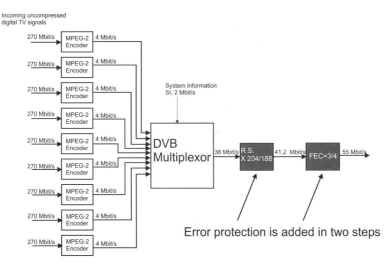

FIGURE

4.25

In the uplink station, error protection is added in two steps before the signal is beamed towards the satellite.

DISH SIZE

The output power of a satellite is spread across an extensive area. The weaker the signal, the larger the antenna required to collect enough signal power for the LNB to produce a useable signal.

In EIRP maps showing the power radiated towards areas on the Earth's surface, it is possible to read what dish size is required at a certain location. You do not have to think a lot about decibels or dBW; instead you may regard the EIRP as a measured value. See Table 4.1.

It is of interest to notice that 6 dB corresponds to a factor of 4 when it comes to the surface of the antenna and a factor of 2 when it comes to the diameter of the antenna. In other words, if the signal strength of the satellite is increased by 6 dB, a dish with half the diameter will produce the same result, while a decrease of power by 6 dB would mean a requirement to double the diameter of the dish.

TABLE

4.1

Suitable antenna diameters at corresponding EIRP levels in Ku-Band which is the frequency band normally used in Europe.

EIRP (dBW):	Antenna Diameter (meters):
41	1.90
42	1.69
43	1.50
44	1.34
45	1.20
46	1.07
47	0.95
48	0.85
49	0.75
50	0.67
51	0.60
52	0.53
53	0.47

Figure 4.26 shows EIRP maps with examples of some important European satellite systems. (Figures 3.28 through 3.30 on page 64 show some others.)

Using these maps with Table 4.1, you can build a quite good view about what dish size is required. More coverage maps may be found in the Web sites of the satellite operators.

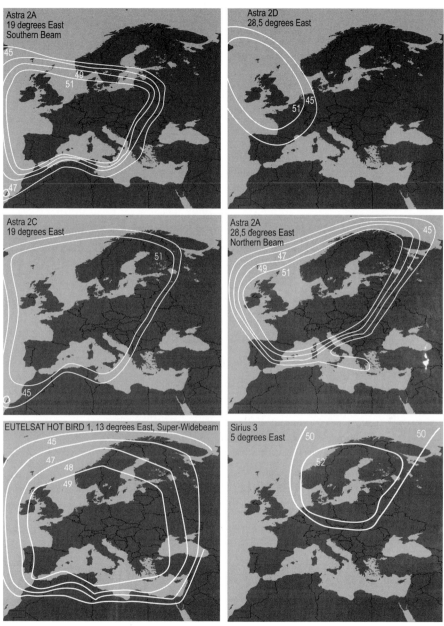

FIGURE

4.26

By reading the EIRP in the maps and the antenna diameter in Table 4.1 identify the dish size required for reception.

MULTI-SATELLITE ANTENNAS

In the beginning of satellite TV, a separate antenna was always used for the reception of each satellite. But soon people wanted to receive signals from several orbital positions. In an ordinary home or on the balcony of an apartment, you don't want to have a dish farm. Times are since long gone when it was status to have a satellite dish.

New kinds of multi-satellite antennas have been developed. By putting more than one LNB in a parabolic dish, it is possible to get a fixed antenna to look in several directions toward different orbital positions.

A parabolic dish actually has several focal points. A signal hitting the dish along its main axis is concentrated in the main focus. This, of course, is the most efficient focal point. However, a signal hitting the dish from a slightly different angle will get concentrated at a secondary focal point. This focal point is not as efficient as the primary, but still useable to locate a second LNB. This LNB can be used to receive signals from a second orbital position.

In Table 4.2, the antenna size required for the use of a secondary focal point at different EIRP values is shown. In comparison to Table 4.1, where the LNB is located in the primary focus, a larger antenna is needed. The values in Table 4.2 are based on an example separation between the primary and the secondary orbital slot of six degrees, such as between Astra 1 at 19 degrees east and Eutelsat HOT BIRD at 13 degrees east.

In the Scandinavian countries, such antennas are used for simultaneous reception of signals from the Sirius and Thor systems that are also at a separation of six degrees.

TABLE
4.2

Antenna Diameter Required for Secondary Focus (six degrees of separation)

EIRP (dBW):	Antenna Diameter (meters):
44	1.90
45	1.69
46	1.50
47	1.34
48	1.20
49	1.07
50	0.95
51	0.85
52	0.75
53	0.67
54	0.60
55	0.53
56	0.47

The "Two-Orbital Position" Dish

The most common multi-focus antenna is the dish covering two orbital positions. Many Europeans are interested in receiving both main positions of the Astra and Eutelsat systems at 19 and 13 degrees east respectively. Six degrees of separation is the magical figure.

There are two ways of designing a two-focus antenna. One way is letting one of the LNBs be in the main focus providing maximum efficiency for one of the positions. The second LNB is located in a way that gives six degrees of separation. Pointing the antenna towards Eutelsat, 13 degrees east, optimize the antenna for this orbital position. Letting Astra use the secondary focus will require better signals from this orbital position. This could be a good compromise, since Eutelsat HOT BIRD, having some of its transponders in a wider European beam, provides some weaker signals than Astra and therefore needs a stronger receiving position. Still, stepping up from a 60- to an 80- or 90-cm antenna will provide good reception of both orbital positions in most parts of Central Europe. However, if you are at the edge of coverage, other solutions might be better.

Another alternative is to put both LNBs in secondary focus with a distance of just three degrees from the direction that is obtained at the main focus. In this case, the dish is pointed towards a direction which is right between both orbital slots. Half of the manufacturers that make multi-focus antennas in Europe use this kind of design for the dual orbital position dish.

However, in multi focus antennas there must be a way for the receiver to switch between the LNBs. The Digital Satellite Equipment Control (DiSEqC) system was initiated by Eutelsat to solve this problem.

The idea is using the 22 kHz tone, which is also used for frequency band selection in universal LNBs, to send short telegrams to remote controlled switches that are placed in the antenna. To be able to switch between Astra and Eutelsat HOT BIRD, we would need a two-way DiSEqC switch (see Figure 4.27). Inside the switch there is a small decoder that reads the messages in the 22 kHz tone. Thus, by using smart addressing the satellite receiver can make the switch to see to that the receiver always get signals from the right LNB.

Earlier tone switches using continuous 22 kHz tones to be able to switch between LNBs cannot be used with modern digital receivers and universal LNBs, since the continuous tone is engaged in switching frequency bands. Therefore all switches need to apply to the DiSEqC standard.

The universal LNB was developed at the initiative of Astra, using a very wide frequency range, while the DiSEqC standard was an initiative of Eutelsat,

FIGURE

4.27

A DiSEqC switch is required to switch in between the LNBs.

which had many orbital slots. Two competing satellite systems and competing strategies have led to the invincible combination of the universal LNB and the DiSEqC-switch, providing the maximum number of channels using only one dish. In a dish for HOT BIRD and Astra, the universal LNB and the DiSEqC-switch are used in combination with each other.

In a dish with two LNBs, the LNB that looks towards the orbital position to the west is actually located to the east of the LNB looking towards to the orbital position to the east and vice versa. In a dish for 19 degrees east and 13 degrees east, the LNB for 19 degrees east is located west of the LNB for reception from 13 degrees east. This is shown in Figure 4.28.

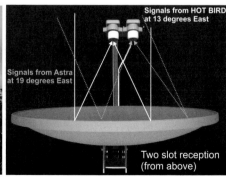

FIGURE

4.28

Reception from 13 degrees east and 19 degrees east using one dish.

The Four-LNB Dish

It is possible to design satellite dishes that can receive signals from more than two orbital slots, such as Figure 4.29. There are DiSEqC switches with four inputs. In many countries, these are used to combine more regional satellite channels with the main European satellite orbital slots at 13 degrees east and 19 degrees east.

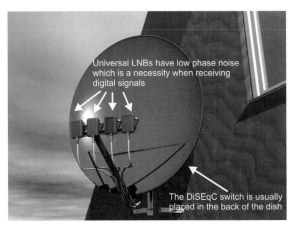

Using a four-input DiSEqC switch, it is possible to combine a wide range of satellite channels in one single antenna. The size of such antennas is about
one meter in diameter.

A parabolic dish with four LNBs may be configured in several different ways. In Figure 4.30, the dish is pointed towards 23 degrees east, which is the Astra 3 slot. There is also a LNB for 28 degrees east (Astra 2 and Eurobird), and one LNB for 19 degrees east (Astra 1) and finally one LNB for 13 degrees east (Eutelsat HOT BIRD).

The other combination in Figure 4.30 is popular in the Scandinavian countries. The dish is pointed towards 13 degrees east (Eutelsat HOT BIRD) and has a second LNB towards 19 degrees east (Astra 1). The third and fourth LNBs are used for reception from Sirius at 5 degrees east and Thor from 1 degrees west.

Of course other combinations are also possible.

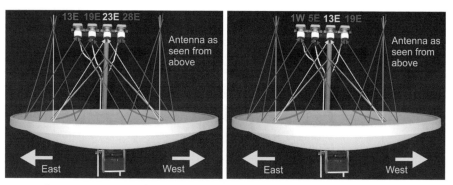

FIGURE

4.30

A popular European configuration for four LNBs on one dish (left) and a popular Scandinavian configuration for four LNBs on one dish (right). (See color plate.)

To get a four-LNB multi-focus antenna to work, a four-way DiSEqC switch, like the one shown in Figure 4.31, is required. The DiSEqC switches are put in plastic housings for weather protection. The switches are generally put somewhere behind the antennas.

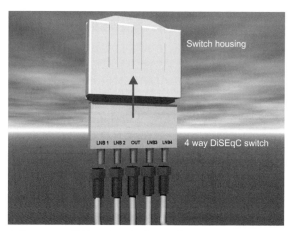

FIGURE

4.31

A four-way DiSEqC switch in plastic housing.

More Advanced Multi-Focus Antennas

It is possible to put even more LNBs into a parabolic dish to be able to receive signals from even more orbital slots. However, there are technical limitations. One such limitation is the mechanical problem of putting LNBs too close to each other. It is hard to receive signals from orbital slots that are separated less than six degrees in ordinary parabolic antennas having a diameter of about one meter. To a certain extent, this problem may be solved using LNBs with separate, specially designed, thin feed horns (the feed horn is the front part of the LNB containing the window that receives the signal). In larger antennas, it is possible to have smaller angular distances in between the orbital slots.

Another problem is that the reception from a certain orbital slot will get less efficient as we move away from the central boresight direction of the parabolic reflector. Therefore, a conventional parabolic dish will only work properly within a limited angular distance from the boresight direction. However measures have been taken in some designs to compensate for this. One way is keeping the parabolic profile in the vertical plane of the dish while changing the horizontal profile from parabolic to a spherical profile. This makes the efficiency in reception more equal from orbital slots within a wider angular range. Figure 4.33 shows a deformed parabolic dish with a fifth LNB.

Using more than four LNBs also means leaving the standard DiSEqC applications. The DiSEqC standard is divided into different levels. At the lowest level, DiSEqC 1.0, two-way and four-way DiSEqC switches are supported. On the next level, DiSEqC 1.1, it is possible to cascade two switches, which means that up to 16 LNBs may be supported if four four-way switches are cascaded with one four-way switch. Less ambitious alternatives are possible, such as cascading two four-way switches with one two-way switch to support 8 LNBs and so on. Cascading DiSEqC switches can be tricky and it is a matter of using the right kind of DiSEqC switches programmed to use the right commands. The first and the second switch in a cascaded chain must use different DiSEqC commands. Therefore the best thing to do is to buy a complete package including a receiver supporting the DiSEqC 1.1 level and the cascaded switches that are to be used. However there is a more modern alternative.

DiSEqC Switches With More Than Four Inputs

There is a way to avoid the problems with cascaded DiSEqC switches. Cascaded switches have two major drawbacks. First the receiver has to support DiSEqC 1.1 which is not very common. Second, the cascaded switches have to respond to different DiSEqC commands; you have to have the appropriate combination of switches.

However there is an alternative. Czech manufacturer EMP-Centauri has introduced a number of switches that have a larger number of inputs (see

Figure 4.32). The most amazing thing about these switches is that they can be set to respond to DiSEqC 1.0 commands as well as the DiSEqC 1.2 commands that are normally used for DiSEqC motor control. DiSEqC 1.2 allows for selection of up to 32 orbital positions using a DiSEqC motorized antenna (which is covered later in this chapter). DiSEqC 1.2 is supported by lots of digital receivers and this makes it as easy to use the multi port DiSEqC 1.2 switch as an ordinary two- or four-input DiSEqC switch.

A switch of this kind is very useful with multi focus antennas that can house a large number of LNBs as the torodial antenna.

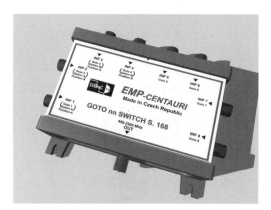

FIGURE

4.32

The eight-input DiSEqC switch from EMP-Centauri responds to DiSEqC 1.1 as well as DiSEqC 1.2 commands.

Note

Receivers that support DiSEqC 1.2 (DiSEqC motor control) also support DiSEqC 1.0 but not necessarily DiSEqC 1.1.

In recent years, new kinds of more advanced antennas have been introduced to improve multi-focus reception. These antennas provide reception that is more equal in performance when it comes to receiving signals from different orbital slots. To obtain this, more advanced antenna techniques have been developed.

The basic idea of this kind of antennas is the torus antenna. This is based on the principle already mentioned of using a spherical profile in the horizontal plane while maintaining the parabolic profile in the vertical plane.

Using dual reflectors opens up new possibilities, both for getting a mechanical design that allows for reception from closer orbital slots as well as improving the performance of reception across the received arc. Up to about 10 LNBs may

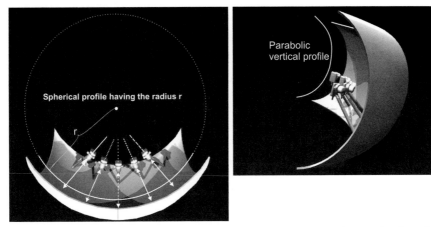

FIGURE

4.33

The torus antenna provides better, more equal reception for multiple orbital slots.

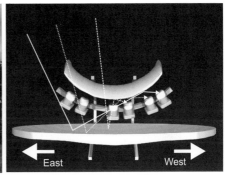

FIG

4.34

The "torodial" antenna is a step even further in getting an antenna with an equal performance across a wide angular range of the geostationary arc.

be housed in the torodial antenna from Wavefrontier. This antenna is sold under several brands in Europe and the U.S. and is available in 60- and 90-cm versions (2 and 3 feet respectively). The 90-cm dish covers an orbital range of 40 degrees allowing as little as four degrees separation between the slots.

Other kind of less conventional antennas are the lens antennas. Lens antennas work more or less like optical lenses focusing radio waves instead of light. The performance is quite equal to the torodial antenna.

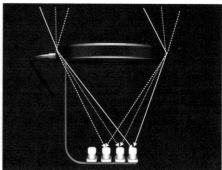

FIGURE

4.35

The "Cybertenna" is a dielectric lens which provides a different looking satellite multi focus antenna.

INSTALLING MULTI-FOCUS ANTENNAS

When installing a multi-focus antenna with more than two LNBs, the best thing to do is to locate one LNB in the center of the dish. Then the dish will have its main boresight direction towards the satellite in the middle of the desired portion of the geostationary arc. Refer back to Figure 4.30, where we have an antenna that uses the LNB in the middle to receive signals from the orbital position of 23 degrees east. In this case, the antenna is first adjusted to optimize the Astra 3 reception using this LNB. After that, we do not have to think anymore about the direction of the reflector. Now we can concentrate on adjusting the positions of the other three LNBs one by one.

In antennas for two orbital positions, it might be a bit trickier if you go for the principle of letting the boresight of reflector point at a location in between the two orbital slots. In some smaller dishes, there is a fixed mount for the LNBs and you do not have to think about adjusting the positions of the LNBs. However this kind of arrangement means that you are stuck with a certain angular distance between the slots.

However, do not forget that the LNB to receive signals from the satellite position to the west should be located east of the LNB that is to receive signals from the orbital slot that is to the west and vice versa.

In multi-focus antennas with a large number of LNBs quite a lot of skill is required. Training makes perfection.

Motorized Antennas

Multi-focus antennas provide easy access to several orbital slots using only one antenna. However, there is always a compromise between convenience and the signal quality as well as possibilities to receive a large number of orbital slots. Multi-focus antennas are convenient since you can immediately switch between different orbital slots without having to wait for the antenna to move as is the case for the motorized antennas. But multi-focus antennas do not cover the entire visible part of the geostationary orbit. If you wish to have access to almost all visible satellites or satellites that are spread widely apart in different slots, and you are eager to receive weak signals, a motorized antenna might be the best choice.

The first motorized dishes were of the center feed (focal feed) kind, as shown in Figure 4.36, but these are not widely used today. If you are looking for very weak signals, there is still a problem in finding larger offset feed antennas. Focal feed antennas might have diameter of 1.5 to 1.8 meters or more. It is easy to know the elevation angle of such an antenna; it is at right angles to the aperture surface, as in Figure 4.36.

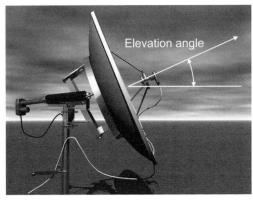

FIGURE	In a symmetrical focal feed antenna, the angle of elevation is at right angles with the aperture of the antenna as is shown in this picture. The actuator, the
4.36	linear motor that makes the antenna move, is on the back of the dish.

We will now take a closer look at the choice between the comfortable multi-focus antenna and the more complicated but more flexible motorized dish.

A multi-focus antenna allows for instant switching between TV channels that are transmitted from different orbital slots. When choosing a channel, the satellite receiver immediately sends the right control signals to the antenna.

This include the correct DiSEqC commands to the switch system, the continuous 22 kHz tone if the upper part of the frequency range is required, and the correct supply voltage to the universal LNB depending on what polarization is to be received. However, the multi-focus antenna can not provide you with optimum signal quality on all slots. The LNBs that are placed in the secondary focal points can not use the entire surface of the dish with full efficiency.

In a motorized antenna, the complete surface of the dish is always used, and antenna can be turned much farther east and west than the angular range of a multi-focus dish. You will also be able to reach orbital slots that are between those you could access with a multi-focus antenna. There are no restrictions to how close to each other the orbital slots might be when using a moveable antenna.

For practical reasons, it may still be impossible to reach the orbital slots that are extremely close to the horizon in either direction even if you have a motorized antenna. In the antenna shown in Figure 4.36, the mechanical restrictions in the mount of the antenna and the length of the actuator limit the range of the adjustment. The actuator is the linear motor that moves the antenna. In an antenna with an actuator, you select the part of the geostationary arc you wish to use by choosing at which side of the mount the actuator is situated and where the actuator is attached (there are usually a number of holes to choose from).

The drawback of using a motorized dish is that you will have to wait for the dish to move between the slots. As a consequence, the channel lists of your satellite receiver might not be arranged as you would have preferred. The order of the channels will probably follow the orbital positions rather than your taste. This is because it is not fun to zap between channels in different orbital locations when you have to wait for the dish to move. It could take 10 seconds or more to move from one slot to another. When you're waiting for a new channel selection, 10 seconds tends to feel like a long time.

As a conclusion multi-focus antennas are best suited for everyday viewing where simplicity comes ahead of technical flexibility and optimum performance. However for the technically interested person a motorized dish has more to give.

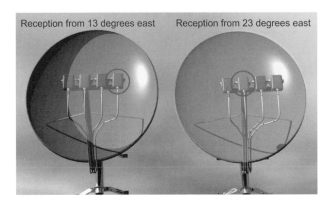

FIGURE

4.37

Comparison between the efficiency in the use of the receiving antenna aperture for the multi-focus versus the motorized receiving antenna. (See color plate.)

DiSEqC-Controlled Motorized Antennas

The large motorized dishes, as you can see in Figure 4.36, to a large extent disappeared from the market by the mid 1990s. At that time, many believed that the motorized antenna story had ended, but turned out not to be the case. An Italian family company, STAB, developed a very small and compact motor that uses the DiSEqC 1.2 protocol commands. The motor really both looks like and works like a part of the antenna mount (see Figure 4.38). Since it is DiSEqC-controlled, the motor uses the existing cable between the satellite receiver and the antenna, as well as the supply voltage for the LNB. No separate control unit or power supply is needed.

For many years the manufacturers of satellite receivers had problems in following the DiSEqC 1.2 standard. This meant that STAB motors, as well as competing motors, required proprietary software in the DiSEqC motors. These days,

STAB DiSEqC
Controlled Motor

Digital Satellite Recieiver
supporting DiSEqC 1.2

NOKIA

22·30

FIGURE

4.38

The STAB motor looks like an integrated part of the dish mount and it does not require any extra cabling or power supplies.

the situation is more stable and you can buy your satellite receiver and DiSEqC controlled antenna motor from different sources and still get it to work.

It would have been possible to design a motorized dish where the antenna could be moved around two axels—one for elevation and the other for the azimuth angle adjustment. Such antennas exist in uplink stations. But for consumer use, there is a lot to be gained from designing a mechanical mount where the antenna only has to be turned around one axle. Using a very cleverly designed mount makes this possible.

The principle of doing this is called polar mount and is based on having the dish mounted on an axle leaning at an angle A in relation to the horizontal plane and letting the reflector lean in relation to this axle with an angle B (the tilt angle). The angles are shown in Figure 4.39. The value of each angle depends on the location of the dish.

To read the angles A and B from Figures 4.40 is easy. To adjust the mount for optimum performance across the geostationary orbit might be harder and will probably takes some time. The manufacturers of antennas suggest different methods and they have their own tricks. However, in my experience, the best way to go is to start adjusting the vertical angles A and B.

It is very important that the antenna mount (STAB motor) is attached to a tube that is absolutely vertical. This may be checked with a level or weighted string.

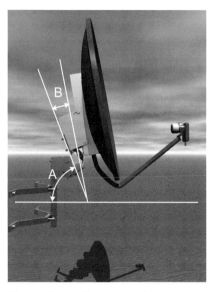

FIGURE

4.39

The main angles in a polar mount.

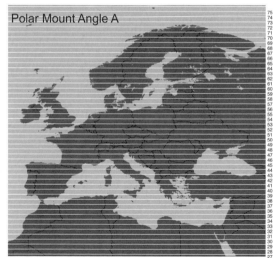

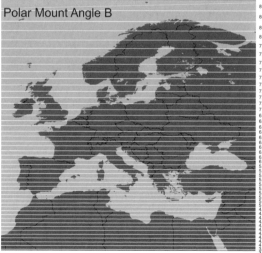

FIGURE

4.40

The A (leaning axle angle) and B (tilt angle) of a polar mount. (The corresponding angles for North America are shown on page 307).

First adjust angle A. This might be done using a protractor and a weighted string. There are also other instruments from the construction business that might do the job. Then, adjust the B angle. In some cases there is a scale on the mount/DiSEqC motor that could be helpful when doing this.

The really hard thing is to get the north to south direction right. If you are lucky you happen to be on the same longitude as a satellite. I am lucky enough to live exactly on the longitude 13 degrees east which means Eutelsat HOT BIRD is directly south of me. If you have a satellite straight to the south you can easily use this to get the north-south line exactly right. Turn the motor so that the antenna is right in the middle position, with maximum elevation. Then just turn the complete mount to get the maximum signal strength from the satellite located directly south.

However if you are not that lucky not having any satellite straight south you have to do it in another way. Choose a suitable satellite as reference satellite. From the maps showing the elevation and azimuth curves, read the elevation angle for that satellite. Then measure the elevation angle of your antenna using a weighted string and a protractor. Now turn the dish using the motor to the east or to the west until the elevation angle of that satellite is achieved. If the satellite is on a longitude to the west of your position you should turn the dish to the west. If the selected satellite is to the east then turn the antenna to the east. Check carefully that the right elevation angle really is achieved. Now, adjust azimuth angle of the complete mount of the antenna (without turning the motor) until you receive an optimal signal from the satellite you selected.

It is not suitable to use a satellite that is in the middle of the orbit. It is better to use a satellite further out since the elevation angle falls steeper farther away from the direction towards the south. This makes the adjustments more sensitive, giving you a better accuracy when adjusting the north to south alignment of the antenna mount.

Still it is not easy finding your way through the satellite jungle. To make it easier to install the system, there might be preset channels in the memory which act as reference channels or thumbprints for each satellite.

If you are having problems in finding certain channels or certain satellites there are sites on the Internet with accurate information on the subject. One such site is *www.lyngsat.com*, which contains detailed information and useful links for almost all satellite channels in the world.

OPTIMIZING PARABOLIC ANTENNAS

Until now, we have concentrated on how to find the approximate alignment of an antenna for satellite reception. The main problem however is that a satellite reception antenna works at very high frequencies. As a result, the antenna requires a very high degree of pointing accuracy. The pointing accuracy required

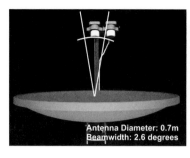
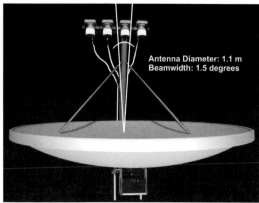

FIGURE

4.41

A 70-centimeter dish has a 2.6 degree beamwidth while a 1.1 meter antenna has a beamwidth of about 1.5 degrees.

is considerably higher than is the case for a terrestrial TV aerial. The angular range, where it is sensitive to incoming signals, the 3 dB beamwidth (the angular range within which the incoming signal is at least half of the maximum on boresight input power) is very narrow. A 70-centimeter dish has a beamwidth of just 2.6 degrees. In a somewhat larger dish (1.1 meters) the beamwidth is about 1.5 degrees. In these cases, you need to be able to measure the strength of the signal when making the alignment of the antenna. Someone informing you about whether or not there is an image on the TV screen is not good enough.

Finding the Optimum Focal Point

In this chapter we have anticipated that there is only one way to attach the LNB in the antenna. There are antennas with a fixed attachment, leaving no adjustment to the installer. However in many antennas, there are possibilities to adjust the position and orientation of the LNB. As we have learned from the multi-focus antennas, the receiving beam direction will change as we move the LNB. Therefore, adjusting an LNB into what we believe is the main focus of a parabolic dish can be tricky. If we move the LNB, the direction of sensitivity also moves. Therefore the search for the optimum focus is an iterative process moving the LNB and realigning the dish several times before the goal is reached (see Figure 4.42).

In a multi-focus antenna, it is only the LNB at the central, main focus that may be adjusted this way. As soon as this LNB works in an optimum way, you should not touch the direction of the antenna any more. The other LNBs

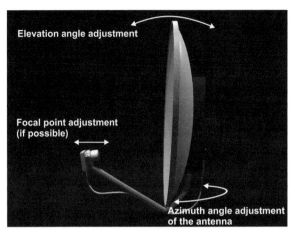

FIGURE

4.42

Iterative adjustment to get the LNB at the optimum focal point of the reflector.

must be adjusted by their individual positions within the antenna itself (see Figure 4.43).

In the previous chapter, we saw that the satellites transmit both horizontal and vertically polarized signals. This makes it possible to reuse the complete frequency range and double the available bandwidth. Therefore it is necessary to orient the LNB in such a way that the small antennas inside are oriented to coincide with the orientation of the transmitted signals from the satellite (see Figure 4.44).

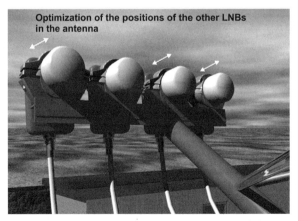

FIGURE

4.43

As soon as the LNB in the centre position of the antenna works at its optimum the orientation of the reflector should not be further touched. Instead it is the individual position inside the antenna of the other LNBs that need to be adjusted.

If the orientation of the LNB is wrong, the signals from both polarizations will get mixed and the reception will not work properly. If this happens, the horizontally and vertically polarized signals will interfere with each other.

Normally the signals from the satellite are oriented in such a way that the horizontally polarized waves coincide with the equatorial plane of the Earth. The vertically polarized signals are at right angles with the equatorial plane.

A satellite that is located on the same longitude (directly south) as the reception site will transmit its horizontally polarized signals parallel with the horizon. And the vertical signals will come in polarized at right angles to the horizon. For satellites located at other slots further to the east or the west, the polarization planes will lean and be in parallel with or at right angles to the geostationary arc at it is seen from the ground in Figure 4.2.

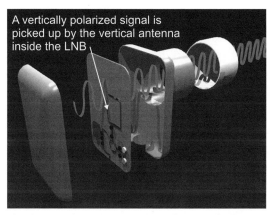

FIGURE

4.44

The internal antennas must align with the incoming signals.

Measuring Digital Satellite Signals

The adjustment of the polarization angle is probably the most difficult part when installing a satellite dish. High-quality measurement instruments are needed to get it all right. The alignment process for a satellite dish follows in three steps: find the signal from the satellite, identify the satellite so that you know what you are receiving, then optimize the antenna for the best reception.

Promax Prodig-1

A good example of a professional measurement instrument for this purpose is the Spanish Promax Prodig-1. Prodig-1 is a pretty small instrument that is used outside at the antenna. It has a built in battery so you do not have to rely on power from the satellite receiver.

There are three buttons and a display on the unit (see Figure 4.45). Pressing the first button triggers the search mode when the instrument just looks for signals using an indication bar on the display and an audio signal with a frequency that gets higher as a higher signal level is achieved. Pressing the second button makes the instrument to go into "fingerprint" mode where you can check different preset transponders to check that you have found the right satellite. The instrument includes half a digital satellite receiver—it is able to demodulate and demultiplex the transport stream. You can add or rearrange the presets to fit your needs as new satellites come along.

Pressing the final button switches the instrument to bit error measurement mode. The quality of the received signal can be measured by checking errors among known bits that belong to the frame structure of the DVB transport stream. By doing this, you can adjust the polarization isolation of the LNB very accurately. It is also possible to adjust for all other errors and problems that may be related to the antenna.

The Prodig-1 is very practical since you can wear on a belt, leaving both hands free. The LCD display is easy to watch even in bright sunlight.

Instruments of this kind cost a few hundred Euros or dollars but the investment will pay off if you install a lot of antennas. The reason for the cost is partly that the instrument contains almost a complete digital receiver. It also comes with software that enables you to put in new presets by connecting a computer.

FIGURE

4.45

Promax Prodig-1 is a small and handy instrument to detect, identify and optimize the reception of a digital satellite signal.

Emitor Digitsat PRO

A more semi-professional instrument is the Emitor Digisat PRO (sold in the United States as Accutrac 22 Pro). This instrument has a very special feature. It has two inputs, so it is possible to monitor the signal level from two LNBs simultaneously. This makes the instrument very interesting when installing two LNB multi-focus antennas. However, it is only possible to measure signal level; it does not measure signal quality. The signal level is not only a product of the strength of the satellite signal but also the length of cable between the LNB and the instrument, the gain of the LNB and a few other parameters. Like many other instruments of this kind, the Digisat PRO is powered by the supply voltage from the satellite receiver.

The Digisat Pro goes at about 100 euros ($130 U.S.).

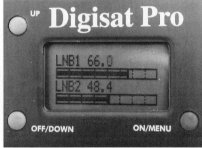

FIGURE

4.46

Digisat Pro from Emitor is a small instrument that can measure the signal level from two LNBs simultaneously.

Spectrum Displays

Technical radio enthusiasts have long wished for a spectrum analyzer, for a graphical display of what a larger or smaller portion of the radio spectrum looks like. But spectrum analyzers are expensive.

Emitor has produced a small, relatively inexpensive device, the Spectralook, which you connect to your TV set. The satellite dish is connected to the device using a splitter (for simultaneous reception with an ordinary satellite receiver). On your screen you can now see all signals that leave the satellite dish in the frequency range 950 to 2150 MHz (see Figure 4.47). Each spike in the spectrum corresponds to a transponder; the longer the spike, the stronger the signal from that particular transponder.

It is not possible to use the Spectralook to make any actual measurements, but still you get a very useful graphical display showing the signals being

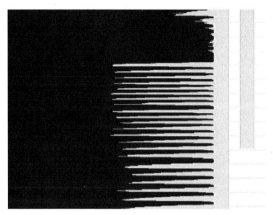

FIGURE

4.47

Spectralook from Emitor converts your TV set to a spectrum analyzer. The spectrum is symbolized vertically where each spike corresponds to a transponder.

received. This instrument is very useful if you have a motorized antenna and you are on the hunt for "new and unknown" signals. When the antenna passes by a satellite you will immediately see its signals on your screen and you can then investigate the signals in detail using your digital satellite receiver. This is an instrument good for finding the needle in the haystack.

Emitor also makes the Satlook Digital (also sold in the U.S. under the same name), a more professional instrument that includes a spectrum display. This very advanced instrument not only produces an image of the spectrum but also performs actual carrier-to-noise measurements based on bit error rate measurements and calculations. A fascinating feature is the constellation diagram display, where you can see samples of the phase angle and amplitude registrations on actual signals—an actual phase diagram of the QPSK signal as is shown in Figure 4.48.

Another great feature of the Satlook Digital is that you can transfer all measured data to an external computer for documentation purposes. This is not an instrument for consumers but could be a goldmine for professional installers and satellite enthusiasts.

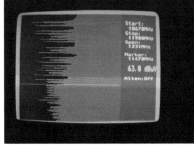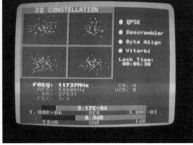

FIGURE

4.48

Satlook Digital from Emitor is both a simple spectrum analyzer and a measurement instrument that decide the signal quality from bit error measurements. It can also display the constellation diagram of a QPSK modulated signal.

Recommendations for Consumers

But what should ordinary consumers do if they want to install the dish themselves? To do the installation without some kind of instrument is not easy. One option is to try to borrow a simple "Satfinder" from the shop where you buy the receiving equipment. Such instruments are not that expensive to buy either. The cheapest instruments in the market are the "Satbeepers" (see Figure 4.49). This is a small device that is connected to the LNB and gets its supply voltage from the satellite receiver. There is a small earphone that indicates the signal strength by a beep. The frequency of the beep corresponds to the strength of the signal. Satbeepers sell at a less than 20 euros ($25 U.S.).

Stepping up to the next instrument will cost 40 to 50 euros ($50 to $65 U.S.) and will provide you with a visual indication of the incoming signal either as meter with a needle on a scale or an LCD indication bar.

The problem in using these inexpensive instruments is that they do not provide you with any identification of which satellite you receive and you are not able to measure the signal quality. The latter means that you will not be able to adjust the polarization because you have to be able to measure the bit error rate in some way.

FIGURE

4.49
Satbeepers and Satfinders are the smallest and cheapest among the large number of instruments that are available in the market.

To do this you have to step up to the professional instruments that generally go at between 500 to 1000 euros ($640 to $1,280 U.S.). All these instruments have in common that they are used outside close to the antenna so you can adjust the dish as you are measuring the signal. A spectrum analyzer is the most professional way to go, but I must say that an instrument like the Promax Prodig-1 is very appropriate to get the job done even though it is not as fancy as a spectrum analyzer.

There is another very cheap way of measuring the signal quality. Your digital satellite receiver is really an advanced measuring instrument. It has the ability to measure the signal strength as well as the signal quality. In many cases, there is a menu that contains measuring bars that show these two parameters. The receiver can measure the bit error rate by counting errors among known bits that are a part of the DVB framing structure. If you see that the signal quality is at a high level you probably have the polarization adjustment done correctly.

For obvious reasons, most dishes are installed when the weather is good. However many times when you watch TV, it is raining. And when it is raining, you may get problems with your satellite signal since that is when the microwave signals are attenuated in the atmosphere. It is quite important to check the signal quality as soon as the installation is done.

In the analog days, you could see from the presence or absence of noise the margins in your receiving system. But digital signals don't provide that. As soon there is a picture it is 100% okay. So, if you have a bad margin you might lose your picture completely when it starts to rain.

Therefore the quality measurement menu is the only way to know the margins. And if it should happen that the signal disappears or get disturbed during a heavy rain shower, it may also be interesting to check the signal quality for future reference. Then you know at what quality level you will lose the picture.

However it is essential to get to know which of the measurement bars in the menu system that measures the signal quality (see Figure 4.50). In some cases, there might be a bar only reporting the signal level. This is not as interesting as the quality since the signal strength depends on several other things, such as the length of the cable in between the LNB and the receiver.

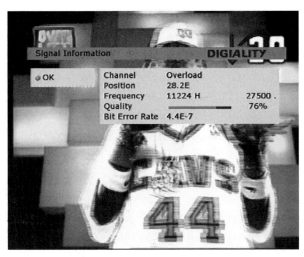

FIGURE

4.50

The menu system of the satellite receiver may contain many useful things. One of the most useful, but also one of the least known, is the built in signal quality metering system. In this receiver from Digitality, the quality is both represented as a bar and in figures providing the bit error rate (BER).

When aligning a satellite dish, it is essential to know that you have found the right satellite. In many cases the receiver is pre-programmed with some known channels on each satellite position. But you always have to start off telling the receiver what the antenna system looks like. Information such as how many LNBs are attached to the receiver and at what inputs of the DiSEqC switch these are connected is necessary for the receiver to find the channels. This is done with the antenna configuration menu in figure 4.51. As soon as this is done, the receiver will be able to search for channels in each slot by itself, provided, of course, that the antenna is properly aligned.

An alternative to automatic channel search is to search for certain channels manually. This may be done by entering the frequency, polarization, symbol rate and FEC of a certain transponder. On top of this you may specify what you are looking for down on service level by entering PIDs. However, manual search is an alternative only if you know exactly what you are looking for and don't want to update an entire orbital slot, which might take some time.

In most cases the automatic channel search preferable. You just select the orbital slot you'd like to update and then let the receiver do the job (see Figure 4.52). The channels are picked up in an automatically generated list. If you have a dish that includes the large European orbital slots, it may take a while to search it all. But afterwards you might have between 2,000 and 3,000 channels in the list. A lot of channels may be unavailable since they are encrypted and only available in other countries. But still there are several hundreds of channels from all corners of Europe available.

FIGURE
4.51

In the antenna installation menu you tell the receiver on which LNB to find a certain orbital slot.

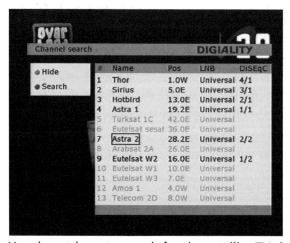

FIGURE
4.52

You do not have to search for the satellite TV channels by yourself. Just pick the orbital slot you like and let the receiver do the job.

Today each orbital slot may contain an almost uncountable number of radio and TV channels. In the 1990s it was still possible to zap between all available satellite TV channels in one night. Perhaps it still is. But almost nobody does that anymore. Figures 4.53 and 4.54 contain the transponder plan for Astra 1 (19 degrees east) and Eutelsat HOT BIRD (13 degrees east). Every transponder may contain up to about 10 TV channels or a very large number of radio channels.

Astra 1, 19 degrees east:

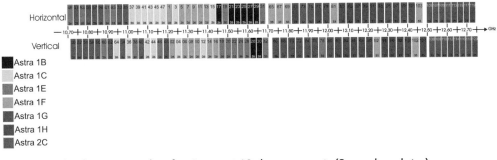

FIGURE

4.53

The frequency plan for Astra at 19 degrees east. (See color plate.)

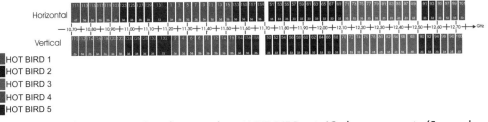

FIGURE

4.54

The frequency plan for Eutelsat HOT BIRD at 13 degrees east. (See color plate.)

Coaxial Connectors

Finally there is a small thing that always needs to be done when installing a satellite dish. You have to bring the coaxial cable from the dish into your house. In order to pull the cable through a hole in the wall, you cannot have a connector on it. For this reason, you will have to put the connector on to the cable by yourself (once that end is in the house), even in a world of ready made cables.

The connectors used for the LNB to the receiver cabling when it comes to satellite TV are the F connectors. They come in many different kinds, but the simplest one to use is the "Twist-On" F-type connector. Figure 4.55 shows how to put such a connector on to a coaxial cable. Remember to use the right size of connector to the dimension of cable that you use. If you have a multi-focus antenna you should take advantage in using ready made cables to connect the LNBs and the DiSEqC switch.

An important issue is weather protection. Nowadays, weather protection of the connector that is attached to the LNB is achieved by using a rubber hose that is attached to the LNB itself and that covers the F connector completely. An old alternative was to use vulcanizing tape that kept the connector moisture-free for a long period of time. Another place where weather protection is necessary is at the connectors for the DiSEqC switch. Nowadays the manufacturers have developed clever solutions for this.

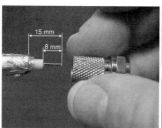 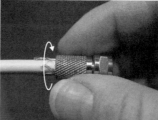 

FIGURE
4.55

The "Twist-On" F type connector is perhaps not the most professional kind of F type connector but it is no doubt the most common one.

5 Digital TV by Cable

FIGURE

5.1

Cable TV is the oldest multi-channel TV media in Europe.

The first cable TV networks were introduced in the United States in order to improve TV reception in areas with poor terrestrial reception conditions. It was also in the U.S. that the idea of using satellites to feed cable TV networks was explored in the late 1970s.

In the beginning of the 1980s, this technology spread to Europe as well. There was a big political debate on this subject in certain countries since television had been a state monopoly for decades. However, as new satellites were launched and the new satellite signals spread across the borders, legislation had to adapt to the new situation. And soon satellite TV started to tie the European countries together in an amazing new way. Who could have thought of being able to watch CNN in a Moscow hotel room 30 years ago?

FIGURE

5.2

Cable TV networks get most of their channels from satellite. But some channels originate from terrestrial transmitters and other local sources.

THE HEADEND: THE HEART OF THE CABLE TV NETWORK

The basic idea of establishing cable television is that the viewer can receive a number of TV channels without any other equipment beyond his existing TV set. Therefore analog TV will live on for a long time in the cable TV networks.

The heart of a cable TV network is the headend, a central utility where all reception is arranged. In the headend, there are a number of satellite-receiving antennas usually a bit larger than is used for individual reception. Another important difference in relation to reception in an individual home using a satellite DTH (direct to home) dish is that the antennas must be able to simultaneously receive both polarizations and both parts of the satellite downlink frequency band. In most individual home satellite receiving systems, you can only receive one channel at a time.

The signals from the parabolic dishes are split up in racks filled with satellite receivers. From the satellite receivers, analog audio and video signals are obtained. These signals are fed to modulators that are comparable with small TV transmitters generating analog TV channels at the desired channels numbers. This converts the digital satellite signals into analog channels, making it possible for the viewer to keep his old analog equipment.

The modulators are connected together to produce the complete package of channels that is fed into the cable TV network. Any encrypted channels will be re-encrypted before they are distributed on the network. The viewers need to have separate decoders to watch the encrypted programming.

In the beginning of the development of cable TV, there was at least one headend in each city. The reception equipment was pretty expensive in the early days of satellite TV since large dishes and expensive satellite receivers were needed. To spread the signals within the city, a large coaxial network was constructed, using existing culverts or buried in tubes. However, the cabling could end up kilometers or miles in length, so amplifiers had to be introduced at certain distances to keep the signal at usable levels.

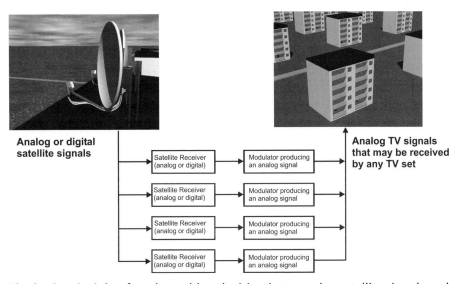

FIGURE

5.3

The basic principle of analog cable television is to receive satellite signals and modulate them into standard terrestrial analog signals that can be received by any TV set.

The early goal of analog cable TV was to connect as many old MATV (Master Antenna TV) systems as possible to the large network that covered the whole city. This was to get as many viewers (customers) as possible. You can say that the cable TV network may be regarded as being divided into three distribution levels. In this book, I refer to them as D1, D2 and D3 levels. D1 is the top level of the network, with cabling to different areas of the city. The D2 level is the level inside the D1 area and the D3 level is the cabling inside the individual building. By the end of the 1980s, receiving equipment started to get cheaper and smaller dishes became possible for satellite reception. Cable TV began to become economical to start up at smaller locations. Even in separate buildings, satellite signals could be introduced into the local net. The large city networks started to get competition from the smaller cabling companies when satellite channels were introduced directly at the D3 level.

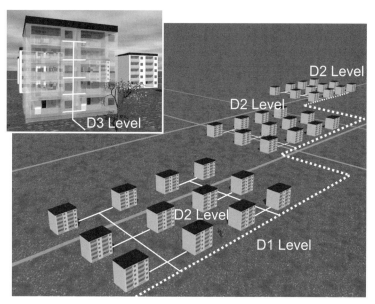

FIGURE
5.4

Cable TV networks may be divided into three basic distribution levels, D1, D2 and D3.

CHANNEL CAPACITY

Still, it did not prove easy to construct cable TV networks that included many TV channels. Figure 5.5 shows the frequency ranges used for European cable TV.

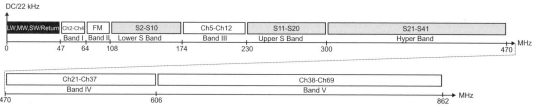

FIGURE
5.5

Frequency bands and channels used for cable TV in most parts of Europe.

The more bandwidth that can be used in the cables, the more channels can be distributed. In terrestrial TV, the UHF band of 470 to 862 MHz may be used. However, at these comparatively high frequencies, the signal attenuation in the cables is quite high. For this reason, early cable TV distribution was restricted to frequencies below 300 MHz. In old MATV systems, the UHF channels were down-converted to lower frequencies before being sent into the network.

Below 300 MHz, not that many channels can be used for distribution. The bandwidth of the channels are 7 MHz wide and in the lowest frequency band, band I (47–64 MHz), there are only three channels: channel 2, 3 and 4. Channel 1 does not even exist. The next frequency band, band II (87–108 MHz) is used for FM radio. The third band, band III, (174–230 MHz) covers the channels 5 through 12. Channel numbers mentioned here applies to continental Europe.

In early cable TV, only every other channel could be used because of filtering problems in older TV sets. This was not so good. The only channels available were channels 3 (band I), 5, 7 9 and 11 (band III) or channels 2, 4 (band I) and 6, 8, 10 and 12 (band III)—not a lot of options. In addition to this, some frequencies could not be used since they were already in use by terrestrial transmitters and would be exposed to interference if used. In some countries, channel 12 was not allowed to be used due to frequency coordination with other kinds of services. Today channel 12 is used for DAB (Digital Audio Broadcasting) in Europe.

To solve the bandwidth problems, two new frequency bands—the S-Bands—that were only allowed to be used in cable networks were introduced. The lower S-Band (108–174 MHz) contains the channels S2 through S10 and the upper S-Band (230–300 MHz) contains the channels S11 through S20.

For quite some time, the larger cable TV networks were restricted to the frequency range below 300 MHz. But as the amplifier technique developed, it became possible to exchange the amplifier for new one that could cover frequencies up to 400 or 500 MHz. The area between 300 and 470 MHz is the hyper band containing the channels S21 to S41 (in most countries only the channels between S21 and S38 are used.) And in this frequency range the channels have the same bandwidth as UHF channels, 8 MHz.

Initially, viewers had to use separate boxes that made it possible to receive the new frequency ranges of the S channels. But after some years, most new TV sets had built in S-channel tuners, even called cable TV tuners. Cable TV became multi-channel and the subscribers could easily receive up to 30 channels.

THE MATV (MASTER ANTENNA TV) NETWORK

In many European countries, cable TV was based on the fact that there were lots of MATV systems that easily could be hooked up the larger cable TV networks. However the quality of MATV networks varies. Most of these networks are cascaded networks (see Figure 5.6). In order to save some cabling, one cable can go from one apartment to the next passing through several outlets. But saving cable comes at a price. The signal level will get lower as the signal pass from one outlet to the next. If you are at the end outlet, your signal might be a lot worse than at the first outlet.

The alternative to the cascaded network is the star-shaped network. Each apartment has its own cable direct from the divider and each unit's signal level is not affected by other outlets. Another advantage is that there is an alternative to encryption of pay TV channels. Instead, the pay-TV content can be filtered so that only people paying would get those channels distributed on their cable.

In the beginning of cable TV, there were some high ambitions about using only star-shaped networks to benefit from these advantages. Economical realities, however, showed that this was not possible. The antenna outlets had to be exchanged and new amplifiers had to replace the old ones. However in many cases old cables were used. And in many cases there was not room for any new cables necessary to get a star-shaped structure in the old tubes and conduits. It was much easier to renovate the old cascaded networks that already existed.

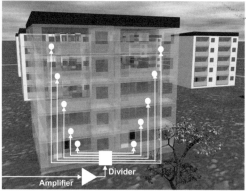 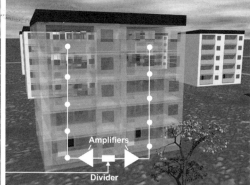

FIGURE

5.6

Cable TV networks with several branches, in this case in star-shaped (left) and cascaded structures (right).

The coaxial cable network within a building may be small or large. There might be a large number of branches each connected to a number of outlets. However there is a large problem. Since the signal has to be split between a numbers of outlets and may be transported in long cables, amplifiers are needed.

In Chapter 4, I mentioned that it is necessary to have only one carrier if an amplifier is to operate in saturated mode and provide maximum amplification. Unfortunately, in cable TV, there are many channels which mean that the amplifiers have to be backed off—i.e., we can only use a portion of the available amplification. The amplifiers have to work in linear mode and if they get into nonlinear mode, it will result in intermodulation and mixing of the channels. If you wish to increase the number of channels the amount of power that can be allocated to each channel will get less (see Figure 5.7).

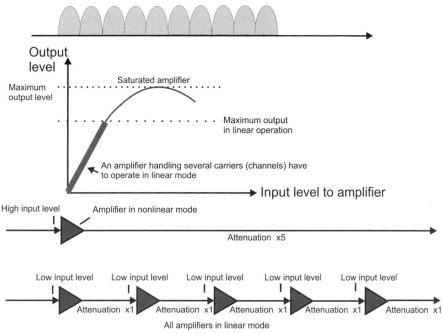

FIGURE

5.7

Amplifiers must operate in linear mode.

This would mean less amplification on each channel, but since a certain amount of amplification is needed on each channel to get the signal to the end outlet of the branch, the number of amplifiers also has to increase as the number of channels increase. By adding more amplifiers and reducing the input level on each amplifier, they continue to function in linear mode and the quality of the signals in the network is maintained.

UHF COAXIAL NETWORKS

Most cable TV networks are limited to the frequency area below 400 or 500 MHz. From a technical point of view, it is possible to design UHF coaxial networks handling frequencies within the 470-862 MHz range. One way of doing this is split-band techniques where the VHF and UHF frequency bands are treated separately. The UHF part of the amplifiers has higher amplification than the VHF parts since the attenuation in the cables increase with increased frequency.

COAXIAL CABLE TV NETWORKS

The MATV systems were the original cable networks. When large-scale cable television was introduced, many of these MATV systems could be reused and integrated in these larger systems. But sometimes the cables were too bad; they had a high attenuation and were too poorly insulated. This meant it was not possible to introduce S channels and avoid interfering with other services that existed in the air. However, the channels in the buildings containing the old cables could be reused for new ones. The old cables could also be used to drag the new cables along the same path in the building. In the 1980s, a lot of work was put into modernization of old MATV networks as they became a part of larger cable TV networks and got more channels. Also at this time, large cable networks covering complete cities were constructed. These networks would integrate all MATV systems into one single system that could be fed from one common headend.

When cable TV was introduced, coaxial cables were used at the D1 level, with amplifiers at suitable distances to compensate for the attenuation in the longest cables even kilometers or miles in length. The major problem is that it is not possible to distribute signals at frequencies above 500 MHz for long distances using coaxial cables (see Figure 5.8). The cable TV operators were forced to upgrade the amplifiers for higher frequency ranges as the technology in the amplifiers developed. A second problem is getting return traffic back from the viewers.

Coaxial Cable Return Traffic

If the cable TV network is to be used to provide broadband connections to the Internet, a return path from the subscriber to the network is required. An Internet connection in a cable TV network is based on using a radio receiver and transmitter for data signals. The cable modems transmit information back to the headend using frequencies below 47 MHz. In some cases, frequencies up to 64 MHz are used for return traffic.

With a lot of subscribers, the return path will get crowded. And if several heavy populated areas are connected, the situation will grow even worse.

Since there is a cable connection to every apartment, traffic in two directions would be desirable. As an example, Internet access can be provided through the cable if the return traffic is handled properly. A large wish among the cable operators was to develop something that would provide two-way communications with unlimited bandwidth at the D1 level in the networks and not have to further exchange amplifiers as development preceded. The solution was to change the coaxial cables to optical fibers.

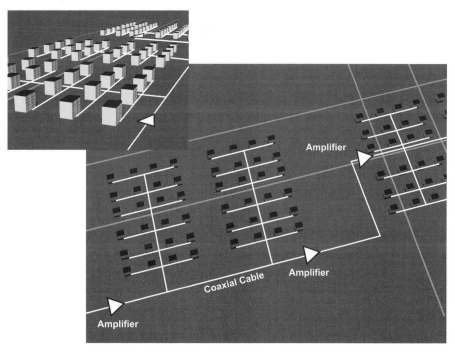

FIGURE

5.8

Old city cable TV networks were based on coaxial cables with amplifiers placed at suitable distances.

HYBRID FIBER COAXIAL NETWORKS (HFC)

Some years ago many people thought that it would be possible to get optical fiber into each household. This is called "fiber to the home." This would provide an electronic highway with unlimited bandwidth into the home. However, the economical reality had proved that fiber to the home is more of a dream than reality. At least until recent developments.

The last part of the cable TV network, the cabling within the building, is the most expensive part to upgrade to fiber. In addition, the coaxial cables already exist and it is very hard to motivate an exchange. There are also practical problems in connecting the fiber to the equipment in the home. Sooner or later you have to convert to an electrical interface before connecting all devices that need to communicate with the outside. Also optical fibers are fed by lasers and may be dangerous to look into if you disconnect them yourself because this kind of laser is often not visible but still dangerous to the eyes.

Optical fibers used to connect digital audio in a home cinema between the DVD recorder and the home cinema amplifiers are not of this kind. They use ordinary LEDs (light emitting diodes) that are completely harmless. The disadvantage is that these kind of light sources only work in short lengths of fibers. Lasers are needed to reduce the attenuation of the light signal in the long fibers that would have been required for fiber to the home distribution.

There are no fibers to the home, but for professional use in the D1 level in the cable networks they have become very popular.

How Fiber Networks Work

As soon as the complete content of the cable TV network has been generated as an electrical signal, the signals are converted into laser light. Instead of distributing the electrical signal, as was done before, the signal is converted into a laser light signal by a laser diode. The laser light is fed into an optical fiber. Light is, in reality, the same physical phenomenon as radio waves. They are both electromagnetic waves, but light is at much higher frequencies. However, light is usually not characterized in frequencies but in wavelengths. One usual wavelength used in optical fibers is 1,310 nm (nanometers). In the terms that are used for radio, this would correspond to a frequency of 229,000 GHz. At these incredibly high frequencies, there is such an immense amount of bandwidth that it is hard for an ordinary human being to understand. The complete content of the cable TV network can easily be converted into a light signal using a laser. At the other end of the fiber, the light signal will hit a photo diode. The photo diode then regenerates the electrical signal.

A fiber of this kind can be kilometers or miles in length without any amplifiers between the laser and the photo diode at the other end.

When the fiber reaches a block of houses, the signal is converted into an electrical signal that is fed into the local coaxial network on the D2 level or directly into the network within a certain building on the D3 level. The lower levels of the cable network can still be used as before distributing the electrical signals.

However the main advantage in using fiber is the possibility to use several wavelengths in the fiber, making it possible to reuse the fiber several times. In the forward direction, as we have already seen, one wavelength is sufficient for all contents.

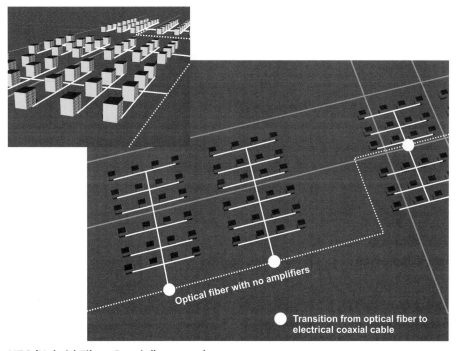

FIGURE 5.9   HFC (Hybrid Fiber Coaxial) network.

HFC Network Return Traffic

One way of solving the return path capacity problem is to collect all the radio signals from all modems within a certain area and convert them into a common optical signal.

From the different areas in the city, different wavelengths are used to carry the return traffic back to the headend. In Figure 5.10, you see four different areas that use the wavelengths 1510, 1530, 1550 and 1570 nm respectively. This way, every area within the city gets its own wavelength and the traffic within the coaxial networks in different areas does not compete with each other. Competition for return capacity within the radio spectrum of the coaxial network is limited to internal competition within that area of the network. If coaxial cable had been used at the higher level of the network, all return traffic for the complete city would have had to fight for the same capacity.

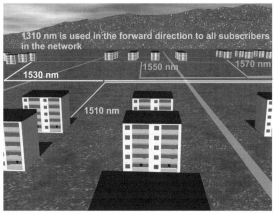

FIGURE

5.10

This HFC network uses different wavelengths for return traffic from different areas in the network. (See color plate.)

Larger cable TV operators often want to connect networks in different cities to one giant network covering a whole country. This may be done using optical fibers. However it is not possible to use the earlier described analog optical signals to do this. Instead, the content has to be digitized before being sent between the cities. Then it is converted into analog optical signals as it arrives to the next city and the end distribution takes place as described above.

DIGITAL CABLE TELEVISION

Until now, we have only discussed distribution of analog signals to the end user in the cable TV network. But of course there are also enormous possibilities to distribute digital TV in the existing cable TV networks.

The major problem related to analog cable TV is that the quality you obtain in your TV set is dependant on where in the branch of your local coaxial network your apartment or house happens to be located. In addition, cable TV subscribers buy DVD recorders and wide screen TV sets and complete home cinema systems. For this reason, there is also a demand for modern digital signals from the cable TV network.

Digital cable TV in Europe is based on the same standard, digital video broadcasting, DVB, as is used for satellite broadcasting. The nucleus of DVB is the transport stream, including the data packets that contain the audio and video information. The main difference between digital cable TV and satellite distribution is the higher level of modulation. The most common kind of modulation is 64 QAM that is a combination of amplitude and phase modulation. There are even higher levels of standardized modulation, such as 128 and 256 QAM that can be used for cable TV. However, these higher modulation schemes would demand higher quality of the signals in the cable TV networks.

Figure 5.11 shows the modulation scheme for 64 QAM. It is not easy to draw a signal, so it is symbolized by its constellation diagram showing the amplitudes and phase angles representing the symbols for each combination of bits.

64 QAM resembles QPSK but has more phase angles. Instead of four possible phase angles there are 52. And on top of this, there are 10 different amplitude levels instead of one as in QPSK. In total, there are 64 different combinations of phase angles and amplitudes that are allowed, to some extent resembling a chessboard. Each symbol then represents a combination of six bits. In other words, six bits may be transmitted simultaneously. Of course, a signal based on 64 QAM is much more sensitive to noise and disturbances than QPSK, since the symbols are located much closer to each other. Despite this, 64 QAM has a large advantage over QPSK because it is possible to get a 38 Mbit/s signal into an 8 MHz channel. 8 MHz channels are used in the hyper band and in the UHF bands. 38 Mbit/s is the same bitrate as the bitrate housed in a satellite multiplex—the content of a satellite transponder.

Setting up a complete installation, including the creation of a complete DVB signal package with MPEG 2 encoders and multiplexing of the signals, is expensive. Adding pay TV encryption services is even more costly. These

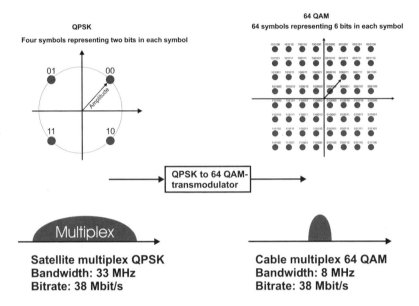

FIGURE

5.11

Transmodulation from QPSK to 64 QAM.

investments are generally limited to large cable TV operators, which spread the costs out to hundreds of thousands of subscribers. A much less expensive way to solve this is by using the satellite multiplexes. However the satellite signals are QPSK modulated, so the signals have to be demodulated to get hold of the transport stream. The transport stream, however, can be modulated again using 64 QAM. Direct transmodulation from QPSK to 64 QAM is cheap but requires that the signal in the cable TV network can be identical to the satellite signal.

A problem of using the same signals in the cable TV networks as on satellite is that pay TV satellite signals are encrypted by the satellite content provider. As a result, the satellite content provider can reach customers in the cable networks. Of course this is not acceptable to the cable TV companies. In order to get the cable TV operators to keep their own encryption systems and program cards, there are different ways of modifying the transport stream before it is modulated to 64 QAM. The costs increase in relation to how much of the transport stream is to be modified. However, these kinds of modifications to maintain the structure of the original transport stream are what make it possible to distribute digital TV even in smaller cable TV networks.

Digital Cable TV Receivers

The difference between digital receivers for cable and digital satellite receivers is the input stage, which covers the input frequency ranges of cable TV. This may include frequencies up to 862 MHz since there might be cable TV operators also interested in using UHF. Also, the cable receiver has a QAM demodulator where the satellite box has a QPSK demodulator.

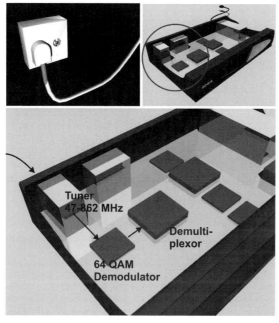

Tuner
47-862 MHz

Demulti-
plexor

64 QAM
Demodulator

FIGURE

5.12

The digital TV receiver for cable has an input stage covering the frequency ranges for cable and uses a QAM demodulator instead of a QPSK modulator prior to the demultiplexor.

Digital cable television makes it possible to get the same content as in a complete satellite transponder into an 8 MHz channel that previously only distributed one analog channel. Today 8 to 10 TV channels in standard resolution may be housed within such a distribution channel. In addition to this, a noiseless picture is achieved in combination with improved audio. The only audio that used to be better is the NICAM stereo sound used in some of the European countries. Most cable TV operators in these countries did never introduce NICAM stereo in the cable networks, except for channels directly fed from terrestrial transmitters into the program content. Otherwise, NICAM encoding in cable networks was quite expensive.

Analog cable TV has become quite old and out of fashion but all this can be easily managed by introducing DVB signals. By using DVB, it is now also possible to introduce multi-channel AC3 audio (Dolby Digital) in the cable networks. In this way, cable TV subscribers get access to the quality and possibilities that previously only have been possible using direct satellite reception.

SMATV, SATELLITE MATV SYSTEMS

In parallel to traditional cable TV there is another kind of satellite MATV systems, the satellite i.f. (intermediate frequency) systems. In these systems, the signal from one or more satellite dish is distributed directly to a satellite receiver placed in each apartment or house. Everyone uses the same kind of satellite receiver as they would if they had a dish of their own. The only common parts are the satellite dishes and a multi-switch system. A drawback is that the households have to be located quite close to each other since distribution takes place in the frequency range of 950 to 2,150 MHz. The advantage is that each household can get the same number of channels as if they had their own dish.

However, this access comes at a price. The coaxial cable in building must be a star-shaped network with one cable to each household from the divider,

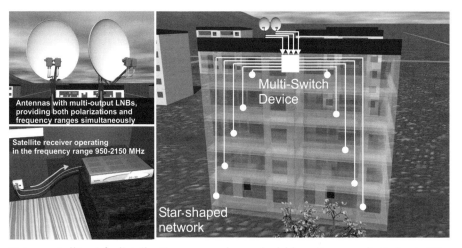

FIGURE

5.13

Using satellite i.f. distribution, every household has its own digital satellite receiver and may receive as many channels as if they had their own satellite dish. This may be regarded as a satellite MATV system.

and the cables have to be of the low-attenuating type. In addition, there has to be a multi-switch device that makes it possible for each viewer to select the correct LNB, polarization and part of the satellite frequency band (10.70–11.70 GHz or 11.70–12.75 GHz) to be able to watch a certain channel. Signaling to the multi-switch device may be used on the 22 kHz tone, the change of supply voltage at the LNB input of the satellite receiver or pure DiSEqC signaling. We will take a deeper look at this technology in Chapter 9, "How to Connect the Devices." The technique described here may be regarded as a kind of MATV based on satellite instead of terrestrial reception.

TERRESTRIAL DIGITAL TV SIGNALS IN COAXIAL CABLE SYSTEMS

There is yet another way to supply a coaxial cable network with digital TV signals. Every household can have a terrestrial digital receiver but share the same antenna system. The drawback (compared to 64 QAM based digital cable television) is that a terrestrial TV channel according to the European DVB-T standard and that is 8 MHz wide only can handle a bitrate of about 22 Mbit/s compared to 38 Mbit/s using 64 QAM. The advantage (compared to the satellite i.f. distribution system) is that ordinary cable TV networks operating at

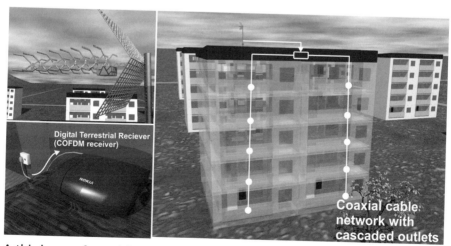

FIGURE

5.14

A third way of supplying a coaxial cable network with digital TV is using signals from terrestrial digital TV transmitters. This technique resembles traditional MATV but in a digital shape.

frequencies in the VHF and UHF frequency bands may be used. It is also possible to distribute the signals in networks having cascaded outlets.

The terrestrial TV signals will be discussed more in detail in Chapter 6, "Digital TV by Terrestrial Transmitters."

The strength of cable TV is that it is possible to let several households share the same signal source. This is ideal for people who do not wish to worry about the reception equipment themselves. The drawback is that programming choices may be limited, relative to having a reception system completely on your own. You have to rely on the signals the cable operator has put into the network and what technology is used for the distribution.

6 | Digital TV by Terrestrial Transmitters

CHAPTER

FIGURE

6.1

Terrestrial digital TV use the traditional TV antenna.

For decades, terrestrial TV was the only way to watch TV. The only exception was MATV systems which could more or less be regarded as an extension of the terrestrial transmitters.

Terrestrial TV is the oldest way of distributing TV and for this reason, all TV sets are equipped to receive these signals without any access to either cable TV networks or satellite dishes. Terrestrial TV is still very popular today. In an astounding way, terrestrial transmissions have been able to withstand the competition from cable and satellite. Even viewers who have access to satellite TV still use terrestrial TV as a complement for reception of the basic free to air channels.

There are even technical advantages in terrestrial TV compared to the other ways of distribution. On top of no need for a cable TV connection, the terrestrial reception is not affected by bad weather conditions such as snow or heavy rain. In other words, terrestrial TV is a very reliable way of distributing TV.

Since the TV signal contains a large amount of information, the analog signals require a lot of bandwidth and rather high frequencies are required for distribution. For this reason, high towers were built to hold the transmission antennas.

The same thing applies to FM radio being transmitted in the range 87–108 MHz. Before the 1950s, when FM radio and television was introduced, lower towers and wires were used for distribution of AM radio in the long- and medium-wave frequency bands. Now 300 m (1,000 feet) towers were introduced to cover an area up to about 50 km (30 miles) or away from the transmission site (see Figure 6.2). The local conditions for reception of the signals still vary a lot from one site to the next due to obstructions such as mountains, hills and even buildings.

FIGURE
6.2

Terrestrial transmissions are often based on 300 m (1,000 feet) towers. At the top there is a red and white cover inside which you will find the UHF transmission antennas. Underneath are the VHF band III antennas and then the FM radio transmission antennas. The antennas are arranged according to frequency with antennas for highest frequencies on top and the lower the frequency the lower antenna position in the tower.

The TV broadcast transmissions that started in Europe in the 1950s used the VHF (Very High Frequency) bands between 47 and 230 MHz. These frequency bands are still used for the first national channel in most European countries except in the United Kingdom where VHF was left when the old 405 line system was shut down. Unfortunately the VHF band does not contain that many channels. In the lower part of the frequency range, band I, covering 47–64 MHz, there is only enough space for three channels: 2, 3 and 4.

Figure 6.3 shows the frequency ranges for terrestrial TV. Band II 87–108 MHz is used for FM radio while band III, 164–230 MHz includes channels 5, 6, 7, 8, 9, 11 and 12. During the 1960s, most countries in Europe wanted to start a second channel. Since the national TV stations had a monopoly in almost all European countries, the development of private TV was restricted and the number of channels was small. It took some time before the UHF frequency bands were brought into operation. In the UHF frequency bands, 470–862 MHz, there are much more bandwidth including channels 21–68.

However, distributing TV at these higher frequencies is much more dependant on a free line of sight between the transmitter and the receiver than is the case in the VHF frequency ranges.

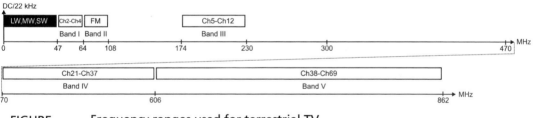

FIGURE
6.3

Frequency ranges used for terrestrial TV.

As a total, there are quite a lot of channels in the terrestrial frequency ranges for TV. But there is also a serious problem. Every analog program channel will require a large number of used transmission channels to cover an entire country. The reason for this is that neighboring transmitters always must transmit at different frequencies (see Figure 6.4). They will interfere with each other even if they transmit the same program content and even if they are synchronized with each other. Since the terrestrial signals may travel quite far during good weather conditions, the necessary distance between two transmitters using the same channel must be quite large.

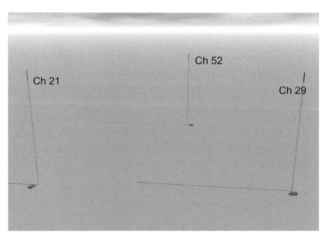

FIGURE

6.4

Adjacent transmitters need to use different transmission channels even though they transmit the same program channel.

For that reason, it is hard to get more than about five analog program channels with national coverage. The conclusion is that right from the start there were large limitations in how many channels could be provided using analog terrestrial transmitters. For many years, the viewers were pretty satisfied with two, three or four channels to choose from.

But during the 1980s, satellite and cable TV offered new possibilities. The analog cable TV networks can handle a much larger number of channels since every channel may be used in one single network. There is also more bandwidth due to the usage of S channels that are not allowed outside the coaxial cables.

ANTENNAS FOR TERRESTRIAL TV RECEPTION

There are three different kinds of antennas for terrestrial radio and TV signals. There are antennas belonging in each of the frequency ranges, band I (channels 2–4), band II (FM radio 87–108 MHz), band III (channels 5–12) and UHF bands IV and V (channels 21–69). Most antennas are based on the classical Yagi design that is well known to everyone (see Figure 6.5).

Yagi antennas are normally designed around a dipole that is half a wavelength wide. A dipole may work as an antenna on its own but will get equally sensitive in both directions. Since directivity in one direction is desired, the lobe in the backward direction may be suppressed with a reflector. The reflector also increases the gain in the forward direction towards the transmitter.

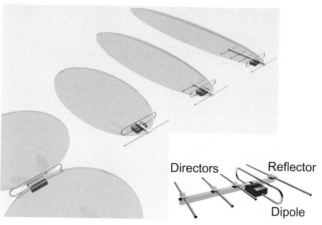

Directors   Reflector

Dipole

FIGURE

6.5

The Yagi antenna is the most common antenna for receiving terrestrial TV signals.

The reflector is a bit wider than the dipole. In terrestrial analog TV, directivity is desired to avoid reflexes. To achieve this, one or more antenna elements can be placed in front of the dipole. These elements are called directors and are less than half a wavelength wide. The larger number of directors the better directivity of the antenna.

In analog terrestrial TV, the reflexes are the largest enemies. Reflexes cause ugly "ghost" images and they are very hard to get rid of. The only way to avoid reflexes is either to live in a place with a clear line of site (no large buildings or mountains in the way) or to use an antenna with a large directivity.

Using an antenna with a large directivity to avoid reflexes follows the same principle that makes satellite TV free of reflexes. In the case of satellite TV, the transmissions are at very high frequencies and the antennas are quite large in relation to wavelength. Therefore parabolic dishes have a much larger directivity than is the case for terrestrial Yagi antennas in the VHF or even in the UHF frequency bands. Even if you use the largest UHF antenna, there is a high likelihood of reflexes in the picture.

Since the dimensions of Yagi antennas are related to the wavelength, there are practical limitations when it comes to the numbers of directors that can be added to obtain greater directivity and gain in the lower frequency bands. For the UHF band it is possible to construct antennas with a lot of directors. Therefore the directivity of UHF antennas is superior to the antennas in the lower frequency ranges.

The In-House Amplifier

In most European countries, the original national channel is transmitted in the VHF bands and the UHF bands are used for the additional channels. Therefore, there is a need to filter together one VHF and one UHF antenna in order to use just one cable to carry the signal from the antennas to the TV set(s). It is necessary to use a filter. If the signals are not filtered, one signal may enter the antenna system two different ways, causing ghost images similar to reflexes on the TV screen. In addition, half of the received power will be lost.

With a filter, it is possible to combine the antennas without compromise. The most common filters have one VHF input (band I or band III) and one UHF input. Sometimes there is an additional input for FM radio (band II). In this case, you must use an outlet that splits the TV and radio signals before they are connected to the TV set and the FM radio.

In many places, the received signal is very weak and it may be necessary to amplify the signal before it is distributed to the TV sets. In most homes, there are several TV sets and the signal is split up before it reaches the sets. Many people choose to use a filtering amplifier instead of a passive filter. The filtering amplifier is a combined filter and amplifier. These amplifiers often have two outputs, making it easy to connect to multiple TVs without suffering any losses (see Figure 6.6).

FIGURE

6.6
Many in-house filtering amplifiers have two outputs, making it easy to connect two TV sets with no losses.

When it comes to amplifiers, it is important to remember that the amplifier only compensates for the cable attenuation and splitting losses you have in the receiving system. It does not resolve problems related to receiving low-quality signals in the first place, so it is still important to have good antennas. Certain amplifiers may give an additional improvement of the reception, since their noise figure may be lower than the input noise figure of a conventional TV set.

No power outlet is needed in the attic or close to the roof since the amplifier can be remotely fed from a power supply placed close to one of the TV sets. The power supply uses the coaxial cable to feed the amplifier in the attic. Figure 6.7 shows an in-house filter amplifier and its power supply.

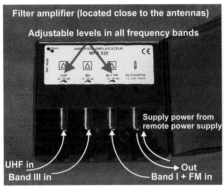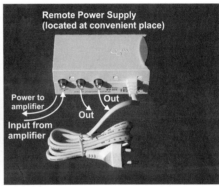

FIGURE
6.7

The in-house filter amplifier is often remotely powered using the coaxial cable to feed power from a power supply located next to the TV set.

Another kind of antenna that is useful is the group antenna, which has four open dipoles and a reflector behind, shown in Figure 6.8. This antenna has a comparatively high gain combined with a large beamwidth and a very large bandwidth. If you are not subject to reflexes and the signals are not extremely weak, an antenna like this might be a good choice. It is also easy to put in an attic where you probably do not have that much space.

A Yagi antenna will not provide full gain across the complete UHF frequency band. This problem is illustrated in Figure 6.9. If you want to have an antenna capable of handling a wide frequency range, a group antenna combined with an in-house amplifier might be a good choice.

In most European countries, only one UHF antenna is needed to receive all channels. However in border areas around Europe, viewers often want to receive the TV channels from the neighboring country. Then UHF receptions from several directions may be needed.

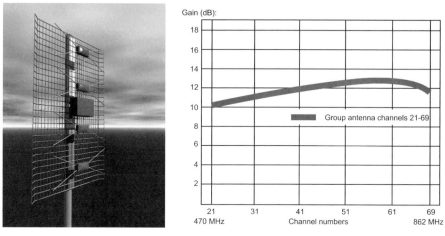

Gain (dB):

Group antenna channels 21-69

21   31   41   51   61   69
470 MHz   Channel numbers   862 MHz

FIGURE

6.8

Typical gain curve showing the bandwidth of a group antenna including four open dipoles.

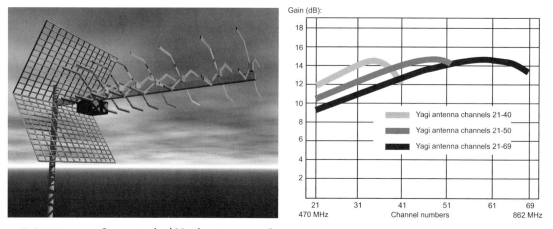

Gain (dB):

Yagi antenna channels 21-40
Yagi antenna channels 21-50
Yagi antenna channels 21-69

21   31   41   51   61   69
470 MHz   Channel numbers   862 MHz

FIGURE

6.9

Some typical Yagi antenna gain curves.

To get this to work when receiving analog signals, you have to use separate antennas for different directions. If you are extremely lucky, you might be in a position where the foreign transmissions are in line or almost in line with the domestic ones, as in Figure 6.10. However this is more likely the exception than the rule.

In all other cases, you must use a combining filter to avoid ghost images when receiving analog signals. This means tailor-made filters for UHF combination for every region. Figure 6.11 shows such a filter. In this case, the filter

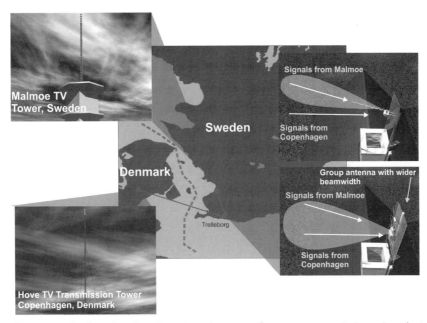

FIGURE

6.10

If you are lucky, the foreign signal comes from a transmission site that is in line with the domestic one. By using an antenna with a broader beam, you may be able to pick up transmissions without a combining filter.

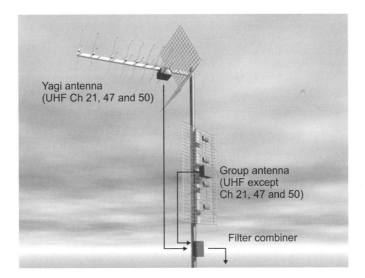

FIGURE

6.11

A Yagi antenna is used for three channels coming in from the left. The rest of the UHF band is available from the group antenna below receiving signals from the other direction.

is designed to let the Yagi antenna (used to receive channels 21, 47 and 50) combine with the remaining parts of the UHF bands that are received by a broadband group antenna below the Yagi.

It is crucial to know which filter is used in the reception system. When you convert to digital reception, a large number of channels are added. Then you will have to know which input of the filter is the broadband input.

DIGITAL TERRESTRIAL TV

Analog TV suffers from two larger problems. One is the lack of bandwidth and the uneconomical ways of using the channels. This means that the number of channels is considerably less than for satellite and cable TV. The second problem is that the picture quality is very dependant upon local reception conditions. Digital terrestrial television, based on the DVB standard, has a very clever way to deal with both these problems.

To begin with, the same basic DVB transport stream is used as for satellite and cable TV. However, the transport stream is distributed using a much more complicated way of modulating the signal. As mentioned earlier, terrestrial signals are exposed to reflexes because hills, mountains and tall buildings interfere with the signal. Reflexes vary due to weather conditions and can also be caused by moving objects such as airplanes. Satellite dishes have narrow beams so the signals are much more stable because there are no reflexes. The secret of digital terrestrial TV is hidden in the way to modulate these signals.

In Europe the DVB-T standard based on, Coded Orthogonal Frequency Division Multiplex (COFDM) is used. This is completely different from the American Advanced Television Systems Committee (ATSC)-standard, which is described in Appendix A.

Coded Orthogonal Frequency Division Multiplex

The COFDM systems have one similarity to the satellite and cable TV DVB signals: It uses amplitude and phase modulation. The standard allows for several ways of modulation. The most common is using 64 QAM just as for cable. What is special, though, is that it is not a matter of one carrier but thousands of carriers, each carrying a small portion of all information to be transmitted.

There are advantages in spreading the information like this. If we use 64 QAM, each carrier may at a certain instant represent a symbol containing six bits. There are two versions of COFDM, 2k (2,000 carriers) and 8k (8,000 carriers). In the 8k system, there are really only 6,817 carriers that contain information to be used for our TV channels. The rest of the carriers have different functions, such as pilot carriers that are used by the receiver to examine the transmission channel. A simple calculation shows that 6,817 x 6 = 40,902 bits may be transmitted (symbolized) simultaneously. This is called a COFDM symbol.

If instead the 2k system is used, 1,705 carriers are used to carry actual data, representing 1,705 x 6 = 10230 bits that can be symbolized simultaneously (see Figure 6.12). Each carrier in a 2k signal will have to be four times wider than a carrier in the 8k system to match the amount of data carried in an 8k system. In this example, consider the same modulation scheme, 64 QAM, to be used in both the 2k as well as in the 8k signal. Each carrier can symbolize six bits every instant. What makes the 2k carrier wider is the fact that it has to change symbol four times faster than a carrier in the 8k system. The important thing is that in the 8k system, the receiver has four times more time to identify the symbol than in the 2k case.

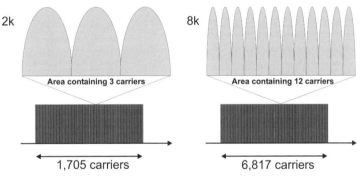

FIGURE

6.12

COFDM using 1,705 and 6,817 carriers.

By using a very large number of carriers you may transmit many bits of digital TV simultaneously giving the opportunity to let each set of bits be on the air for a quite long time.

The receiver will always receive a signal that gets directly from the transmitter. If there is also a reflected signal, this signal will arrive at the receiver a bit later. If the symbol can be transmitted for quite some time, there is a chance that the reflected signal will contain the same symbol as the direct signal. This is the basic idea of creating a system that is not sensitive to reflections—letting everything happen so slowly that the direct signal and the reflections have the same content. Since everything happens four times slower in the 8k system than in the 2k, the 8k system can handle reflections that are four times longer than in the 2k system.

In both systems, each symbol (set of bits) is transmitted for a bit longer than is really necessary to keep the bitrate at the desired speed (see Figure 6.13). This extra time is called the guard interval, and it provides extra time for the receiver to identify the symbol while the same symbol is available in the directly received signal as well as in the reflected signal. The symbol is also surrounded by a cyclic prefix that helps the receiver synchronize several signals that are delayed in relation to each other.

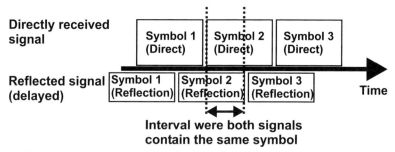

Each symbol contains a guard interval and a cyclic prefix
that are not shown in this figure

FIGURE

6.13

Two signals are entering the receiver. There is quite a long interval where both signals contain the same symbols. The main task for the demodulator is to detect this interval and to decide the value of the transmitted symbol during this interval.

In Figure 6.13, the direct signal and the reflected signal are shown as they enter the demodulator of the receiver. The secret of COFDM is to detect the symbol while the same symbol is still contained in both signals.

Some of the transmitted carriers are pilots containing known information. These pilots are used by the receiver to calculate the actual reflection properties of the channel. This provides additional information that is used to select the correct time for identifying which value (which set of bits) is being transmitted.

Single Frequency Networks (SFN)

We have already seen that in the analog world, two adjacent transmitters distributing the same program channel have to use different transmission channels operating at different frequencies. This consumes an enormous amount of bandwidth. Digital systems do not work that way, fortunately. Using the capability of the COFDM receiver to receive signals that are delayed in relation to each other, it should be possible to receive signals from two transmitters simultaneously. However, in order to get this to work, the receiver has to experience the second signals as if it was a reflection of the first signal. If we let both transmitters distribute exactly the same signal and see to that they are absolutely synchronized, this condition can be fulfilled. Then the receiver can not distinguish a difference between a reflection and the "interfering" signal from the adjacent transmitter.

The possibility to use the same frequency in a larger area (including several transmitting sites) saves a lot of frequencies. An interesting comparison is that in satellite TV, as well as in cable TV, only one frequency is used for each service. By using SFN techniques, a similar situation applies for a digital terrestrial network as well.

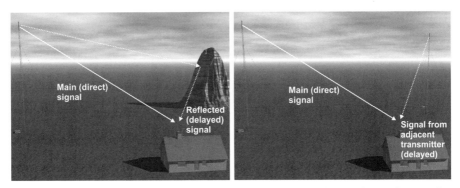

FIGURE

6.14

The basic principle for single frequency networks (SFN) is making the receivers believe that the interfering signals are really ordinary reflections by giving them the same technical properties.

Choosing 2k or 8k

The choice between 2k and 8k is due to the distance between the transmitting sites. We have already seen that everything is four times slower in 8k than in 2k, making the 8k system capable to handle reflections that are four times longer than in the 2k system. If we regard an interfering signal as a reflection, the allowed distance between two interfering stations must be four times larger for an 8k system than a 2k system (see Figure 6.15). In some countries, such as the Untied Kingdom and Germany, the distance between stations is short. Therefore, the 2k system has been selected. In other countries, such as Spain and the scarcely populated Scandinavian countries, the 8k system is used because the distances between the existing transmitting stations are longer.

Using the 2k system, the distance between the transmission sites can be up to 17 km (11 miles) in order to get SFN to work. However, with the 8k system, the distance between the SFN transmission sites increases to a maximum of 68 km (42 miles).

From a receiver point of view, the selection between the 2k and 8k systems does not matter any more since most receivers nowadays are equipped to receive both systems.

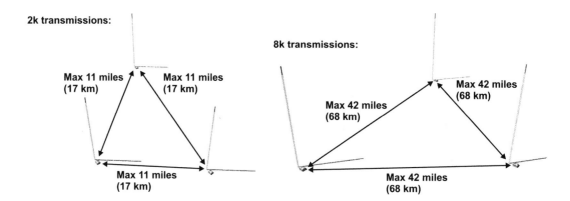

FIGURE

6.15

Since the symbol rate is less when using the 8k system, the time interval where both the direct signal and the reflected signal contain the same symbol will be longer. For this reason the distance in between two adjacent stations may be longer than is the case when using the 2k system.

The Pre-Echo Problem

The basic premise of COFDM is to handle reflections. SFN is a later invention based on the resistance to reflections that is built into the system. In order to choose the right instant to identify the symbol, many COFDM reception chips assume that the first signal to arrive at the receiver is the strongest. When handling reflected signals this is always true. However in an SFN, that is not always the case. If transmitters always have equal transmission power, this would probably be a very minor problem, but frequency coordination issues complicate matters a bit. In Figure 6.16, you can see such a case in Sweden. The Malmö transmitters are coordinated at a power level that is one-fourth of the power transmitted from Hörby TV transmission station. The Malmö and Hörby transmitters are in the same SFN network to preserve frequencies. This is important in this area, due to a tough coordination situation at the border area to Denmark.

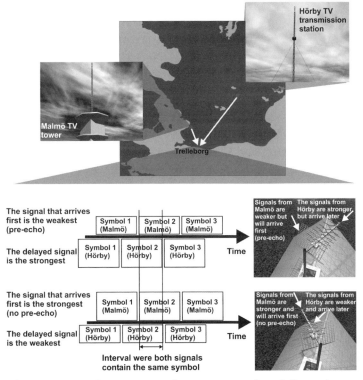

FIGURE

6.16

Always see to that you get the strongest signal first when receiving signals from a COFDM Single Frequency Network. Otherwise the receiver might not work due to the pre-echo phenomenon.

In the small town at the bottom of the map, Trelleborg, people have used the signals from Hörby instead from Malmö for decades since the Hörby analog signals contain all channels in the UHF band and you will only have to use one antenna for all channels. When introducing digital TV this is not a good choice of reception.

The problem is that the signals from Malmö will come in first but will be weaker since the antennas are turned towards Hörby. The Hörby signals will be stronger both due to the fact that the antennas are turned there and that the transmitters are stronger. There will be a pre-echo effect, making it hard for the receiver to keep track of which symbol to compare to which when trying to get the right instant for symbol identification.

A way to solve this problem is to turn the antenna towards Malmö instead. Now the Malmö signal will be stronger since the antenna is pointing in that direction. The Hörby signals will continue to interfere but will be weaker than the signal that is first to enter the receiver and the pre-echo effect is cancelled.

MULTI-DIRECTIONAL ANTENNA SYSTEMS

Digital TV using the COFDM technique is almost completely insensitive to reflections. And the reflections will never cause any visible problems in the picture. In analog terrestrial television, reflections were the most disturbing problem and therefore antennas with a high degree of directivity have been prioritized. Since we don't have to put priority on directivity for antennas used for digital TV, we might use omni-directional antennas. This may solve problems where we wish to both receive signals from several directions and signals that are spread over the entire UHF bands. Omni-directional antennas for TV have existed for many years but the use has been limited to caravans and boats where ease of operation has been more important than picture quality.

From a theoretical point of view, it is also possible to combine two antennas using a broadband combiner without filtering. However if you do that, it is essential to see to that it will not cause any pre-echo effects. In Figure 6.17, a scenario for combining two antennas without using any filters is shown. Half of the received power is lost, but the pre-echo problems are avoided by carefully selecting the location of each antenna and keeping track of cable lengths. The important thing is to be aware of is that both antennas will receive both signals and you will have to ensure that the strongest signal always arrive at the receiver before the weaker signal from the other antenna.

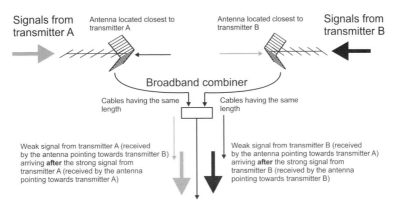

FIGURE

6.17
When combining two antennas without filtering for multi-directional COFDM digital TV reception, the strongest signal should always arrive before the weaker, undesired signal.

INDOOR ANTENNAS

Indoor antennas can be used if you live very close to a transmitter. If you have a weak signal, like most people, you must still use an outdoor antenna. But if the signal strength is enough, an indoor antenna will provide full picture quality much easier than was the case for analog transmissions.

For these reason, lots of new active (antennas that contain an amplifier) indoor antennas have been designed for indoor digital TV reception. The antenna may be connected directly to the receiver, like the early model from Nokia in Figure 6.18. This antenna is fed by 5-volt power supply at the antenna input of the receiver.

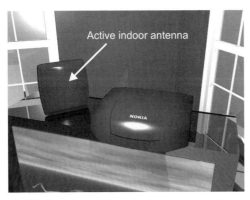

FIGURE

6.18
Nokia 212T connected to an early active broadband antenna from that same company.

Omni-Directional Antennas

Figure 6.19 shows another solution that is suitable for digital TV. This is an outdoor broadband active and omni-directional antenna. This is a way to receive signals from different directions across the complete UHF band. Since it can be located outside, it will work even at low signal levels. It is much better to use an outdoor antenna, since walls and roofs tend to significantly attenuate the UHF signals, especially the higher channel numbers that are at 800 MHz or more.

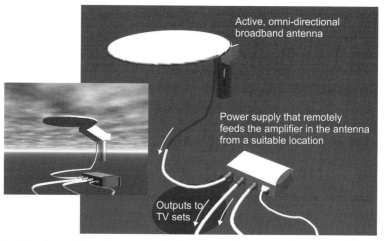

Active, omni-directional broadband antenna

Power supply that remotely feeds the amplifier in the antenna from a suitable location

Outputs to TV sets

FIGURE

6.19

Active, broadband and omni-directional antenna from Danish manufacturer Triax is suitable for digital reception.

DIGITAL TERRESTRIAL RECEIVERS

The digital terrestrial receiver is different from the corresponding satellite and cable receivers when it comes to the input stage, the tuner and the demodulator. The tuner covers the UHF bands and, in some cases, the VHF bands as well. In some European countries, the VHF bands have been abandoned and only UHF will be used for further distribution. However as the analog transmissions cease, it might be possible that even the VHF bands will become popular again for digital distribution, because mobile reception is much easier at lower frequencies. Another situation where VHF is preferable is for MATV systems where the coaxial cable network is not suitable for UHF distribution. Then incoming UHF channels may be converted to VHF before being sent into the coaxial network.

After the tuner, we have a COFDM demodulator and after this the 22 Mbit/s transport stream is regenerated (see Figure 6.20). This transport stream usually contains about five standard definition TV channels. The rest of the receiver is quite identical to satellite and cable TV DVB receivers.

Note

22 Mbit/s is an approximate figure. By using different modulation parameters, the bitrate in a transmission channel may vary. However the 22 Mbit/s choice is a good compromise between capacity and channel robustness.

To compete with satellite and cable, it is essential to get as many channels as is possible into the terrestrial networks. Statistical multiplexing is often used to increases the number of MPEG-2 TV channels from four to five in one terrestrial multiplex.

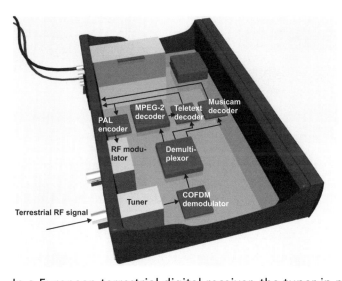

FIGURE

6.20

In a European terrestrial digital receiver, the tuner in most cases operates within the UHF band, 470–860 MHz. The tuner is followed by a COFDM demodulator.

DVB-T RECEIVERS

The introduction of terrestrial digital TV is complicated because in the long run this means closing down the analog transmitters. This will force all viewers to buy digital receivers either as separate boxes or integrated receivers in the TV sets.

To make the transition to digital TV easier, a wide variety of small STBs (set-top boxes) have been developed. These small units can be placed on top of the TV set, hence the name. Earlier designs have had to be placed on a shelf underneath the TV set. The new devices are not much larger than an ordinary VHS video cassette.

FIGURE

6.21

Small size STBs from Swedish manufacturers Emitor and Tevebox.

TERRESTRIAL TV FOR MOBILE DEVICES; DVB-H

The latest addition to the DVB family of standards is DVB-H. "H" stands for Handheld. This standard is optimized for distribution of TV signals to hand-held devices such as cell phones or other mobile devices.

The DVB-H standard is based on adding special signals to an ordinary DVB-T multiplex. These signals are special in several ways. First, the DVB-H signal is based on IP Internet Protocol Packets and thus similar to IPTV (covered in Chapter 6). Another difference is the signal is split into signal bursts instead of being a continuous signal. The idea of sending small bursts of information is that the receiver part or the mobile phone can be switched off between the bursts to preserve battery power. Since the receiver quickly learns the rate and length of the bursts, it knows when to switch on and off.

Another thing that is different from stationary DVB-T reception is that the mobile device only can have a small antenna. This is compensated by even more powerful error protection (adding extra bits for restoring destroyed packets) than is the case for the DVB-T signal.

DVB-H is distributed at considerably lower bitrates than DVB-T for stationary reception. In a cell phone, there is no need for HDTV, since the mobile units use very small displays. Therefore bitrates in the range of 300 kbit/s might be considered for each TV channel. This is to be compared to 3 to 4 Mbit/s per channel for an ordinary standard definition TV channel or up to 16 Mbit/s or more for an HDTV channel.

An interesting aspect of mobile television in cell phones is that there is a return channel, which is not always the case for stationary TV. This means that the broadcaster, the transmission service operator, the mobile phone operator and Internet service providers can work together in completely new ways.

FIGURE

6.22

DVB-H is the latest addition to the DVB family of technical standards for distribution of TV.

7 Digital TV by Broadband

FIGURE

7.1

By using optical fibers that interconnect the continents, it is easy to spread TV at low cost all over the world. NASA TV, one of my personal favourites can be received even in Europe via the Internet. (Screenshots from NASA TV inserted in picture).

The digital television distribution systems described in this chapter are not DVB. However they are related to DVB, since most of them are based on MPEG compression. There are two different kinds of broadband-related TV. First, we have TV transmissions that are streamed on the Internet, Internet television. Secondly, in recent years, the telephone companies have started to compete with the cable operators by providing multi-channel TV services, quite similar to cable TV using IP distribution of TV, IPTV.

BROADBAND IPTV

Instead of coaxial cables, the telephone companies are using the copper wire that was once used for the telephone only. It is the recent advances in Asymmetric Digital Subscriber Line (ADSL) technology that has made this possible. By using ADSL modems, it is now possible to reach connection speeds of about 24 Mbit/s on an ordinary copper wire.

The telephone company starts by establishing a headend that is quite similar to those used in cable TV networks. However instead of distributing analog and digital DVB signals, they encapsulate the TV signals into IP packets. This is the same protocol as is used for general data on the Internet. People who already have Internet access through ADSL can get an IPTV subscription that has the same picture quality as digital cable TV.

Figure 7.2 shows the IPTV set-top box connected to the home IP network switch just like a computer. After this, it works just like a cable TV set-top box. However there is an essential technical difference. When you press the button on the remote, a signal is sent to the telephone company telling them which channel you want to watch. Then they send IP packets containing just that service to your box. In cable television, all channels are available in the cable and your receiver just selects the channels to receive.

In broadband IPTV, you can, in most cases, only receive one TV channel at a time because of the limited bitrate. However it is obvious that in the future, the telephone companies will have to provide several simultaneous TV channels. If you have an 8 Mbit/s connection and you ask for a TV channel of 4.5 Mbit/s, then more than half of the capacity on your connection will be used so this will decrease the speed available for surfing on the Internet.

Triple Play
The telephone operators have a new weapon, called Triple Play (telephony, Internet and TV, all based on IP delivery) to win customers. To use Triple Play, you have a special Triple Play ADSL modem with an integrated IP switch. This modem has separate RJ.45 connections for your computer, your IP telephone and a set-top box for IPTV. In a Triple Play situation it is very easy to establish interactive TV services and so on.

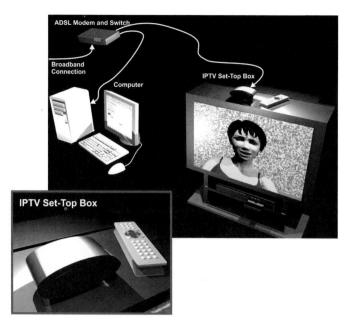

FIGURE

7.2

Broadband IPTV, with IP delivery of a desired channel through an ADSL modem, is a competitor to cable TV.

These broadband IPTV services do not have anything to do with the Internet. The broadband provider, who actually is a telephone company, uses the broadband connection to supply TV channels in more or less the same way as cable TV operators do.

Set-Top Boxes for Broadband TV

A set-top box (STB) for broadband TV is very similar to other kinds of STBs. The same development as for satellite, cable and terrestrial receivers can be expected. These boxes are getting support for HDTV and there are also boxes with hard discs making it possible to store TV programs easily. Already today there are HDTV boxes and MPEG-4 boxes.

INTERNET TV

Another kind of Internet Protocol-based TV, IPTV, is Internet television. Internet television is a way to distribute TV all over the world at quite low cost. This media developed quite early and some of it is based on the assumption that the receiver consists of an old telephone modem.

Broadband TV as described above is quite similar to ordinary cable TV when it comes to quality. But when you start watching TV over the Internet you can not expect the same quality as in ordinary TV. However Internet-based TV is fascinating by providing quite different possibilities for the TV media.

Internet TV is more or less adapted for the computer screen instead of the TV set. It could be regarded as some kind of desktop TV. Often, Web sites include a streamed video clip or a live Internet TV broadcast. Since the TV signals being distributed across the Internet require less bandwidth than all other forms of distribution, where each channel may occupy 4 or 5 Mbit/s. At distribution rates below 1.5–2.0 Mbit/s, MPEG-2 can not be used efficiently. Instead MPEG-1 and MPEG-4 or Windows Media is used to compress the signals.

As covered in Chapter 2, "What Is Digital TV?", MPEG-1 is a predecessor of MPEG-2. The disadvantage in using MPEG-1 is that is has no motion compensation that is needed in order to get soft movements in the reconstructed video signal. This is one cause of the instable movements that are typical in Internet-distributed video. Another problem is that the frame rate often is less than in conventional TV.

Since Internet-based TV uses less resolution than ordinary TV, the picture cannot be enlarged too much on the computer screen. Full screen viewing is more or less hopeless if the signals are not extremely good and you use a broadband connection. In most cases, people watch the transmissions using matchbox-sized windows to keep the picture quality acceptable. It is interesting to compare these small viewing windows viewed close-up against conventional TV at a normal viewing distance. In the picture on the right of Figure 7.3, you see a TV picture that is received through the Internet and presented on a conventional TV set. On the left, you have the corresponding desktop media player picture. In both cases, the image appears about the same size in your field of vision.

Note
   Conventional European TV using 625 lines, of which 576 lines are visible, is designed for a distance between the screen and the viewer that is equal to six times the picture's diagonal.

FIGURE

7.3

The picture of a conventional TV set will fill about the same amount of your field of vision as when you watch a picture on in a small or medium window on your computer screen.

Connecting Your Computer to Your TV

A good way to get the Internet TV picture at a suitable viewing distance is to connect the computer to your TV. There are two basic ways of doing this. The older method is to transfer audio and video from the computer to the TV set using a connecting cable. This requires the computer to have composite video out which today applies to most graphics cards. The graphics cards then usually have a very nice feature—when using a software media player, the graphics card extracts the video content and converts it to full screen video on the composite video output even though the player is only presented in a small window on the computer screen.

However the problem is very often that the computer is not in the same room as the TV set. Then some kind of wireless link is required to solve this geographical problem.

Figure 7.4 shows a wireless system to transfer audio and video signals. In this case the Philips TV NET system is used. In the TV NET system, audio and video is fed from the computer to a 2.4 GHz transmitter/receiver that transmits signals to a device placed by the TV set. This device is connected to the TV set using the scart connector and it also receives infrared signals from an infrared wireless keyboard. These signals are sent back to the device at the computer. In this way, complete control and monitoring of the computer can be achieved using the TV set and the wireless keyboard. Systems like the TV NET are originally thought of as a solution to transfer and control signals from a satellite receiver box to other TV sets in the house that are not directly connected to the box. This kind of devices may actually be used for any kind of audio and video transfer between different parts of your home.

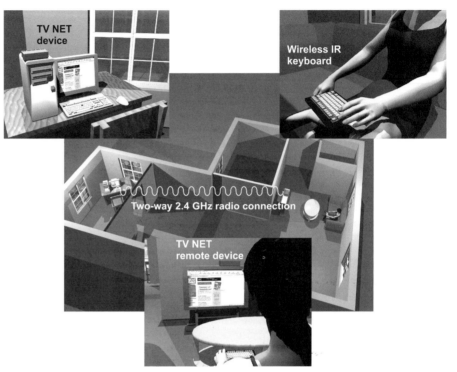

Wireless transfer and control system for using the audio and video signals from a computer in a TV set. There is also a return path from a wireless keyboard.

Unfortunately, the audio and video quality when using this kind of systems is not that good. Most devices like this use analog transfer of the signals. Another problem is that radio propagation in the 2.4 GHz frequency band is quite sensitive to people moving around in the house, thick walls and metal objects that are in the line of propagation of the radio waves.

Another possibility is to have a computer that is directly connected to the TV set. This might be an expensive solution since it may be a dedicated computer for use together with the TV. There are special media computers, called media centers, that are adapted for the media environment and such a computer might be the right choice if you which to have a dedicated computer for media.

However there is a second, more modern, way of combining your computer and your TV set. Several manufacturers such as Hauppauge and D-Link offer media players that are IPTV boxes very similar to the IPTV broadband STBs, including an ordinary remote control. The only real difference is that instead of getting the IP content from the telephone company, you get the files from your own computer using your own home network. This is a good way of connecting your TV set with your computer, since the transfer of the signals is digital, which ensures high picture and audio quality. There are also wireless media players of this kind (WLAN). The IP media player is definitely the most convenient way to get hold of Internet TV as well as the full content of your computer such as digital photos, movies and MP3s.

What Kind of Internet Connection Is Required?

In order to get TV over the Internet, some kind of Internet connection is required. For the best results, you want a high bitrate broadband connection with good quality. However, it is actually possible to watch TV using an ordinary telephone modem. Though broadband connections are increasingly common in Europe and North America, in many parts of the world, the telephone modem is the only way to get Internet. Therefore there are still many streaming TV stations on the Internet that use low bitrates.

In South America and the Arab countries there are lots of TV stations that operate at low bitrates, like those in Figure 7.5, all received using a telephone modem. Note the net congestion warning in the picture from Bahrain TV. Net congestion is the largest problem in Internet TV distribution.

Globo News: 19 kbit/s   **TV Bahrain: 14 kbit/s**   **Fox News: 20 kbit/s**

FIGURE 7.5   Screenshots from Internet TV channels; Globo News at a bitrate of 19 kbit/s. Bahrain TV at 14 kbit/s. Fox News at 20 kbit/s. (See color plate.)

Broadband Connections

In the last few years everyone has talked about broadband, but the definition of broadband varies. For many years, a conventional broadband connection has been 512 kbit/s downstream (from the Internet towards the user) and 128 kbit/s upstream (from the user towards the Internet). However, in order to make high-quality broadband IPTV a reality, bitrates comparable to DVB broadcasting, 4 to 5 Mbit/s, will be required. If you also want to be able to use your broadband connection for simultaneous Internet surfing, you will need still more bandwidth. Bitrates between 8 and 20 Mbit/s have become quite common in some countries, but to connect at these bitrates, you must live quite close to the telephone station. The distance for high speed broadband is limited to a few kilometers or miles.

In order to make broadband radio and TV interesting, you must either have an IPTV subscription with a fixed monthly rate or watch Internet-based TV paying a flat rate for your connection. If your connection is using a telephone modem or using ISDN, you have to pay by the minute. This does not promote the use of this new media.

Internet Connection Options

There was a time when people had good hope for an optical fiber into each household. But this has not yet become a reality but at certain places (See Chapter 5, "Digital TV by Cable"). So, there are only two realistic ways of connecting to the Internet: through the copper wire for your phone or through the coaxial cables for your cable TV. The cable TV Internet connection has been discussed in Chapter 5.

ADSL stands for Asymmetric Digital Subscriber Line and is based on putting radio traffic on the existing copper wires for telephony. This makes this technology very economical. In addition to this, it is a matter of a star-shaped network which makes it easy to establish two-way communications.

Using the audio spectrum in a telephone line makes it possible to use modems that provide about 56 kbit/s maximum in the downstream direction. Upstream is limited to even less, about 34 kbit/s. By putting radio carriers above the audio spectrum, it is possible to extend the bitrate to several Mbit/s, depending on the distance to the telephone station. However in rural areas, it could be hard to get broadband and you will have to find other ways of getting Internet access.

Building Your Own Local IP Network

As you get your broadband connection, a lot of new possibilities are presented to you. The first advantage is that using broadband you will be able to surf the Internet and still be able to use your telephone. However, you will have to find a way to explore many other advantages and possibilities. One of the best ways is to build your own home network. By having a local network at home, you will be able to connect more than one computer to the Internet.

In order to connect several computers you will need a switch, which in most cases, also contains a firewall (see Figure 7.6). Even though you have several computers connected to your local network, the switch sees to that only one IP address is exposed to the outside. Most switches of this kind have four connections, but you can increase this number with an extra switch. Wireless equipment (WLAN) can also take away the tedious work of cabling all around the house.

The firewall is very important because it makes it harder for intruders to get into your computers. All computers communicate through a number of ports. The firewall ensures that just the ports you are actually using are open. Since broadband is fast, there might otherwise be an opportunity for an intruder to get into your computers without you knowing it, spoiling your files or copying valuable or private information.

Another advantage in having your own local network is the possibility to communicate between your computers, sharing printers and other devices. Not to forget the possibilities to use multiplayer computer games between several computers.

FIGURE

7.6

An ADSL modem connected to a combined firewall and switch.

However there is yet one more possibility that we have already discussed, the possibility to connect media computers and media players to your network and making the Internet and the contents of your computers a part of your TV environment. We will take a closer look at this in the next chapter.

Required Bitrate for Picture Quality

As already been discussed, it is possible to use an ordinary telephone modem operating at bitrates below 20 kbit/s for TV distribution. But the video quality will not be impressive. If a broadband connection is used the quality will improve considerably. If you have a broadband connection, you can select higher bitrates. Many Web sites give you a choice of streaming services according to what kind of connection you have. This also gives you an opportunity to compare the picture quality at different bitrates, as in Figure 7.7.

In Figure 7.7 a comparison is made between the picture quality at different bitrates used for modem or broadband reception of low bitrate TV. The pictures are screenshots made using Windows Media Player.

At 56 kbit/s, the picture is quite blurred but a lot better than the previously shown pictures at bitrates below 20 kbit/s. At 96 kbit/s, the picture is considerably better. At bitrates above 221 kbit/s the improvements are less and at 346 kbit/s, the picture quality improves to that of a bad VHS level.

The worst problem in Internet-based TV is not the picture quality itself. The major problem is the risk of getting interruptions due to net congestion somewhere on route between the streaming server and your computer.

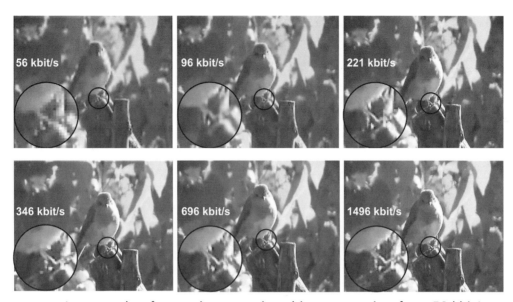

FIGURE

7.7

An example of reception at various bitrates ranging from 56 kbit/s to 1496 kbit/s using Windows Media Player. (See color plate.)

SOFTWARE MEDIA PLAYER OPTIONS

Listening to radio and watching TV over the Internet is different from conventional media through cable, satellite or terrestrial transmitters. These three ways of distribution involve buying a specific hardware receiver for that media. When buying the receiver, you can choose which features you want in the device.

Watching TV or listening to the radio through the Internet starts off with a computer. The media player(s) to be used is or are downloaded into the computer. In essence, the STB has been replaced by a computer and software. When a new player is released, you do not have to buy a new box; you just have to download the new software version.

There are three main software media players that dominate the market: Real Player, Windows Media Player and Quick Time. As a user, you should install all three of them because different radio and TV stations use different players.

Real Player

Real Player has existed for a long time and has always specialized in transfer of low bitrate TV. Real is still a dominating player when it comes to TV in particular. Real is available in a free version which is enough to watch TV on the net. However there is also an improved pay version of the player. Visit *www.real.com* for more information.

FIGURE   C-Span received using Real Player at 100 kbit/s.

7.8

Microsoft Media Player

From the start, Real dominated the market for software media players, but Microsoft Media Player is now perhaps the most common program. Media Player is a part of Windows and therefore comes standard on most computers.

I would especially recommend Media Player when it comes to listening to radio stations. The audio quality is excellent in relation to the bitrates used.

FIGURE

7.9

French news channel BFM TV received using Windows Media Player at 327 kbit/s.

Apple QuickTime

The third major media player is Apple QuickTime. QuickTime is used primarily as an integrated part of Web sites for animations and so on. However during recent years, the program has developed a wider usage, more or less equal to Real or Microsoft Media Player. However QuickTime is seldom used for distribution of radio channels.

> **Streaming Video**
>
> Players for Internet-based low bitrate TV have yet another area of usage. Digital cameras now also record short video files with audio. However the flash memories in cameras of this kind are not yet large enough for full video quality comparable to cassette or disc storage. For this reason the camera manufacturers use the same video file formats that these software media players use.
>
> This means the camera can be used to create short video sequences that may be used for Internet download applications. The viewer then has to first download

the file and then play it in the computer. This technique for distributing short films is suitable for individuals with personal Web sites.

Streaming live TV is much more complicated and expensive. Then you need to have an agreement with a Web hosting operator that provides streaming services, and you will likely have to pay for the traffic to your site. This depends both on the chosen bitrate and on the number of simultaneous viewers that receive your transmission. It is not for free to have your own TV station on the Internet. However this is by far the least expensive way to have a TV station that can be received in all corners of the world.

FIGURE   CNN International received using Quick Time.

7.10

Winamp

Most people relate Winamp to MP3 files rather than listening to radio channels. Winamp is the classic MP3 player and its MP3 capabilities have made the program known worldwide.

But the more recent versions of Winamp have impressive features for listening to radio stations over the Internet. The player contains a very good stand-alone Web browser that may be used to find suitable radio stations. In the latest versions it is also possible to play video and to watch TV.

FIGURE

7.11

Italian 3Web.tv received with Winamp at 331 kbit/s.

Finding Internet Radio and TV Stations

A good way of finding stations is to use the built-in search features in the players themselves. Both the Media Player and Real Player are full featured in this respect. Winamp is a very good tool for finding radio stations. Another source is www.lyngsat.com, which contains listings of almost all satellite channels in the world and also links to radio and TV channels that broadcast live over the Internet.

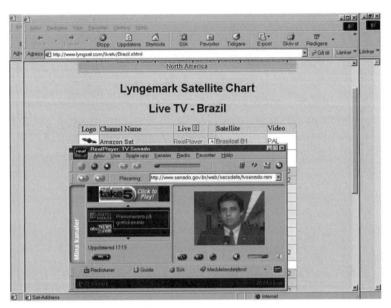

FIGURE

7.12

TV Senado, Brazil found through www.lyngsat.com.

INTERNET VIA SATELLITE

Internet connection via satellite is a special area that perhaps deserves a chapter of its own. Everyone can access Internet with a telephone modem. Broadband connections using ADSL or cable, however, are not available everywhere. The possibilities are depending on where you live. If you live in rural areas without any possibilities to get ADSL or cable, the only remaining alternative is satellite. There are two ways of getting broadband through satellite.

The simple solution is to use a telephone modem to send information to the Internet which means a limitation to 34 kbit/s in the upstream direction (when using telephone modems, 56 kbit/s is only available when going downstream). Therefore in the downstream direction, the IP packets are distributed via satellite instead. The bitrate might be 512 kbit/s or even more, thus comparable to a cable or an ADSL connection. It's in the downstream direction that people need the higher bitrate to download different kinds of files.

The equipment to be used is simple. You can either put a satellite receiver card in the computer or connect an external satellite receiver to receive the IP packets. The receiver is capable of extracting IP packets that are encapsulated into an ordinary DVB transport stream. The drawback of this solution is that in addition to having a low bitrate in the upstream direction, you also have to pay per minute for the telephone modem. Plus, your telephone line is occupied while you are surfing the net.

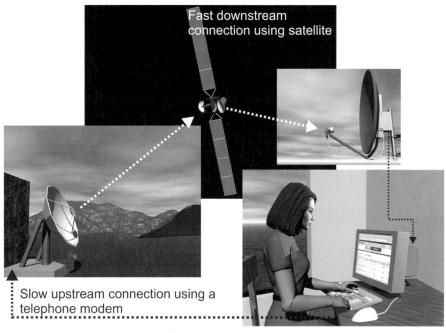

FIGURE

7.13
Internet via satellite where the return traffic (upstream) uses an ordinary telephone modem.

Two-Way Internet Using Satellite

In the United States and Europe, there are ways to connect to the Internet using satellite alone. Figure 7.14 illustrates the American StarBand system. In Europe there are three similar systems: TiscaliSat, SatLynx and Hughes.

The problem with two-way satellite communication is that the user must have an uplink of his or her own. Uplinks are considerably more complicated and harder to install than conventional satellite reception dishes and must be done by a professional installer. In addition, a frequency permit is required in some countries. But still it is interesting to see that StarBand and its European colleagues have been quite successful in offering an Internet access that is comparable to ADSL with a bitrate around 512 kbit/s in the downstream direction and 128 kbit/s upstream at a cost of less than 100 euros (US $120) as a flat rate. However there is a difference compared to terrestrial Internet—the amount of data allowed for download each month is limited to 1 Gbyte.

The terminal equipment in Europe is still expensive as this is written (2006), between 1,600 and 2,000 euros, (US $2,000–2,500) including installation. Internet via satellite is more expensive than an ADSL or cable Internet connection. However there are places where satellite is the only option, so there is a large market for satellite Internet within the coverage areas of the European satellites.

The North America market is more competitive than Europe. The most well-known operator, StarBand, has a flat rate that is below its European counterparts. This is probably due to and interesting new Satellite Internet provider, WildBlue that offers satellite Internet acces at a low rate. This system use brand new Ka-band technology using multiple small beams in the 20/30 GHz frequency bands. This is one of the reasons why they offer a less expensive alternative.

As with other Internet operators, StarBand, TiscaliSat, and SatLynx cannot guarantee a certain bitrate at all times. Therefore they work according to the principle of "best effort." This means that at traffic peaks, the bitrate may decrease slightly or fall to a very low rate. Satellite broadband connections give an impression of being broadband connected, but there are certain things that do not work via satellite, such as online gaming where player reaction time is critical. The trip to the satellite and back takes approximately 0.26 seconds and makes these kinds of applications impossible.

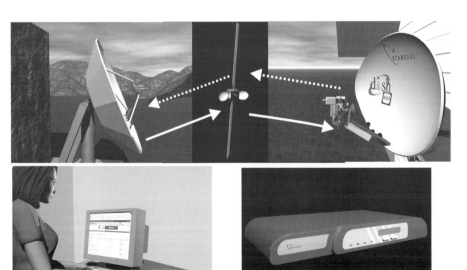

FIGURE

7.14

Two-way Internet connections via satellite do not require terrestrial links or telephone lines.

8 | Choosing the Right Box

FIGURE

8.1

Consumers can choose from a wide range of boxes for digital reception.

In this book, I have described how different kinds of digital TV work. There are four different kinds of set-top boxes: satellite, cable, terrestrial and IPTV. In addition, computers can be used for receiving TV, primarily via the Internet.

DIGITAL RECEIVERS

However, there are also other dimensions in digital TV. The basic principles for satellite, cable and terrestrial STBs are quite alike. But there are other differences. Digital technology also gives us options for lots of new features at different levels. There are digital receivers ranging from very simple featureless boxes to advanced media gateways equipped with hard discs.

Free to Air

The simplest receiver is the FTA, free to air, STB, like the one in Figure 8.2. It can only be used to receive unencrypted signals. In many European countries, such as Germany and Italy, and for terrestrial reception in the United Kingdom, this is enough for many people. If you have a multi-focus satellite dish, there are hundreds of unencrypted channels to watch for free.

FIGURE

8.2

There are lots of small and low cost STBs, including the German Maximum FTA 100. This receiver is smaller than a VHS cassette.

Pay TV

In recent years, pay TV has become more popular and people are quite interested in more specialized channels. But in most European countries, the state owned public service channels still hold a strong position along with the basic commercial general entertainment channels. Still, there is a lot of money to be made from direct payment from the viewers.

Pay TV is based on encrypting the channels and the viewer will need a receiver capable of decrypting the signals. In addition, most encryption systems require a smart card with keys and subscription information. The pay TV business is based on people buying or renting these cards. In certain cases, even commercial and public service channels are encrypted to avoid copyright problems when signals cross a country border, which often is the case in Europe. This problem especially applies to the Netherlands and Scandinavian countries where movies are broadcast in their original language with subtitles. In Germany, France and Italy, most movies are dubbed and this is considered as a kind of "encryption," ensuring that a certain movie is only of use in a certain country.

However, encrypting pay TV channels is not that easy. There are a number of encryption systems available, and the pay TV operators have not selected or wanted to select one common standard for this. The most common systems in Europe are Irdeto, Nagravision, Viaccess, Mediaguard, Cryptoworks, Betacrypt and NDS/Videoguard. There are some other smaller systems, such as Conax as well. All these systems have evolved through several versions in their struggle against pirates. These systems are used in satellite as well as cable and for terrestrial transmissions.

Common Interface

In all this mess, there is something common to at least some of the systems—the "common interface," where it is possible to put a common interface module for a certain encryption system into a common receiver.

Among the advantages of using CA (conditional access) modules is that the same receiver can be sold in many markets, bringing up volumes and lowering prices. Another idea is that it would be easy to exchange encryption system if it has been cracked by pirates. The CA system is put into a PCMCIA module and the receiver has a PCMCIA slot. In the module there is a card reader for the smart card, as shown in Figure 8.3.

When buying a receiver, it could be wise to buy a device that might be equipped with a CA module in the future. This especially applies to more expensive devices that might have hard discs and so on. However some of the systems, such as NDS/Videoguard, are not compatible with CA modules. Instead these systems are embedded in the receivers and the receiver has an internal card reader.

Receiver including a Common Interface for CA modules

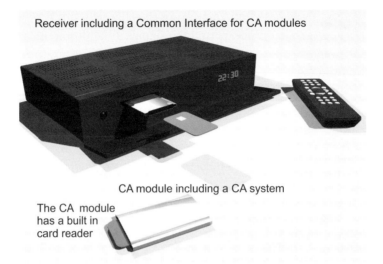

CA module including a CA system

The CA module
has a built in
card reader

FIGURE

8.3

FTA receiver with two common interface slots for CA modules.

Figure 8.4 shows a receiver from Nokia that has a common interface slot
and a built-in card reader for an embedded CA system. A receiver like that can
handle two different CA systems. There is usually no need to handle more than
two CA systems in the same receiver. However, there are exceptions where people move to other countries and want to watch channels from both countries.

FTA channels and encrypted
channels

Common Interface
slot

Card reader for
embedded CA system

FIGURE

8.4

Receiver with both embedded CA and common interface slot.

Proprietary Receivers

Pay TV operators are interested in tying their customers to their services. For this reason, digital receivers are often subsidized and the boxes are adapted in one way or another to the specific technical system used by the operator. You may get the receiver for free if you sign up for a subscription for a certain amount of time. These "free" receivers are more or less proprietary and they might not work at all if you cancel your subscription. There might also be limitations in receiving FTA signals or the possibilities to arrange the channel lists as you which.

Proprietary receivers can be very advanced in some respects and completely featureless in other ways. There might be limitations in handling different CA systems at the same time as advanced interactive services. It is essential to the pay TV operator that you can use all its services. For return traffic from the box to the operator, a telephone modem might be used, and another option is using the mobile phone.

If you only wish to receive channels from one specific operator, a proprietary box might be a good deal. On the other hand, if you change your mind and want to have channels from another operator or two operators simultaneously it might be better to buy a more flexible "retail" box.

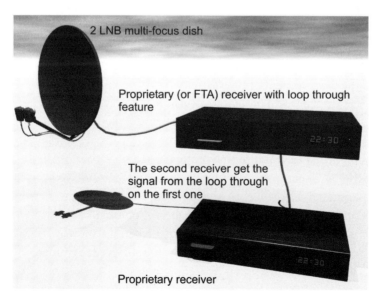

FIGURE

8.5

Connecting two boxes to the same dish using the loop through feature.

If you have a proprietary satellite box and wish to add another proprietary box or a FTA box, there is a clever way to connect two boxes to the same dish. Using the "loop through" feature on one of the boxes, you can let the signal pass through the first box and into the next. If the receiver closest to the dish is in operation, it controls the LNBs in the dish. If the first receiver is switched off the signal is fed to the second receiver which then takes full control.

It may be a drag to use two remote controls, but still it will be possible to receive channels from two operators using one single dish.

DIGITAL TV WITH INTERACTIVE SERVICES

A few years, ago there was a lot of talk about interactive TV. These services are based on the assumption that the viewer will sit in front of his or her TV set and order services and make different kinds of purchases.

However, interactive services are not that new. The first interactive service in Europe was teletext. In this case it was only a matter of interacting with the TV set itself.

The nest step is interacting directly with some kind of operator. This may be done using a telephone. The first truly interactive services were based on this simple principle shown in Figure 8.6. It may seem inconvenient to have to handle both the telephone and the TV remote at the same time. However, this concept has one big advantage. People already own a telephone and a TV set. Later, it would be proved that the technical equipment would be of crucial to the development of interactivity.

In the world of digital television, it is easy to include the telephone modem in the receiver and let the viewer handle the return path through the remote control to participate in contests or to buy services and products.

Most of the interactive ideas became a part of the IT crises in the late 1990s. The interest for interactive services was not as big as had been expected. Some services still exist and work well. But today, most interactive services are not made in front of the TV. Instead they are made in front of the computer. It is hard to compete with the Internet when it comes to interactivity.

Among the things that have really survived are Video On Demand (VOD) services or more precisely Near Video On Demand (NVOD). NVOD means that you have a selection of movies that start once every hour to choose from. Once you select the movie, you may have to wait for the next starting time. Real VOD, where the movie starts the instant you select it, is probably only

FIGURE

8.6

Early interactive services in Europe were based on teletext to reach the viewer and the telephone as a return path.

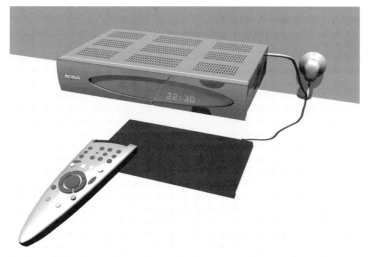

FIGURE

8.7

In the digital receiver the telephone can be replaced by a modem and the interactivity can be handled through the remote.

possible using IPTV, since you can go into the video achieves of the Web sites and fetch small video clips on demand. In the future, it might be possible to go into the archives of the movie companies and buy a personal showing of your favorite movie whenever you want. This may be the way for the telephone companies to win over the satellite, cable and terrestrial operators.

DIGITAL RECEIVER FIRMWARE

A digital receiver is more or less like a computer. There is a processor a bunch of memory and a lot of software. The master software—the firmware—controls most functions of the receiver, what the menus look like, and so on. Different manufacturers use different processors and other hardware and therefore they have different firmware as well. However, the firmware can be exchanged over the air, so the viewer to upgrade the receiver in the future. This is a large advantage, especially to the pay TV operators who recognized that it would be easier to introduce new services and even to make improvements on the encryption system.

This lead to the development of a process called the boot load was introduced. The boot load is a small nucleus of software that cannot be changed. This software contains the code that is needed to download new firmware to the receiver using the on-air signal. Getting new firmware is more or less like getting a new receiver.

Getting a new receiver this way is, of course, nice for the viewer. However this system has a drawback. In the analog ages, the manufacturers were very careful not to put unproven products on the market because it would lead to consumer dissatisfaction, which meant the next version of the product might not be well-received. Today, competition makes it necessary for the manufacturers to start selling new products as quickly as possible. Since software bugs can now be fixed by issuing a new firmware, manufacturers are not as careful as they used to be. For this reason you might get a receiver with a large number of bugs.

Many receivers have proven to have a significant hang rate. There is a cure for that is to pull the plug. But there is one occasion when you should not try to pull the plug—when the receiver is downloading new firmware to be automatically installed.

When you ask the receiver to search for new firmware, it checks what version number is on air and puts it in relation to the firmware currently installed in the box. If there is new firmware on air you will get a question about if you wish to proceed with the upgrade or not.

When trying to upgrade a satellite receiver, you must see to that the receiver is tuned to a certain channel, transponder or at least a certain program package in order to download the new firmware. These problems are not that large in cable and terrestrial receivers. Of course, different brands of receivers and different models need their own specific download streams from the satellites, cable or terrestrial transmitters.

THE APPLICATION INTERFACE

In order to make interactive services fancier than was possible using teletext, better graphics are required. Also, more complex functions are needed when it comes to handling commands sent by the user through the remote control. Why not take advantage of the fact that a digital receiver is more or less a computer? It contains a processor as well as memory.

Software is required to make things work, and if the same application could be run in all receivers, regardless of brand or model, even better. However in order to get this to work, a common operating system, or application interface, is needed.

A part of the firmware therefore has an interface to external applications, called the application interface, or the API. Figure 8.8 shows how the API of the firmware is like a layer between firmware and the applications that may be downloaded into any receiver using the same API.

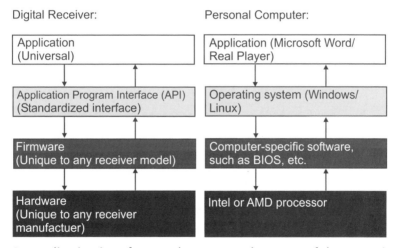

FIGURE

8.8
An application interface can be compared to parts of the operational system in a computer.

Just as in a computer the system is divided into layers with the hardware at the bottom, then the firmware including the API on the upper end. Then finally on top is the application. The most common application is the Electronic Program Guide (EPG).

It could be a nuisance that applications have to be downloaded each time they are going to be used, but in this case it is an advantage. When you change to a channel that belongs to a different operator, you will have to change EPG anyhow.

FIGURE

8.9

An Open TV EPG application made by German public service channel ARD.

THE API OF THE FUTURE

The fact that different operators use different APIs makes it very expensive for the program companies to develop interactive applications. A public service provider that distributes their programs on satellite as well as on cable and by terrestrial transmitters might have to make each application in three different versions in order to get distributed everywhere.

There have been strong demands from the networks and program companies to get a more standardized API. One such possibility is MHP, Media Home Platform, which should provide possibilities to develop cheap applications that would fit everywhere. The drawback is that the MHP requires more processing than the previous APIs.

However there is an even more simple way of creating an EPG that is really standardized. This is by simply using the basic functionalities in the DVB standard. A good example of this is the information on the current and next programs. Figure 8.10 shows an example of what can be made with the DVB standard information. There are tables within the frameworks of the DVB standard that can be used to show more information about programs over a longer period of time. However, each receiver manufacturer has to build his own EPG to use this information as a guide on screen.

FIGURE

8.10

An example of program guide information based on the event tables of the DVB signal. (Screenshot from German commercial channel SAT 1.)

THE MEDIA GATEWAY DREAM

Obviously, there is a dream to put all contents of the radio and TV broadcasting worlds into the same box with Internet and personal computer technology. The digital receivers are not real computers (yet) and the computers are not real digital receivers, so they are still parts of separate worlds.

Those who still want to try to combine the broadcasting world and the Internet world can try to do so by buying separate parts to build their own media computer. To get the computer to work as a full-featured digital TV receiver, a gaming platform and access to the Internet—a complete personal computer—the device has to have enough processing power. Currently, these functionalities cannot be implemented in ordinary STBs. There must not be any compromises when it comes to the processor power or the amount of available memory. You may want to choose between adopting the computer for terrestrial and satellite reception. But in reality you could do both. The port towards the Internet world could be a telephone modem but why not a broadband connection?

Figure 8.11 demonstrates an ordinary computer with a satellite reception card replacing the STB to provide all these things. This is a media gateway.

There are small computers that are better adapted to the living room. But these smaller units do not have the same number of slots you will need for the different kinds of cards making all these features possible. You have to determine the number of extra cards you will need before choosing the box. There

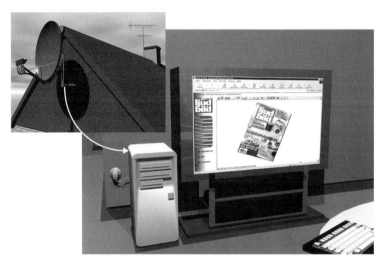

FIGURE

8.11

A media gateway may be based on an ordinary personal computer to provide access to many types of programming.

are even PCI cards with common interface slots so you can theoretically handle several CA systems, provided that there are CA modules available for the encryption standards that you wish to use. Some receivers that are made for installation in computers have their own remote. Otherwise a wireless keyboard might be a more general solution to this problem. If the computer is located close to the TV set, it is really a complete replacement for the digital STB. Using a wireless media player as mentioned before, you will only have one remote and still be able to reach most of the features that are included in your media computer. Another advantage in using media players is can put the computer anywhere in the house; with several media players, you may also use the computer to feed information to several TV sets around the house.

Do not forget the S/PDIF digital audio output of your sound card. This make the computer an interesting program source, even for the home cinema, which will be further discussed in Chapter 11, "The Home Cinema." Finally, the computer may also be used as a DVD recorder and player and the hard disc can be used to pause and store TV programs. A computer may replace most other devices that you use with your TV. The only disadvantage is the work to make all these considerations and decisions. And finally it will be a tech freak device that is quite complicated to maneuver. But still, some people are really tech freaks and want this kind of stuff.

THE MEDIA TERMINAL

After reading the description of the things to think about when designing your own media gateway, most people might wonder if there are no ready-built boxes of this kind. The answer is that there are commercial media computers available. The problem is that you must check that these devices really contain everything that you want. And remember that if the computer has a fan it may be disturbing, just as noisy hard drives might be.

It is essential to remember that a media terminal is not really a replacement for the personal computer. You do different things in front of the TV than you do at your desktop. This may be the simple explanation why there still is a difference between boxes on your desktop and boxes close to the TV. By the TV, you have this "lean backward" attitude and want to relax. Conversely, in front of your desk you intend to work (even though sometimes the work consists of playing a computer game). At desk, you are in the "lean forward" position.

The latest contribution to this is the Microsoft Media Center based on Windows XP. But the idea is not new. In 2001, Nokia tried to introduce a set top box that was really a Linux computer combined with a digital satellite receiver. However this product was probably too early for the market and disappeared six months later. However the Nokia box had the intention of combining satellite reception with a broadband connection, to be able to play MP3 files and store TV programs and digital photos on the hard disc.

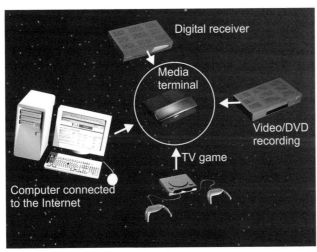

FIGURE
8.12

A media terminal combines a number of features in one single device.

As you join together all these features, you get a lot of new features created by the synergies of the others. As an example, being able to reach the Internet from your digital receiver suddenly turns the Web sites of the program companies into very advanced electronic program guides. This is much better than conventional EPGs and much, much better than the old teletext. Actually you can also read newspaper articles on your TV.

The Nokia media terminal Mediamaster 510S was ahead of its time, and we can see that the idea still lives on. A challenge in the late 1990s and early 2000s was that it became a part of the IT crises. But the features of this device can be found in several other receivers and computers today. All manufacturers today have a hard disc digital box, personal video recorder (PVR), at the top of their product range. And there are receivers with flash card readers to take care of your digital photos that may be easily shown on your TV set.

But including a 500 MHz Pentium Celeron processor and a 40 Gbyte hard disc it was a solution without compromise when it was presented in 2001.

One of the major problems in introducing digital TV has been the many possibilities. This makes it hard for the viewers to understand and adopt all new ideas and ways to use all new features. A computer with appropriate software allows for almost whatever you may ask for, or perhaps evens more.

9 Connecting the Devices

FIGURE

9.1

There is a lot to say about connecting devices to the TV set.

After a while, all TV viewers will discover their personal preferences for connecting the electronic devices in their homes. This may require several different communications networks in the home.

The oldest communication network in the home is the telephone connection. Another network that has been around for a very long time is the cabling from the TV antenna to the TV sets. Nowadays, there is a third network in most homes, the IP network which serves the computers with Internet connection as well at tying the computers to each other.

191

In this chapter, we will take a deeper look at how these three kinds of networks can be designed and improved. As the digital signals are introduced, it may be a good idea to check everything and see what can be done.

Lots of viewers have combined their terrestrial TV system with satellite reception. The satellite signals are fed from a satellite dish to a receiver installed on the most-used TV set in the home. If the viewer instead is connected to cable, he might do with just one means of reception. The cable TV network contains all important channels and there might not be a need for additional signals.

However, it is not just a matter of bringing the signals into the house. Modern homes are stuffed with electronic devices that require signals from satellites, cable, terrestrial transmitters and the Internet. The next step is distributing these signals around the home.

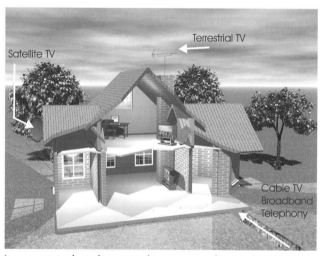

FIGURE

9.2

In most modern homes, there are radio and TV signals either from terrestrial transmitters, satellite, cable or broadband.

THE ANTENNA SYSTEM FOR TERRESTRIAL SIGNALS

The traditional antenna system for TV in a home is based on antennas that are located on the roof, in many cases on a tube attached to the chimney. The antennas are combined to one coaxial cable which uses either a passive filter or an in-house amplifier, performing the filtering and amplifying the signals to suitable levels for further distribution within the building (described in Chapter 6, "Digital TV by Terrestrial Transmitters").

Coaxial Cabling

In many cases, there is a cable from the antenna system to the living room. Coaxial cables are often housed in the same kind of plastic tubes used for the electrical cabling. Even in older houses, there might be plastic tubes in the walls where this cable is located. If you are lucky there are tubes even to other rooms in the house. When constructing a new house it is essential to see to that there are tubes from the attic to all rooms from the start. Even if there is no need for cables to all room in the beginning, such needs will occur sooner or later. Otherwise cabling to different rooms later might be very difficult and time-consuming.

In-house amplifiers usually only have one or two outputs. The supply voltage to the amplifier is usually done using the coaxial cable. This allows the power supply to be at a convenient place, such as the living room, and no electrical outlets are required in the attic. Then the outputs of the amplifier system are on the power supply. But there is a problem with this. It might not be wise to have cables go from the living room to the other rooms; it would be better if the cables went straight from the attic to the different TV sets in the house. This means putting the power supply in the attic. Then it is easier to split the signals to the different antenna outlets of the house. After the outputs of the power supply we do not have to care about supply voltages in the cables.

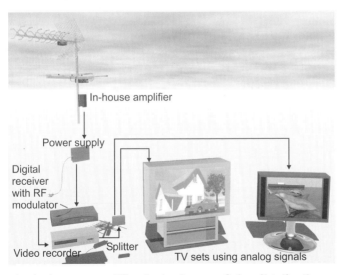

FIGURE

9.3

The in-house amplifier is the heart of the distribution system for terrestrial signals. It is also an easy and classic way to spread RF modulated signals from digital receivers and video and DVD recorders, with built in RF modulators, around the house.

The terrestrial signals are at frequencies below 862 MHz and are distributed using coaxial cables that, in reality, can handle even higher frequency ranges. Therefore, the same cables can be used to distribute the satellite signals from the satellite dish to the satellite receiver. These signals are in the range 950–2150 MHz. But the higher frequency, the higher is the attenuation in the cables.

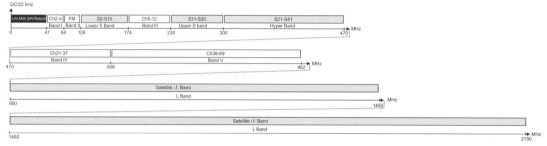

FIGURE 9.4 In practice, all frequencies from DC up to 2150 MHz can be used to distribute signals between various antenna systems and set top boxes and TV sets.

Splitters

Splitters can be attached at the output of the power supply of the in-house amplifier. There are different numbers of outputs from the splitters but most common are two- or four-way splitters. But the loss in the splitter will increase with the numbers of outputs. The splitter is a small box which contains a printed circuit board where the coaxial cables are connected using screw attachment. We can't just attach the cables to each other in a pure galvanic way without the printed circuit in the splitter because the input and the outputs have to be matched to each other. The signals are electromagnetic waves and all connections have to be matched to avoid the waves from getting reflected. As a comparison, we can look at a wave in the ocean as it approaches the beach. The sandy beach is a thicker media than water and therefore the wave is reflected back into the ocean. The same thing applies to a radio wave which is entering a change in the media as when traveling through a cable and coming to a split point. If we just split up a signal without first making arrangements so that the wave does not feel the media change, we get reflections. In analog TV signals, we will see these reflections as ghost images. The splitter matches all the signals so no reflections are created.

Another reason for using splitters is that the outputs should be isolated from each other. TV sets and receivers contain oscillators creating internal radio signals that are used for frequency conversion of the incoming signals. These local oscillator signals may cause problems if their signals leak out in the wrong directions. Spurious signals that may be radiated from the antenna input of one TV set can affect the received signals in another TV set that is connected to the splitter, unless properly isolated. Small, cheap splitters do not provide any isolation between the outputs while more advanced (and costly) splitters contain directional couplers that sometimes may be needed quite badly to get sufficient isolation between the connected sets. Figure 9.5 shows examples of each.

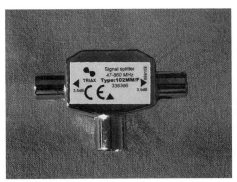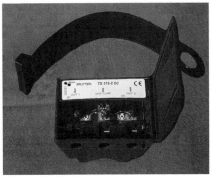

FIGURE

9.5

The simple splitter (left) provides matched input and output but no isolation between the ports. The splitter to the right provides matched connections and also offers isolation between the inputs.

It may also be good to know that it is possible to use a splitter in the reverse direction, as a combiner of two and more signals. We will return to this subject later on.

Outlets and In-House Networks

The signal that is obtained from the output of the power supply of the amplifier may be connected straight to the antenna input of a TV set. However, in most cases, a wall outlet is put in each room partly for aesthetic reasons, but there are also technical reasons. In the outlet, a filter separates the FM radio (band II) from the TV bands so one cable connects to the radio and the other to the TV set. In addition, it might also be practical to be able to use a shorter cable inside the room. This might be practical if you move the TV set. Then it is just a matter of choosing the right length of cable between the outlet and the set.

It is preferable to design an in-house network as a star-shaped network (see Figure 9.6). Remember that you should use outlets designed for star networks, which only have one connection to the antenna system. The other kind of outlets, for cascaded networks, also has an output connection to continue the cable to the next outlet. Really, cascaded outlets are splitters dropping off a small portion of the signal in the outlet and feeding most of the signal on to the next outlet. The relationship between the signal dropped off and the signal that is fed on to the next outlet varies. The first outlet in a branch might have just one-tenth of the signal while the outlet before the end outlet has half of the remaining signal power. The last outlet must be the star outlet kind since we want to terminate the signal.

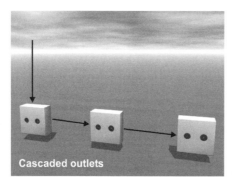
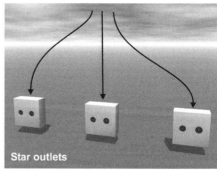

Cascaded outlets

Star outlets

FIGURE

9.6

Cascaded and star-shaped networks require different kinds of outlets.

Mounting IEC Connectors

A coaxial cable consists of an inner conductor, dielectric insulation material and an outer coaxial conductor, which is the reason for the name. On top of that there is an outer insulation protecting the cable. The outer conductor is usually connected to ground and acts as a shielding against signals from the outside.

When an IEC is to be mounted on a coaxial cable, about 1 centimeter (0.4 inch) of the outer insulation is removed. Then the outer shielding is pulled back over the outer insulation. Finally, five to seven millimeters (0.2 to 0.3 inches) of the inner insulation is removed. In Figure 9.7, you can see what it all looks like after this. In the IEC connector, there are two screw attachments for the inner and outer conductor respectively.

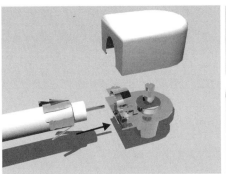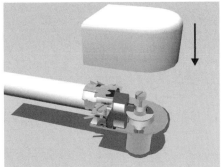

FIGURE

9.7

Mounting an IEC connector to a coaxial cable.

Note

When working with the cabling from an in-house amplifier be sure to unplug the power supply before you start. A short circuit on the input or outputs of the amplifier system may destroy the amplifier immediately.

Another important thing is to avoid bending the coaxial cables. You have to allow a certain minimum radius of the cable when passing corners. If the cable is bent too much, there will be a mismatch and a reflection in the bend. Of course you should not press cables in closed windows since this will also cause reflections and, in the long run, completely destroy the cable.

The antenna cable to the TV antenna input requires a female connecter in the TV set end.

Some more modern in-house amplifiers don't use screw attachments but F connectors instead. This is the same kind of connectors that are also used for the cabling between LNBs, DiSEqC switches and satellite receivers.

CONNECTING THE DIGITAL RECEIVER TO THE TV AND OTHER VIDEO DEVICES

When the first commercial video recorders for consumer use showed up at the end of the 1970s, it was necessary to connect the video tape recorder through the antenna input of the TV set. In those days, most TV sets had no audio and video inputs at all. For this reason, the built-in RF modulator, essentially a miniature TV transmitter, became popular in all video devices. The modulator converts the audio and video signals into a common analog TV channel that can be received by any TV set. In the beginning, all such European modulators were delivered tuned to channel 36 in the UHF band. In order to get the whole thing to work, the video recorder also needed an antenna input of its own.

At the output of the video device, the internally generated TV channel is added to the incoming signals from the aerial.

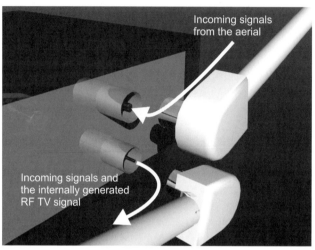

Incoming signals from the aerial

Incoming signals and the internally generated RF TV signal

FIGURE

9.8

In devices with a built-in RF modulator, the incoming signals are combined with the internally generated TV channel that contains the signals from the video device.

As time passed, more and more devices, such as TV games, started using internal RF modulators. The analog satellite receivers got the same feature when they were introduced during the 1980s. Nowadays, all TV and video devices in Europe have scart connectors (more on scart in the next section). This is also the most common way to connect the TV to digital receivers and so on. But the built-in RF modulator still exists in most devices, primarily because it's easy to bring the signals on to other TV sets around the house.

Figure 9.3 showed how a digital receiver and a video recorder (or a DVD recorder) could be cascaded before the combined signals from both devices are distributed to the TV sets. In Figure 9.9, the modulated signals from a digital satellite receiver are sent back up to the attic to be combined with the other signals at the in-house amplifier.

The digital receivers are usually designed to let the signals from the attached video device (DVD recorder) use the built-in modulator if the external source is turned on. In this way, you can use the modulator of the digital receiver to distribute the signals from the video device to the other TV sets in the house. However, it is essential to connect the devices exactly as is shown in

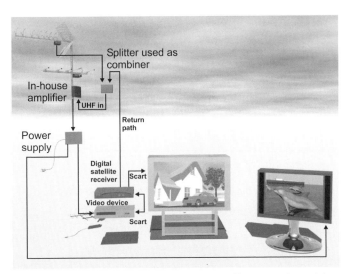

FIGURE

9.9 The RF signals generated by the satellite receiver (the satellite dish is not shown in the picture) are sent to the attic and the in-house amplifier to make them available in other TV sets in the house.

Figure 9.9 to avoid sending a modulated signal goes the whole way around the system and back to the device where it was created. Then the complete system begins to oscillate and this won't work. At the in-house amplifiers, the signals from the antenna and the modulated RF signal from the satellite receiver are connected using a reversed splitter as a combiner.

USING SCART CABLES

SCART is French and stands for Syndicat des Constructeurs d'Appareils Radiorécepteurs et Téléviseurs. The connector is also called a Peritel connector or Euroconnector, but most people in Europe today just call it "scart." It was accepted as the standard for cabling in the 1980s. Before we dig deeper into the scart connector we will take a closer look at the alternative way of connecting the devices; using the built-in RF modulator.

RF modulators still exist because they are an easy way to distribute signals around within buildings. The point is that the existing coaxial cables that still have to be used or the signals from the aerial system can be reused. However if the coaxial cabling carrying modulated signals is used between the digital receivers and the TV sets, the audio and video quality will be lower than if using a scart connection.

Another limitation is that the built-in modulators do not allow for stereo audio distribution. There is only one low-cost consumer product in Europe that allows for RF modulated NICAM stereo distribution (and by low cost, I mean in the range of 350 euro). That is the three-channel digital Multibox receiver by Swedish manufacturer A2B. This receiver takes three digital terrestrial free-to-air channels simultaneously and modulates them to conventional analog channels. This product solves the problem of terrestrial analog closedown that has started in some European countries such as Germany and Sweden. The smart thing about the Multibox is that the viewer can still use all TV sets and video devices along with the remotes without thinking about that the analog terrestrial network has been shut down.

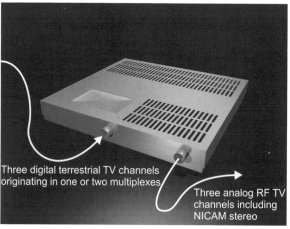

Three digital terrestrial TV channels originating in one or two multiplexes

Three analog RF TV channels including NICAM stereo

FIGURE

9.10

The Multibox provides three modulated analog TV channels, including NICAM stereo from three digital terrestrial channels.

With the exception of the Multibox, the only way to get stereo audio is with scart cables or separate audio and video cables. Outside Europe, cables with RCA connectors are commonly used to interconnect TV sets and video devices. Digital receivers made in the United States or in Asia frequently use these connectors. In Europe, RCA connectors are used primarily to connect external audio systems such as stereo- or home cinema amplifiers. There are also digital ways to connect the audio from the digital receiver or DVD recorder, which we will return to in Chapter 11, "The Home Cinema."

As shown in Figure 9.12, there might be a bunch of devices to be connected to the TV sets, including digital receivers, analog receivers, video recorders, DVD players and recorders, etc., so using the scart connections economically is important.

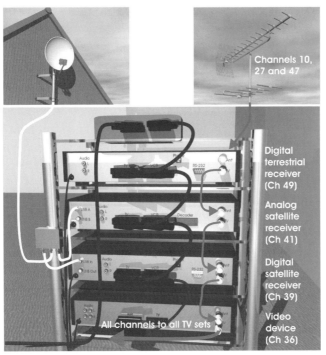

Channels 10, 27 and 47

Digital terrestrial receiver (Ch 49)

Analog satellite receiver (Ch 41)

Digital satellite receiver (Ch 39)

Video device (Ch 36)

All channels to all TV sets

FIGURE

9.11

The RF modulated signals from several receivers and video devices can be combined by cascading the RF inputs and outputs. (See color plate.)

TV NET

Digital terrestrial receiver

DVD recorder

Digital satellite receiver

Video recorder

FIGURE

9.12

Quite easily you will get a whole rack of receivers and players.

The Scart Connector in Detail

The scart connector has 21 pins. There is a reason for the large number of connections. The scart connector was introduced in the early 1980s to make way for the television of the future (the television of today). Two things were considered as important. First, it needed to be able to handle stereo audio connections. Secondly, it should be able to connect component-encoded signals, the R, G and B signals. And it was also quite natural that conventional composite video should be handled using the new connector. A video recorder can not handle RGB signals. The video recorder records a modified version of the composite PAL or SECAM signal. Finally, there are pins that may be used for different kinds of signaling between the devices.

There are two kinds of scart connections on the devices. Those marked "TV" are one-way connections to connect a TV set. The other kind is marked "VCR" (Video Cassette Recorder) and allow for two-way traffic, since a video recorder (or DVD recorder) must be able to receive as well as to deliver signals.

The oldest usage (around the end of the 1980s) for the scart cables was to connect stereo video recorders to the TV sets. A scart cable to connect to the video recorder uses the composite pins and the audio pins (see Figure 9.13). This kind of scart cables is a bit thinner than those where all pins are connected.

DVB signals are component-encoded and RGB connection should be used. For this reason a "full" scart with all 21 pins connected is the only option if you

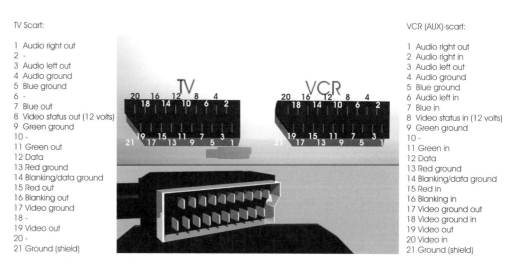

TV Scart:

1 Audio right out
2 -
3 Audio left out
4 Audio ground
5 Blue ground
6 -
7 Blue out
8 Video status out (12 volts)
9 Green ground
10 -
11 Green out
12 Data
13 Red ground
14 Blanking/data ground
15 Red out
16 Blanking out
17 Video ground
18 -
19 Video out
20 -
21 Ground (shield)

VCR (AUX)-scart:

1 Audio right out
2 Audio right in
3 Audio left out
4 Audio ground
5 Blue ground
6 Audio left in
7 Blue in
8 Video status in (12 volts)
9 Green ground
10 -
11 Green in
12 Data
13 Red ground
14 Blanking/data ground
15 Red in
16 Blanking in
17 Video ground out
18 Video ground in
19 Video out
20 Video in
21 Ground (shield)

FIGURE   The pin configuration in the scart connectors on a set-top box.

9.13

wish to enjoy full picture quality. The same thing applies when connecting a DVD player or recorder to your TV set. The signal stored on DVDs is also based on MPEG-2 compression and component-encoded signals. Strangely enough, there are still some cheap DVD players available without component video.

Simple Scart Connector Configurations

The most common way to connect a video device and a digital receiver is shown in Figure 9.14. The video recorder or DVD recorder is connected using a scart cable to the VCR scart connection on the digital receiver. The digital receiver is then connected to the scart connector on the TV set. It is important that the cable between the digital receiver and the TV set is of the "full" scart type, with all 21 pins connected. When connecting a DVD recorder, the "full" scart is also important, since the DVD recorder may take full use of component video (unlike the VHS machine).

To play a recording from the VHS recorder or the DVD recorder, the signals travel through the digital receiver and then on to the scart cable that is connected to the TV set. In most cases, the digital receiver also sends the signals to the built-in RF modulator, as discussed earlier. The digital receiver handles all the traffic from the video device to the TV set. On the other hand, to record a program from the digital receiver, the recorder must be set to the AV input position (Audio Video). The signals are taken through the scart cable and the program will be recorded with stereo sound. Connecting the video recorder this way is the same as in the analog years, when the receiver was an analog satellite receiver.

To get the different devices to understand how to react when the user wants different connections to be established there are control signals in the scart. The pin configurations shown in Figure 9.13 are in the scart connectors of a set top box. When there is a video signal available, 12 volts is sent through pin 8 to the TV set from the TV scart to tell the TV set to change from RF to video input and start listening to the digital receiver. The VCR pin 8 input is used in the same manner to let the digital receiver detect a 12 volts from a video or DVD recorder and to route the video/DVD recorder audio and video output signals on to the TV set when needed. Pin 12 can be used for data exchange between recorders and TV sets. To use this you usually need devices of the same brand.

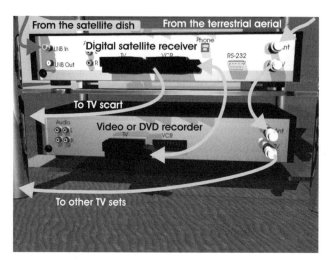

FIGURE

9.14

The most common way of connecting a video recording device to a digital receiver.

The cabling illustrated in Figure 9.14 is probably sufficient for most home situations. But in many cases, there are more devices to be connected to your TV set than there are scart connectors on the set. It is always better to choose a TV set with more scart connectors than you think you need.

Chaining Devices with Scart Connectors

If you only have one scart connector on the set, Figure 9.15 is what you may end up with—a scart "chain" where the devices are connected one after another.

The most important thing is to note that scart connectors on digital receivers marked "TV" can only deliver signals, not receive signals as connectors marked "VCR" can. This means your chain may place limitations on which devices you will be able to make recordings from. In Figure 9.15, for example, the video recorder is at the bottom. Except from recording analog TV using its own built-in receiver, it can only make recordings from the digital satellite receiver, which is located right above it. The two upper devices may be watched on the TV set but cannot make any recordings. Of course, all devices have to be either turned on or in stand-by mode for this chain to work.

If you find the simple or chaining methods insufficient or undesirable, external switch boxes provide an additional option. Switch boxes enable you to

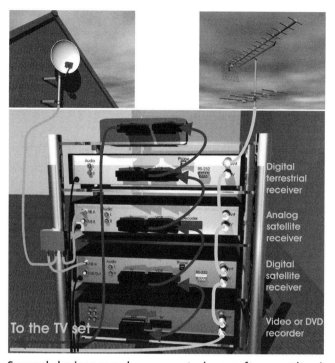

Digital
terrestrial
receiver

Analog
satellite
receiver

Digital
satellite
receiver

Video or DVD
recorder

To the TV set

FIGURE

9.15

Several devices may be connected one after another in a scart "chain." But there are compromises to be made since it is a matter of one-way communication. (See color plate.)

make recordings from any device. However, you also have the inconvenience of not being able to make the switch using your remote control(s).

Wireless Scart Connections

Another case for extra accessories is transferring audio and video to a TV set in another room and you want to have the audio in stereo. It might not be appropriate to use scart cables that are 10 to 20 meters in length since these cables are as thick as your pinkie and not very beautiful to look at. They do not exist in standard lengths that are more than 5 meters (about 16 feet). Wireless solutions like the devices discussed in Chapter 7, "Digital TV by Broadband" offer a good solution. In that case, it was connecting a computer to a TV set in another room, but the same solution can apply to connecting a digital receiver or DVD recorder to a TV that is at the other end of the house.

As shown in Figure 9.16, the wireless system serves as an invisible scart cable. Both units have a scart connector as an interface and are connected to the digital receiver and the TV set using short scart cables at each end. In many cases, wireless systems like these may be a very good solution to avoid actual cabling. However systems of this kind have a few drawbacks. First, the audio may become a bit noisy because of the analog FM modulated transfer of the signals. The same may happen with the video, because it is in composite PAL format and not component-encoded. Additionally, you may end up in problems if the 2.4 GHz signal has problems penetrating the walls in your house. Metal objects and people moving around may obstruct the signals.

It should be noted that the system's own transmitter is connected between the devices to which signals are distributed and the TV set, so the unit does not consume any of the scart connections itself.

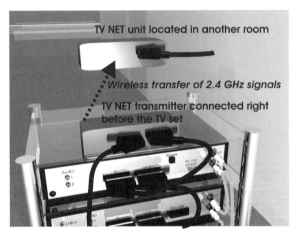

FIGURE   The basic principle for a wireless scart extension system.

9.16

Figure 9.17 shows a very compact version of the wireless scart extension system. This is the Philips TV NET-300 and it also contains a return channel for the IR commands that are picked up from the remote control in the other room. It is also possible to use additional receivers to supply even more rooms with signals from the transmitter unit. Today, there are quite a lot of different brands of this kind of product.

The scart cables and connectors will probably be history in some years. HDTV receiver and the new flat-panel TV sets and other display systems require digital connection instead of the analog scart. In Chapter 12, we will

FIGURE

9.17

The Philips TV-NET wireless scart extension system also include a return path for the commands from the remote control that is used in the other room. In this picture the signal is transferred from a computer.

take a closer look at the DVI (Digital Video Interface) or rather the HDMI (High Definition Multimedia Interface) that is about to replace the scart and other analog means of connecting the receivers with the display systems.

CONNECTING A SATELLITE DISH TO MULTIPLE RECEIVERS

Most people today have just one satellite receiver connected to their satellite dish. As were discussed in Chapter 4, "Digital TV by Satellite," satellite reception is primarily based on the assumption that only one TV channel is received at a time. The satellite receiver sends DiSEqC commands to a single DiSEqC switch to choose the desired orbital position, and a 22 kHz control signal and an LNB supply voltage (14 or 18 volts) are sent to tell the LNB in what part of the frequency band and at which polarization to find the desired channel.

However, in a modern home there might be different opinions about which channel to watch (see Figure 9.18). There are lots of ways to distribute the signal from one single digital set-top box to different rooms in the house. You can even control the digital receiver from wherever you are using the remote and the return channel of a wireless scart extension system. But still you can not receive several channels simultaneously.

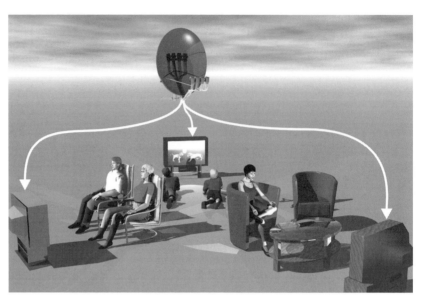

FIGURE

9.18
To split the signal from one satellite dish to several TV sets may be quite complicated if flexibility is important.

FIGURE

9.19
A conventional satellite dish only has one output from each LNB and one DiSEqC switch allowing only one channel to be received at a time.

Two satellite receivers may be connected to the same satellite dish if an external smart switch is used. The smart switch has one input for the satellite dish and two outputs, master and slave. If the receiver connected to the master output is in operation, it is in control of the antenna system, and if it is switched off, the receiver connected to the slave output may use and control the antenna system. The smart switch can be located anywhere (except near any of the receivers) so you can be "smart" about your cabling as well (see Figure 9.20).

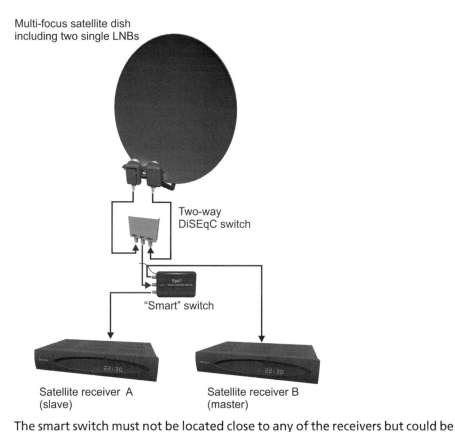

Multi-focus satellite dish
including two single LNBs

Two-way
DiSEqC switch

"Smart" switch

Satellite receiver A   Satellite receiver B
(slave)   (master)

FIGURE

9.20

The smart switch must not be located close to any of the receivers but could be placed at a suitable location to minimize the cabling that need to be done.

If any of the receivers have a "loop through" feature (discussed in Chapter 8, "Choosing the Right Box"), no external smart switch is needed. The smart switch is an integrated part of the receiver. You may still want an external smart switch to reduce your need for external cables.

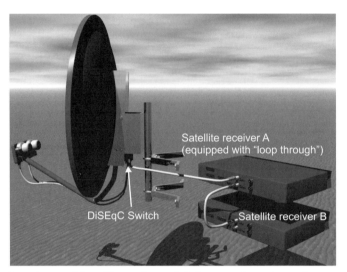

Satellite receiver A
(equipped with "loop through")

DiSEqC Switch

Satellite receiver B

FIGURE

9.21

Receivers with a "loop through" feature do not need an external smart switch.

Fully Flexible Satellite Receiver Connections

In our modern time with universal LNBs, it's the DiSEqC signaling that controls the choice of received orbital slot, a 22 kHz tone that controls what part of the frequency band is to be received, and the choice of supply power to the LNB that controls the polarizations of the received signals.

To connect several satellite receivers that can work completely independent of each other, both parts of the satellite downlink frequency band, as well as both polarizations, have to be received simultaneously. More advances types of LNBs make this possible.

Quattro LNB

Reception at European cable TV headends has long demanded this type of connection. There, access to both parts of the downlink band as well as both polarizations is necessary to enable reception of any channel needed in the network. The Quattro LNB (also called just Quad) can handle this because it has four outputs, each dedicated to one part of the frequency band (10.70–11.70 GHz or 11.70–12.75 GHz) and one sense of polarization (vertical or horizontal). Using a Quattro LNB, four or more channels, located anywhere in the downlink frequency band and in any polarization from a certain orbital position, can be received simultaneously.

Figure 9.22 shows a block diagram of a Quattro LNB. It has a low noise amplifier for each polarization. On top of this, both local oscillators, 9.75 and 10.60 GHz, are always in operation to get four mixers going. Finally, there are several i.f. amplifiers in operation.

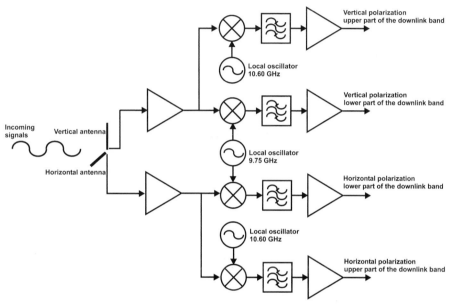

FIGURE

9.22

Block diagram showing the principles used in Quattro LNBs, suitable for satellite reception in cable TV headends.

In one way, the Quattro LNB is simpler than an ordinary single LNB. It does not have to handle the 22 kHz and dual voltage (14/18 volts) control signals from the satellite receivers. Instead it has its four outputs each delivering its part of the received signals from the satellite. A Quattro LNB is more or less four LNBs in the same casing.

Twin Universal LNB

The Twin Universal LNB is an extension of the Quattro LNB, where dividers and switches have been added to accept two separate satellite receivers on each of the outputs. These receivers can then work completely independently from each other, as if each receiver has its own LNB.

In Figure 9.23, two LNB multi-focus antennas are shown. Each receiver has its own two-way DiSEqC switch. Each switch is connected to one of the outputs on each LNB. This configuration is the same as if each satellite receiver was connected to its two of its own LNB multi-focus satellite dishes. The setup can be used either to serve two satellite receivers in the same home or to serve two separate households with satellite TV.

Figure 9.24 shows a block diagram of the Twin Universal LNB. This LNB has to take care of the control signals from each receiver.

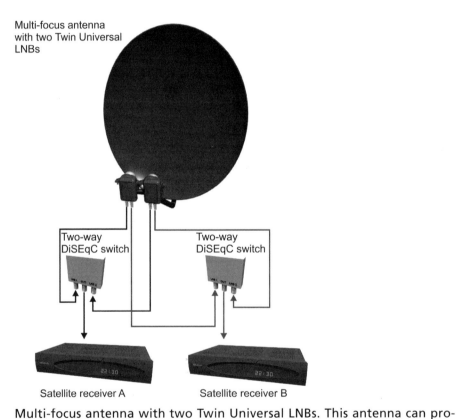

Multi-focus antenna with two Twin Universal LNBs

Two-way DiSEqC switch

Two-way DiSEqC switch

Satellite receiver A

Satellite receiver B

FIGURE

9.23

Multi-focus antenna with two Twin Universal LNBs. This antenna can provide signals to two satellite receivers that may operate independent of each other.

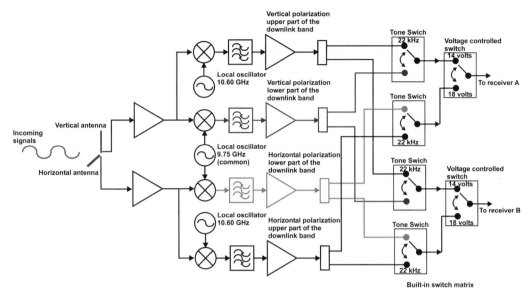

FIGURE

9.24

The principles for a Twin Universal LNB.

Quattro Universal LNB

The Quattro Universal LNB works very much the same as a Twin Universal LNB, but with an even more complicated switch matrix. It has four outputs that can control four separate satellite receivers (see Figure 9.25).

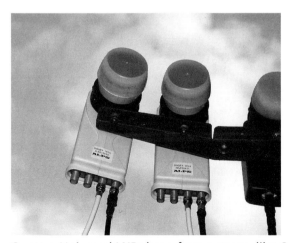

FIGURE

9.25

Quattro Universal LNBs have four outputs, like Quattro LNBs.

It is now possible to connect four independently operating LNBs to one single antenna (see Figure 9.26). You might say that there are a whole bunch of switches and dividers have been integrated in the LNB. (Yet another example of what you can do with micro electronics!) However, the DiSEqC switches, used to select the orbital position, must still stay outside the LNBs.

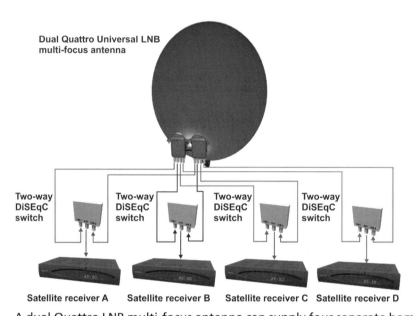

FIGURE

A dual Quattro LNB multi-focus antenna can supply four separate homes with satellite signals from two orbital positions.(See color plate.)

9.26

There are ready-made package solutions (see Figure 9.27) where four two-way DiSEqC switches are combined in a common case. The connection cables are delivered complete with F-type connectors mounted on the cables. This will give you a very compact and comparatively cheap solution for four households. One dish instead of four dishes is a big advantage. However, the households must be quite close to each other. A solution like this can also be useful in a single home where four different satellite receivers that are to be operated independently from each other.

Using four Quattro Universal LNBs in a four-slot multi-focus antenna makes it possible for four receivers to reach four separate orbital positions independent of each other (see Figure 9.28). The Quattro Universal LNBs are followed by four four-way DiSEqC switches. One switch is needed for each receiver.

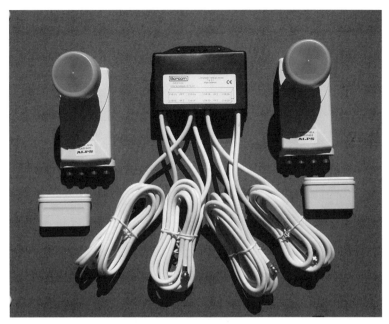

FIGURE

9.27

A complete set of equipment to build a dual Quattro LNB multi-focus antenna. All switches are contained in the same casing and the cables are ready-made, complete with F-type connectors.

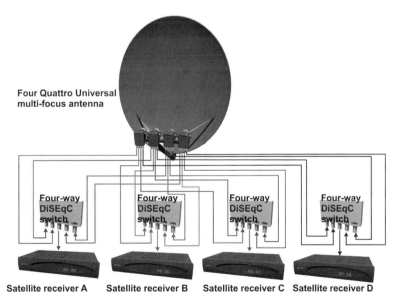

FIGURE

9.28

A four Quattro LNB multi-focus antenna can supply four separate homes or receivers with satellite signals from four orbital positions completely independently. (See color plate.)

But isn't there a simple solution for anyone with one two-slot multi-focus antenna who do not want to buy more expensive Twin or Quattro Universal LNBs? Yes, there is. Figure 9.29 shows what can be done if you have, for example, two proprietary receivers with operators that use one of the orbital slots each. Remove the DiSEqC switch and let each receiver be used for just one satellite position.

The advantage in doing this is that you may use both satellite receivers simultaneously and independently from each other. The disadvantage is that each satellite receiver can only receive signals from one orbital position. It is up to you to decide whether this might be something useful for you. It all depends on the receivers you have and what channels you want to watch and in which orbital positions these channels happen to be.

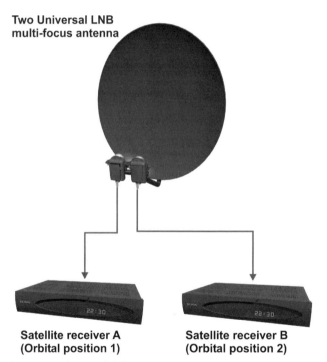

**Two Universal LNB
multi-focus antenna**

**Satellite receiver A
(Orbital position 1)**

**Satellite receiver B
(Orbital position 2)**

FIGURE

9.29

In a two-slot multi-focus antenna, you can use one receiver for each orbital position to receive two satellite channels simultaneously using single Universal LNBs.

AVOIDING UNNECESSARY CABLES

When installing a satellite dish, it can be quite tedious to pull a separate cable from the attic to the living room. There are combining filters that make it possible to use the same cable for the satellite i.f. signals as for the terrestrial signals from the aerial on the roof.

At the other end, in the living room, a special wall outlet can be used that contains a filter that separates the signals again. However, there is one disadvantage in doing this. It is not possible to supply the terrestrial in-house amplifier with power from a remote power supply in the living room. This is because the DC connection in the cable has to be used for the DC supply and polarization voltage control to the LNBs. Therefore the in-house amplifier, if any, must be supplied with power using a power supply that is located ahead of the combination filter for the satellite signals.

Figure 9.30 shows a combining filter and the outlet with the separation filter. The outlet looks like an ordinary wall outlet, but there is an extra F-connector connector on top of the two other connectors for terrestrial TV and FM radio. This new connector contains the satellite signals as well as the DC connection needed to operate the LNBs.

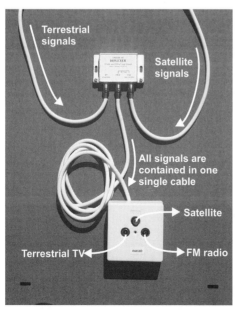

FIGURE

9.30

A separate combination filter for the satellite and terrestrial signals. The wall outlet separates the satellite and terrestrial signals again.

Figure 9.31 contains a combination filter that is also a combination filter for the terrestrial VHF and UHF channels.

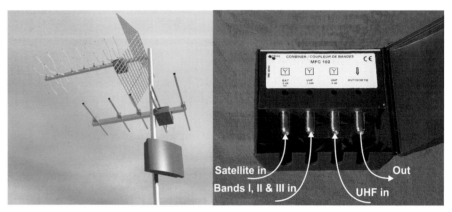

FIGURE

9.31

A combination filter from Danish manufacturer Triax that also combines the terrestrial VHF and UHF signals.

As shown here, there are possibilities to reuse existing cables. However remember that the satellite signals require low attenuating cables. If the existing cables are low–quality, you may have to exchange them for new ones. In addition, if there are severe problems, such as the need to use the cable for remotely powering the in-house amplifier, a separate cable will have to be added to the system.

THE TELEPHONE AND COMPUTER NETWORKS

The telephone network once was only used for the telephones. But now the telephone lines are used for computer modems as well as broadband ADSL modems (see Figure 9.32). Another application is for the modems built into the digital receivers for ordering NVOD (Near Video On Demand) movies from pay TV operators, even though such services also may be ordered using the mobile phone. A problem might be to extend the telephone line so that you get a cable that reaches all the way to the digital receiver. Today it is quite easy to connect an extension cable to the telephone line since telephones use RJ11 connectors and the extension cables use the same kind of connectors. The simple trick is to buy a female-female RJ11 connector that allows two extension cables to be connected together.

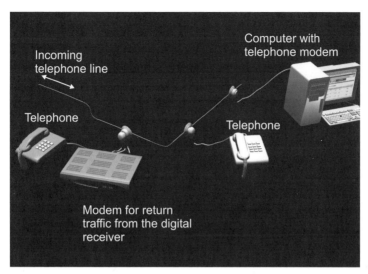

FIGURE

9.32

The telephone cabling in your home may be used for computer modems as well as modem-equipped digital receivers and, of course, for the telephones.

The broadband ADSL modem is also connected to the telephone line. This technology uses radio signals that are above the spectrum used for speech in the copper wire telephone line. These radio signals are sensitive when traveling through a medium and the copper wire is not that well suited for radio waves. There is a filter that is used to separate the radio signals from the telephone signal that must be placed at the first telephone outlet. Otherwise, the cabling in your house will affect the ADSL signals and reduce the maximum bitrate you can get from your Internet connection. Another reason is that in some countries in the outlets, there is a secrecy function disconnecting the following outlets as you pick up the phone. This is to prevent people from listening to a phone in the other room. And of course, if you connect your ADSL modem to one of the following outlets, your Internet session might interrupted if someone else uses the phone.

THE HOME COMPUTER NETWORK

Following the ADSL modem the next home network, the Ethernet computer network begins. The Ethernet connection on your ADSL modem is normally connected to a combined firewall and switch. In some cases, the modem may have these functions integrated.

Sooner or later, you get a bunch of computers in your home. As you buy a new one, which probably happens quite often, the surplus computers are still in use somewhere in the house. Therefore the switch associated to the ADSL modem quickly becomes very important. You want to reach the Internet from everywhere in your house. At the same time you also get the opportunity to interconnect your own computers.

I will not go into all details about how to design a home computer network. But as has been discussed in Chapter 7, "Digital TV by Broadband," the computer network and the Internet connection opens up a lot of new possibilities as adding media players and media centers that are connected to your TV sets as well. There are also other special devices in the market, such as IP radio sets that are really audio-only media players. In many cases it might also be interesting to use a wireless LAN solution, at least if you are not interested in pulling cables everywhere. Perhaps the future is not optical fiber in the home but no cables at all. WLAN and Blue Tooth solutions are probably only the first steps in that direction.

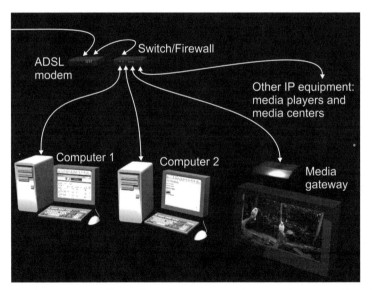

FIGURE

9.33

The home computer network can connect computers as well as different kinds of media centers, media gateways and media players.

FIGURE
7.7

An example of reception at various bitrates ranging from 56 kbit/s to 1496 kbit/s using Windows Media Player.

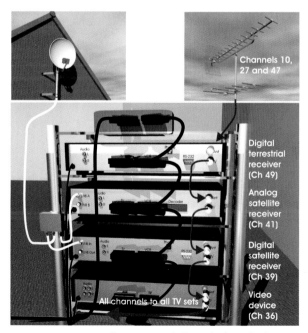

FIGURE
9.11

The RF modulated signals from several receivers and video devices can be combined by cascading the RF inputs and outputs.

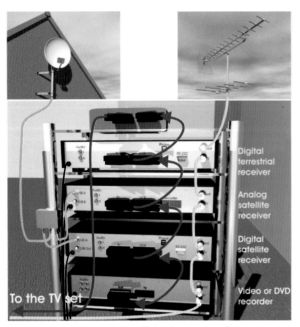

FIGURE 9.15   Several devices may be connected one after another in a scart "chain." But there are compromises to be made since it is a matter of one-way communication.

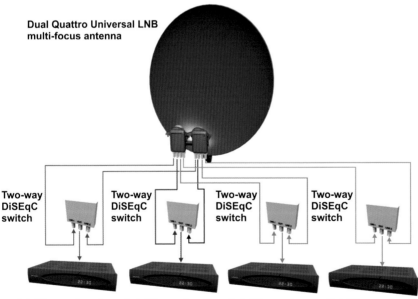

FIGURE 9.26   A dual Quattro LNB multi-focus antenna can supply four separate homes with satellite signals from two orbital positions.

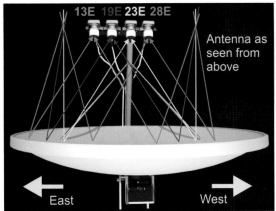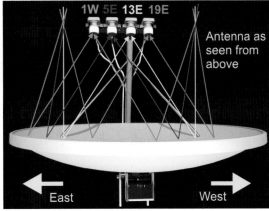

East West East West

FIGURE

4.30

A popular European configuration for four LNBs on one dish (left) and a popular Scandinavian configuration for four LNBs on one dish (right).

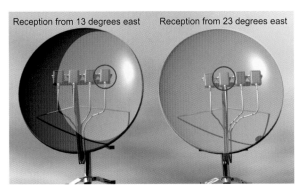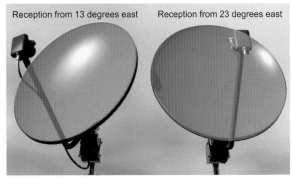

FIGURE

4.37

Comparison between the efficiency in the use of the receiving antenna aperture for the multi-focus versus the motorized receiving antenna.

Astra 1, 19 degrees east:

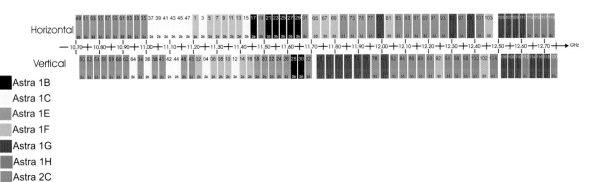

Astra 1B
Astra 1C
Astra 1E
Astra 1F
Astra 1G
Astra 1H
Astra 2C

FIGURE

4.53

The frequency plan for Astra at 19 degrees east.

EUTELSAT HOT BIRD   13 degrees east:

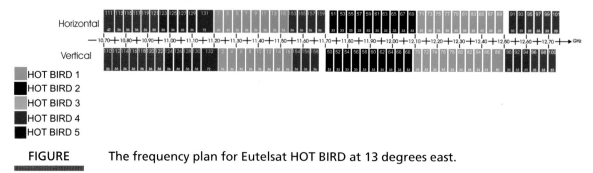

HOT BIRD 1
HOT BIRD 2
HOT BIRD 3
HOT BIRD 4
HOT BIRD 5

FIGURE

4.54

The frequency plan for Eutelsat HOT BIRD at 13 degrees east.

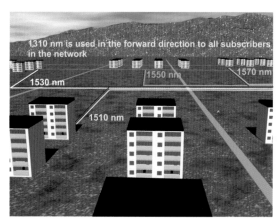

Optical signal:

1310 nm
Forward traffic

1510 nm 1530 nm 1550 nm 1570 nm
Return traffic

Wavelength (nm)

FIGURE

5.10

This HFC network uses different wavelengths for return traffic from different areas in the network.

Globo News: 19 kbit/s

TV Bahrain: 14 kbit/s

Fox News: 20 kbit/s

FIGURE

7.5

Screenshots from Internet TV channels; Globo News at a bitrate of 19 kbit/s. Bahrain TV at 14 kbit/s. Fox News at 20 kbit/s.

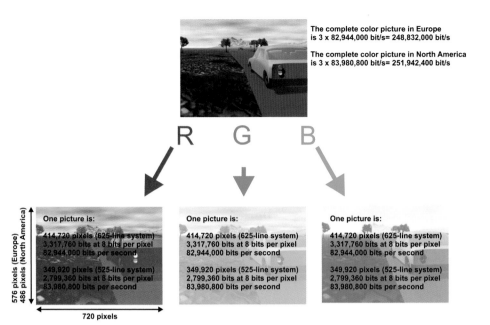

The complete color picture in Europe
is 3 x 82,944,000 bit/s= 248,832,000 bit/s

The complete color picture in North America
is 3 x 83,980,800 bit/s= 251,942,400 bit/s

R   G   B

576 pixels (Europe)
486 pixels (North America)

One picture is:

414,720 pixels (625-line system)
3,317,760 bits at 8 bits per pixel
82,944,000 bits per second

349,920 pixels (525-line system)
2,799,360 bits at 8 bits per pixel
83,980,800 bits per second

One picture is:

414,720 pixels (625-line system)
3,317,760 bits at 8 bits per pixel
82,944,000 bits per second

349,920 pixels (525-line system)
2,799,360 bits at 8 bits per pixel
83,980,800 bits per second

One picture is:

414,720 pixels (625-line system)
3,317,760 bits at 8 bits per pixel
82,944,000 bits per second

349,920 pixels (525-line system)
2,799,360 bits at 8 bits per pixel
83,980,800 bits per second

720 pixels

FIGURE 2.3 A color pictue really consists of three pictures (red, green and blue). Alternatively, the picture may be represented by the black-and-white Y signal along with the U and V color difference signals.

FIGURE 2.5 MPEG algorithms are based on using only the difference in information between the original pictures in the video file. In this example only one of every 12 pictures is saved or transmitted (marked in red).

FIGURE
2.9

Statistical multiplexing takes advantages of the variations in motion and capacity demands across the channels in a multiplex.

Original Picture:
-No distortions

Analog terrestrial
TV signal:
-White Gaussian noise
and reflections

Analog satellite
TV signal:
-Spike noise, "sparks"
 but no reflections

Digital TV signal:
-Block errors and
the picture freezes

FIGURE
2.11

Digital TV is different from analog TV when it comes to distortions. Either you have a perfect picture or no picture at all. However there is a very narrow range between acceptable reception and loss of signal where you will see blocking effects in the picture.

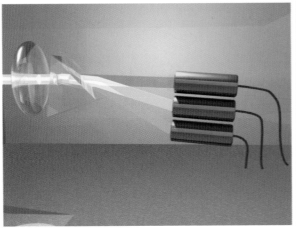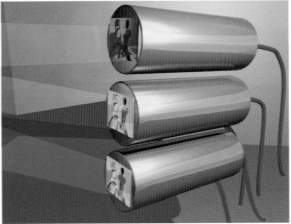

By using color filters or a prism, a picture can be separated into its three basic color components.

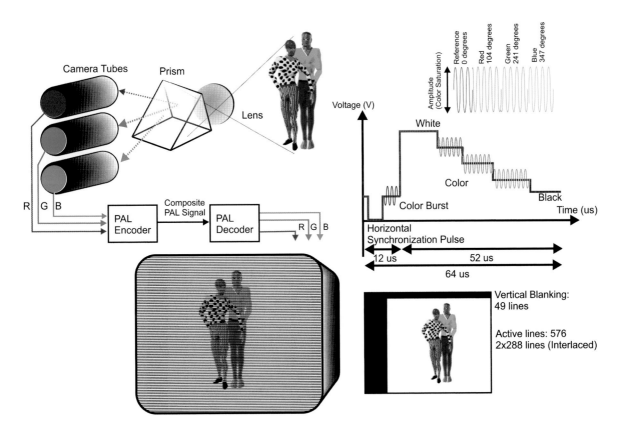

In the European analog system for color television, PAL, the color information is coded in a phase modulated subcarrier at 4.43 MHz. The phases of the carrier indicate the color tone and the amplitude symbolizes the saturation of the color.

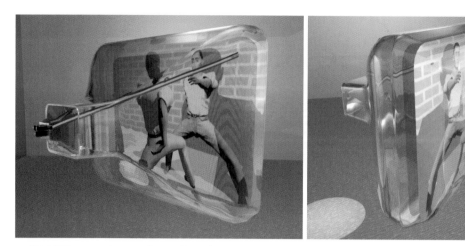

FIGURE

1.9

In a color tube, there are three electron guns instead of one as in a black and white tube.

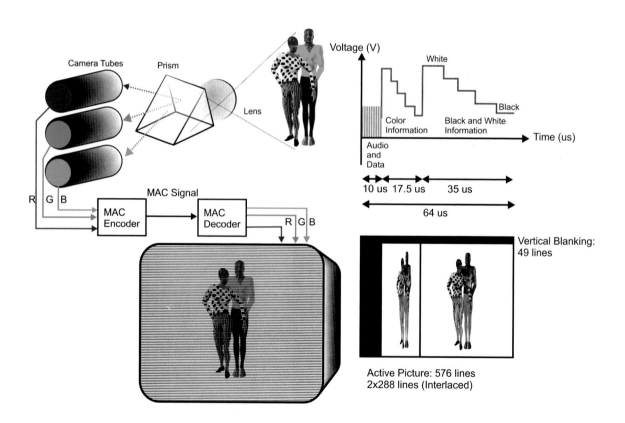

Camera Tubes

Prism

Lens

R G B

MAC Signal

MAC Encoder

MAC Decoder

R G B

Voltage (V)

White

Color Information

Black and White Information

Black

Time (us)

Audio and Data

10 us 17.5 us 35 us

64 us

Vertical Blanking: 49 lines

Active Picture: 576 lines
2x288 lines (Interlaced)

FIGURE

1.11

In the MAC system, the color components of the picture were separated by transmitting the black-and-white part of the picture in the beginning of each line and the color information was sent in the later part of each line.

FIGURE

12.3

Fast horizontal movement in interlaced scanned images will cause weaving effects.

Plasma 852 x480   LCD 1,366 x 768 (HD Ready Flat-Panel)

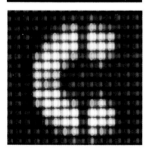 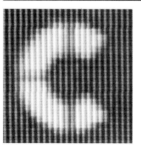 

HDTV channel C More HD received in HD-format. The video signal is converted from 1,920 x 1,080 to 852 x 480 pixels by the plasma display system

C More HD received in HD-format The video is converted from 1,920 x1,080 to1,366 x768 pixels by the LCD display system.

SDTV channel Canal + received in standard format 720 x 576 pixels and converted to 1,366 x 768 pixels by the LCD display system. (SDTV=Standard Definition TV)

FIGURE

12.6

Comparisons at pixel level between different screen resolutions and different signal resolutions (detail screenshots from Scandinavian pay TV operator Canal Digital channels C More HD and Canal+).

FIGURE
12.24

The future of 3DTV depends on the development of an inexpensive display system that does not require glasses for viewing.

Wireless Virtual Reality (VR) glasses

FIGURE
12.26

The future audio and video technologies may give us completely new experiences such as augmented reality.

FIGURE

12.14

MPEG-2/DVB-S HDTV promotional transmission received from French pay TV operator Canal Plus. Sports events with audience pictures become more believable than ever before. Check the resolution in the enlarged part of the received picture from Canal Plus (Screenshot from Canal Plus, France).

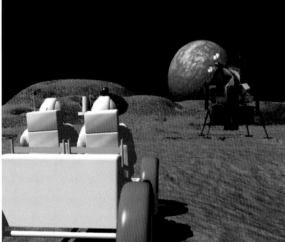

FIGURE

12.17

The stereo pair of picture on top can be experienced as a three dimensional picture if you focus at a distant and then quickly look down in the book without defocusing.

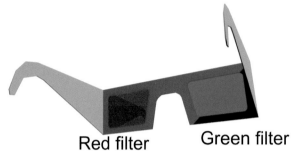

Red filter   Green filter

FIGURE

12.20

The first 3D movies used color filters on the projector's cinema audiences.

Horisontally
polarized filter   Vertically
polarized filter

FIGURE

12.21

The next generation of 3D movies was based on polarization rather than color.

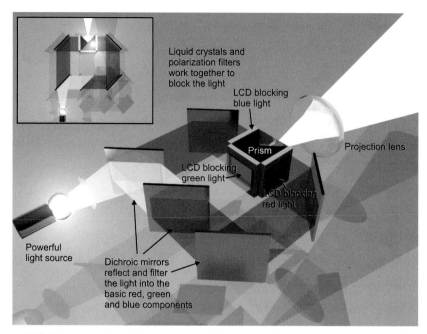

FIGURE 11.6   In LCD projectors, there are often three separate LCDs for each color.

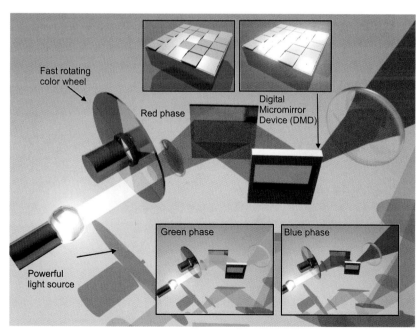

FIGURE 11.7   The DLP is based on a small chip with micro-mirrors. Controlling the angle of the mirrors determines whether a certain pixel will be bright or not.

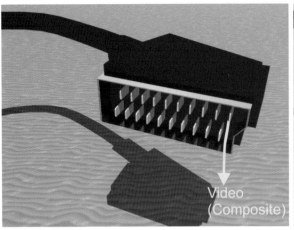
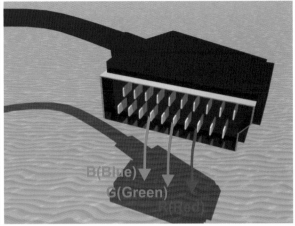

FIGURE

11.16

The composite and component RGB signals are available in the scart connector. The RGB signal provides the best picture quality.

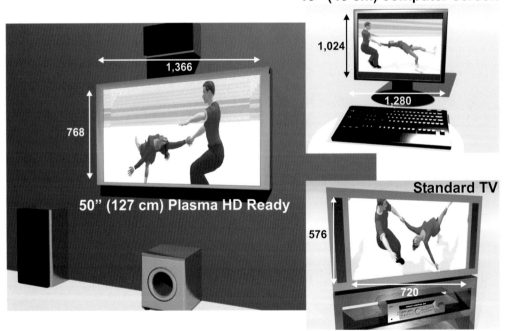

FIGURE

12.2

Comparing common screens and resolutions.

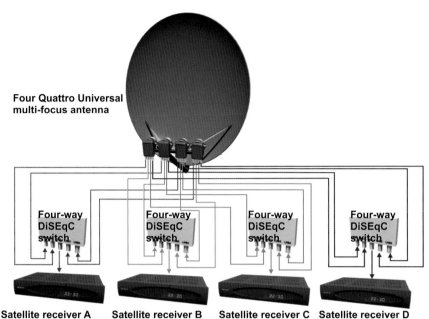

Four Quattro Universal multi-focus antenna

Four-way DiSEqC switch

Four-way DiSEqC switch

Four-way DiSEqC switch

Four-way DiSEqC switch

Satellite receiver A   Satellite receiver B   Satellite receiver C   Satellite receiver D

FIGURE

9.28

A four Quattro LNB multi-focus antenna can supply four separate homes or receivers with satellite signals from four orbital positions completely independently.

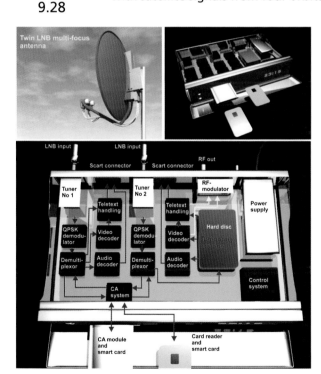

FIGURE

10.8

If the multi-focus satellite dish has twin LNBs, two sets of DiSEqC switches and is connected to a twin receiver, the same smart card may be able to decrypt two simultaneously received TV signals. One of the signals might be used for instant viewing and the other might be stored on disc for later use.

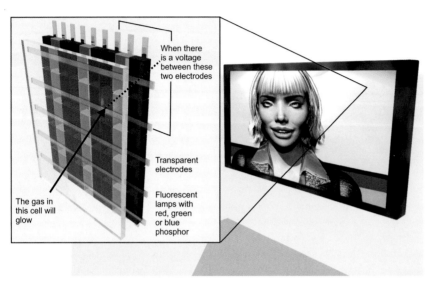

When there
is a voltage
between these
two electrodes

Transparent
electrodes

Fluorescent
lamps with
red, green
or blue
phosphor

The gas in
this cell will
glow

FIGURE 11.3   The technology behind a plasma display.

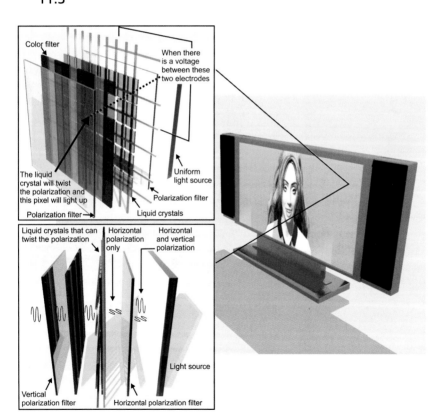

Color filter

When there
is a voltage
between these
two electrodes

Uniform
light source

Polarization filter

The liquid
crystal will twist
the polarization and
this pixel will light up

Polarization filter

Liquid crystals

Liquid crystals that can
twist the polarization

Horizontal
polarization
only

Horizontal
and vertical
polarization

Light source

Vertical
polarization filter

Horizontal polarization filter

FIGURE 11.4   The technology behind an LCD display.

10 | Digital TV on Disc

FIGURE

10.1

The video recorder provided the viewer with a new freedom of viewing. Digital television combined with laser discs and hard discs give still more freedom and possibilities that are largely undiscovered.

The first video recordings ever made were stored on an old 78 rpm gramophone record. This was done sometime during the 1920s or 30s. The recorded signals were the same signals as were broadcast to the mechanical televisor, the predecessor of the TV. It wasn't until the 1950s that the first professional video recorders that could record "ordinary" electronic TV became useful.

By the end of the 1970s, it became possible for ordinary consumers to buy their own video recorder and watch recorded TV programs whenever they wanted. In 1979, I bought my first video recorder, the Philips Long Play VCR, which I had read had the best picture, best audio and the lowest price. But it all became wrong since the VCR cassettes were the wrong ones. After yet another Philips try, the Video 2000, undoubtedly the best system from a technical point of view, I finally bought my first VHS machine in 1985. This VCR even came with a video camera!. I was sure this would be the optimum solution. But still wrong! As a home video recorder, the device lacked many important features—it had no remote had to stand vertically, so I could not put it on a shelf. As a portable system, it was designed for body builders. If I wanted to go outside to record something with the video camera, I had to carry along the receiver, the timer system and the power supply (since the battery did not last that long).

From all this, I learned two things which I would like to share with you. Choose the standardized product even if it not the best from a technical point of view and do not underestimate devices specialized for different applications. Remember that a Swiss multifunctional knife does many things tolerably well but does not excel at anything. This also very much applies to electronics, where it might be better to buy two specialized pieces of equipment, rather than one that claims to do both.

SOLVING THE NEED FOR ANALOG RECORDED VIDEO

The VHS recorder is today a well-proven technology and fulfills all the basic needs of consumers. Since these needs are the same in the analog as well as in the digital world, we will dig deeper into this. There are three basic tasks most common for VHS recorders:

- Viewing pre-recorded movies and programs
- Time shifting or storing temporarily
- Storing permanently

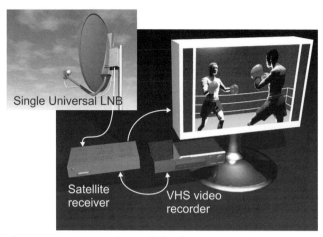

FIGURE

10.2

The VHS cassette solves all the basic needs for recorded video.

Viewing Pre-Recorded Movies and Programs

In the early days of home video recorders, the availability of pre-recorded cassettes was very important. You might very well say that it was the large number of pre-recorded VHS movies that led to the victory of VHS in the standards war against Philips VCR, Video 2000 and the Sony Betamax systems that also existed in the early years of video recording equipment. Today, this need is handled by the DVD players. VHS still exists but is decreasing all the time and will soon disappear completely. It is probably only a matter of a few years before you don't find any more pre-recorded VHS cassettes in the shops.

Time Shifting or Storing Temporarily

The most common way to use a video recorder is for temporary storage or timeshift—recording a show at its original broadcast so you can watch it later, at a time that's more convenient for you. To be able to move a TV program to a more suitable time of viewing is very fundamental. For this reason, even the first video recorders had a built-in TV receiver, which made it possible to watch one TV channel while recording from another. Or you could record programs when you were not at home, had guests or other activities planned.

Though the earliest VHS recorders had tuners, they were only for terrestrial analog signals. As soon as you connect a satellite receiver, you will run into problems. You may let the satellite receiver be on at a selected channel while you program your video recorder to record from the scart connection at a certain hour. However this will only work if you only want to record from one single channel. This challenge led to the development of video timers to program the satellite receiver to jump between several channels according to the timer. Unfortunately you will have to program two devices—the satellite receiver and the video recorder. This is tedious and the risk making a mistake and recording the wrong thing is substantial. The manufacturers have made big efforts to synchronize the devices, but this has not proved to be very successful since you will have to have the right brands of equipment to get compatibility (using the data signals in the scart connector that were described in Chapter 9).

One of the worst problems in using the VHS recorder for temporary storage is that you must have an empty tape at home or know where on your existing tapes you have the empty space that you need for immediate use.

Storing Programs Permanently

The movies and films that we find important may be stored permanently on video cassettes. In this category, we find your home video recordings containing precious memories that you wish to save for future generations, such as weddings, birthday parties and graduations. However copying from 8 mm, Hi 8 or DV format (the media on which these events are most likely recorded) to a VHS tape will cause quality degradation. Further analog copying will make the quality problems even worse.

DIGITAL VIDEO RECORDING

Digital techniques provide completely new ways of recording video. The primary advantage is that the quality of the recorded material is much better that analog recording. The explanation for this lies in the possibilities of copying without any quality losses. Another advantage is that digital data is easy to store on discs rather than on tapes. This makes it much easier to find and to retrieve the recordings.

DVD: The Solution for Pre-Recorded Material

DVD stands for Digital Versatile Disc and the technology has quite quickly come to dominate the market for pre-recorded movies, since a wide range of titles are available and the audio and video quality is superior to anything ever available on cassettes. No matter how many TV channels you may have coming into your home, pre-recorded movies are very important. You are able to watch much newer movies and you can be much more specific when it comes to choosing what to watch. This is quite obvious, since there has always been a big market for renting VHS cassettes and DVD records.

A DVD record may be played hundreds or thousands of times without showing any signs of degradation. After about being played for just 20 times, the degradation of a video cassette recording is quite evident, which makes the DVD much more suitable for the renting business. What pushed the adoption of the DVD technology forward was also the fact that more and more people are buying home cinema systems. Only the DVD can provide the audio and video quality that is expected from such systems.

FIGURE
10.3

Today the DVD player is as common as the VHS recorder in most homes.

To record audio and video in digital format was a big challenge only a few years ago, primarily due to the enormous quantity of data that has to be stored if the signals are not efficiently compressed. To be able to record in digital format is very important to avoid the noise that is always involved and unavoidable in analog recording on tape.

The introduction of MPEG-2 made it possible to compress the video signals so DVDs could contain hours of video. As with DVB distribution, it become much easier to have several versions of subtitles going in parallel with the audio that also might be multilingual. There might also be different multi-channel audio versions, such as Dolby Digital 2.0, Dolby Digital 5.1 and DTS 5.1 and higher levels of these formats stored in parallel on the discs. All these signals are completely separated from each other and there is no crosstalk whatsoever as is normal in analog systems. Of course all this is necessary to achieve high quality home cinema performance.

The DVD is closely related to the digital television system regarding the compression systems for audio as well as for video. You could say that they belong to the same era while the VHS recorder belongs together with the analog TV systems that are now being abandoned.

Digital Recorders with Hard Discs

In order to time-shift a TV program in digital format, you have to be able to make digital recordings yourself. One very practical way of doing this for temporary recordings is by integrating hard discs, as in Figure 10.4.

The digital TV signals arrive at the digital receiver in compressed state. The DVB signals for standard definition TV contain MPEG-2 encoded video and

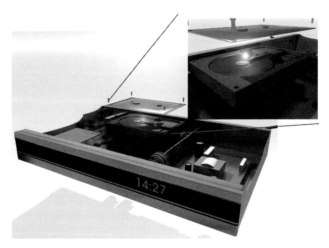

FIGURE

10.4

Hard discs in digital receivers provide unprecedented capabilities for temporary storage (Digiality VC-CI 624S Hard Disc satellite receiver).

consist of packets containing the compressed components of each TV signal. In the demultiplexor of the receiver, the packets for the selected TV channel are selected. This data is sent to the decoding circuits that retrieve the original video and audio signals.

Putting a hard disc in between the demultiplexor and the decoding circuits (see Figure 10.5), achieves a kind of delayed reception. And it is really a matter of delayed reception. The picture quality will remain intact as if the signal was decoded immediately after reception.

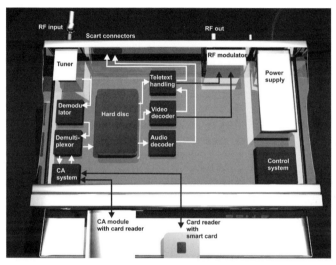

FIGURE

10.5

The hard disc is located between the demultiplexor and the decoding circuits, allowing for "delayed" reception.

Another fantastic feature of the hard disc is the possibility to record at the same time as playback. This means you can pause a live broadcast. If you pause the program for one minute, the hard disc continues to record. When you press play, the program playback resumes where you left off, while the recording continues.

In reality, the pause feature is a new fourth functionality in recording that is not available in a VHS recorder.

The storage capacity on a hard disc is quite large using today's compressed signal. A 120 Gbyte hard disc can store up to 45 hours of standard definition TV in MPEG-2 format. The quality of the recording playback is exactly the same as the live reception and is decided by the compression equipment used by the broadcaster. The higher the bitrate, the more storage capacity is used. The total capacity of the disc depends on what bitrate is used for the various recordings on the disc.

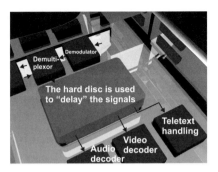

The pause feature requires simultaneous recording and playback

Hard disc

FIGURE

10.6

The possibility to pause live broadcasts is perhaps the most impressive feature in hard disc receivers.

If you make your own MPEG-2 recordings using a video camera on a small DVD disc or if you make a recording from an analog source using a DVD recorder, the quality will not be the same as for a hard disc recording from live reception. The reason is that when you make the hard disc recording, you are actually using the program company's professional compression equipment. This equipment has a higher quality than the low-end consumer MPEG encoders that are available in DVD recorders and in digital disc based video cameras for consumer usage.

In short you could say that professional equipment will allow for lower bitrates while maintaining the same picture quality as consumer encoder working at much higher bitrates.

DVD Formats

Even if the hard disc is the perfect media for time shifting TV programs, there is a limitation. Sooner or later the hard disc will become full and you will have to remove some recordings. If you want to save some of those recordings, you will need a media for permanent storage.

One solution is to make copies of the digital recordings on VHS cassettes. However, this will decrease the quality, and you will get all the well-known disadvantages typical for VHS storage, such as tape winding time when look-ing for recordings, degradation of recording quality after repeated playbacks, and so on.

Permanent storage is much better done using a DVD recorder. The normal recording media is a two hour, 4.7 Gbyte disc. However, recording time can be decreased to one hour with improved quality or extended to up to six hours at the cost of picture quality. There is big difference compared to hard disc recording. Hard disc recording is based on storing files that are compressed by the broadcasting company. DVD recorders of today only have analog inputs and you have to compress the signals yourself. As said before, the quality of consumer MPEG-2 low-cost encoders is not as good as professional equip-ment. Therefore you also have to make a choice of quality versus recording time when you make your copies or record directly to a DVD. This is very similar to choosing between the short play and long play modes of your old VHS recorder.

However there is another consideration to keep in mind. Though there is only one kind of VHS cassettes, there are five kinds of recordable DVDs: DVD-R, DVD-RW, DVD+R, DVD+RW and DVD-RAM. DVD-R and DVD+R are not erasable and you can only record once. The three other formats are more expensive but can be used almost as many times as you like. If you have a hard disc receiver, you probably make only temporary recordings on that machine and can probably do with just the DVD-R or DVD+R formats, since the DVD recorder will only be used for permanent recordings. The best thing of course is to have a DVD recorder supporting as many formats as is possible, especially the most popular +R and −R formats. Still, you will always have to put the right kind of disc into the right recorder. In computer DVD writers most for-mats are supported.

Another important thing is that DVD recorders may support one or two layers. Conventional DVD recorders use only single-layer discs with a capacity of 4.7 Gbyte. The latest recorders also support dual-layer discs with 8.5 Gbyte capacity. As with all other new technology dual-layer media is more expen-sive than single-layer media. But prices will drop as dual-layer recording will become more widely used. Most new computer DVD writers also support dual layer-media.

DVD recorders for HDTV increase the storage capacity even more. There are two competing formats—HD-DVD (developed by Toshiba) and Blu-Ray (developed by Sony). The HD-DVD disc can store 15 Gbyte in each layer and Toshiba has announced that they will create discs capable of holding up to three layers The single layer Blu-Ray disc can store 25 Gbyte and 50 Gbyte on the dual-layer version. There is obviously a standards war going on about the future of home HDTV recording formats. Much like VHS versus Betamax, most likely only one technology will achieve widespread acceptance and the other will disappear into the brief mention in books like this one. Or perhaps something different will happen and we will get DVD players and recorders that can handle both formats. Already the DVD players for standard definition signals can handle a wide variety of formats. In a world were a large portion of a device's functionality is actually just software, this might really happen. Most certainly the consumers will demand players that can handle both formats. The future will tell.

INTERCONNECTING DEVICES

To get the highest quality transfer from the hard disc to a DVD, you need a purely digital connection between the hard disc receiver and the DVD recorder. Since both the digital receiver and the DVD recorder are based on MPEG-2 technology, the best thing would have been to directly transfer the compressed data packets to the DVD without decoding the digital signal. This would make the transfer to the DVD lossless, from a quality perspective. However, these are interfaces that the movie industry does not accept. But in the long run, we will probably get these kinds of interfaces just with some kind of copy protection system on top.

In the long run, we will probably get devices where digital reception, hard disc storage and DVD recording are integrated in the same unit, as shown in Figure 10.7. This functionality does not exist today, but it will be developed, and some years from now, you might even be able to buy these devices even for HDTV.

Computer as Receiver and Recorder

It is, as discussed earlier, possible to reconstruct a computer into a digital receiver. There are digital satellite reception cards that can be put into the computer PCI slots and so on. Those who have tested solutions like this know that is will be a more or less tech freak project, not as streamlined as using a commercial set top box or media center. However a computer provides some advantages.

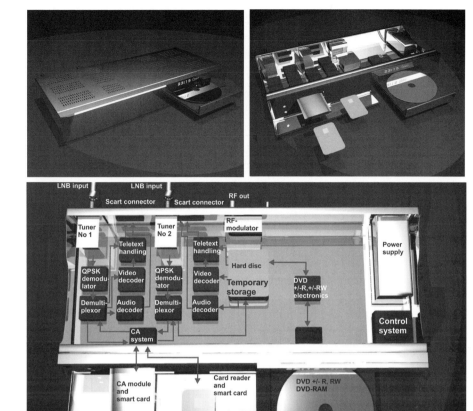

FIGURE
10.7

Future devices may be a combination of dual digital receivers, hard disc storage and DVD recording. This would fulfill all expectations regarding temporary and permanent storage of TV programs.

If a satellite reception card is added to the computer, it is possible to use the computer hard disc to store the received programs and movies the same way as in a satellite receiver with a hard disc. Then using the right software, you could transfer the MPEG files to a DVD record without passing through any analog interfaces. This is a possible solution to transfer the content to the permanent storage on the DVDs in a lossless way. Playback of the DVDs may be done in the computer or using a conventional DVD player.

Other Digital Video Recording Formats

In the digital world, it is quite easy to introduce new standards. Today the ruling standard is MPEG-2. HDTV formats such as MPEG-4 and Windows Media 9 are coming soon. But already there are well-known standards of the past, such as VCD and Super VCD. These formats are based on using conventional CDR discs for storage. These standards do not provide the same quality as DVD since there is only capacity for about 45 minutes of standard quality video on a CDR providing just 700 Mbytes of storage. Most modern DVD players handle these kinds of formats. A more important format today in DVD players is DivX. DivX uses MPEG-4 compression techniques that allow for considerably more video recording time on a DVD than MPEG-2.

However DivX, just like VCD and SVCD, is not a commercially used format, though they all represent interesting technical possibilities. Further commercial developments will instead be based on the previously mentioned HDTV disc storage standards.

TWIN TUNER RECEIVERS

In order to be able to receive two simultaneous TV channels, some things need to be considered. In addition to having two or more receivers, you will need a satellite dish with Twin or Quattro Universal LNBs and two or more DiSEqC switches (if you have a multi-focus antenna). All this was explained in Chapter 4, "Digital TV by Satellite." However, there is yet another problem to be solved: the need for several smart cards from the program provider in order to decrypt several pay TV channels simultaneously.

Using two receivers and two smart cards will solve the problem, but there are some smarter solutions. There are twin receivers which have twin tuners and twin demultiplexors (as well as a hard disc), so they are able to decrypt more than one channel from the same smart card simultaneously.

All this was easy in the analog world, using a VHS recorder and a TV set. In the digital pay TV world, the most advanced digital satellite receiver in the world is required to do the same thing.

Finally there is an important remark. It is necessary for the recordings on the hard disc to be decrypted before being stored there. The reason for this is that if the packets were still encrypted on the disc the viewer would not be able to watch the recordings after a while when the pay TV program provider changes the decryption keys.

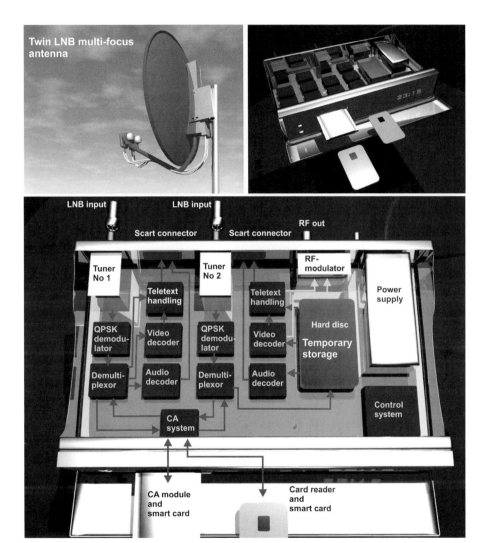

FIGURE

10.8

If the multi-focus satellite dish has twin LNBs, two sets of DiSEqC switches and is connected to a twin receiver, the same smart card may be able to decrypt two simultaneously received TV signals. One of the signals might be used for instant viewing and the other might be stored on disc for later use. (See color plate.)

11 | The Home Cinema

FIGURE

11.1

For some, the dream scenario for a home cinema might be a high definition projection system combined with a 7.1 multi-channel audio system.

By the end of the 1990s, the development of the TV set had gone so far that the home entertainment electronic industry started to search for something new and different. The more TV channels, the more movies. Movies are a good way of filling program hours. But movies are at their best at the cinema. Why not try to create a more cinema-like environment at home, one that is adapted to movies rather than conventional TV? The basic ideas behind the home cinema were born.

HOME CINEMA DISPLAY COMPONENTS

A home cinema is a system of devices or you may even regard it as a system of sub-systems of devices. First, we have to have some kind of display system. To get as close as possible to a cinema configuration, a projection system is the best choice.

However it has to be dark in the room for a project system to perform adequately. The alternative is a back-projection TV set, but the picture is not as bright and sharp as in a cathode ray tube. The solution that will be most common in the future is probably large plasma or LCD screens. As of today, these screens are quite expensive for the general public.

Therefore, the cathode ray tube is still the most common display system since it provides a sharp and intense picture with good contrast ratio at a low price.

Cathode Ray Tubes

Cathode ray tubes, CRTs, have been used since the late 1930s and have developed considerably since then. The black and white CRT became the color CRT, and the latest developments have been 100 Hz tubes that remove some of the typical flickering in CRTs. Another important development was the introduction of 16:9 format, (widescreen) CRTs. The 81-cm (32-inch) size has become especially popular, since it is regarded as a replacement for the old 74-cm (29-inch) 4:3 set.

Of course it is possible to build your home cinema based on an 81-cm (32-inch) CRT TV set. But it is hard to get a larger picture. There are also used to be 91-cm (36-inch) 16:9 CRT sets, but they were very big, bulky and heavy. Conventional CRTs are not the way of the future. To get a larger picture we have to try to find other means, such as flat-panel sets and home projector systems.

Flat-Panel TV Sets

For decades people have dreamed about a flat television that can be hung on the wall like a painted picture. That seems to have become a reality at a price that is getting more and more affordable. The larger sets are mostly plasma

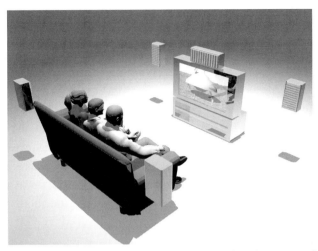

FIGURE

11.2

This 81-cm (32-inch) CRT TV set combined with a 5.1 multi-channel audio system, including two rear channels, has been a very common home cinema system.

screens, where each pixel consists of one red, one green and one blue fluorescent lamp that is very tiny. Each pixel is in reality just a small cell containing an ionized gas that lights up when an electrical field is built up around it by a grid of electrodes that reach all pixels of the screen (see Figure 11.3).

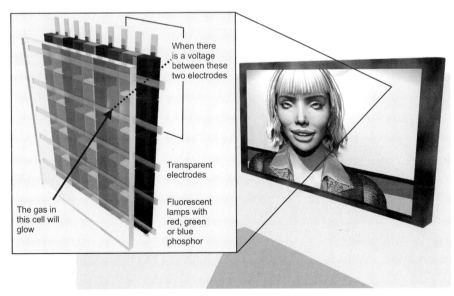

When there is a voltage between these two electrodes

Transparent electrodes

Fluorescent lamps with red, green or blue phosphor

The gas in this cell will glow

FIGURE

11.3

The technology behind a plasma display. (See color plate.)

The competing technology is the LCD, Liquid Crystal Display, which is based on having a giant fluorescent light source behind the screen (See Figure 11.4). In front of the lamp, there is a polarization filter that makes the light have just one polarization. Then there is a second grid of tiny liquid crystal polarization filters. The light polarization angle of these crystals is changed when there is an electrical field put on the crystals. This electrical field is created by a grid that reaches all the liquid crystals (similar to the grid in the plasma display). As the polarization angle changes more and more to get at right angles to the light from the rear fluorescent lamp, it is possible to block the light at a single red, green or blue part of a pixel. There is also a filter in the rear, giving each part of each pixel a red, green or blue color.

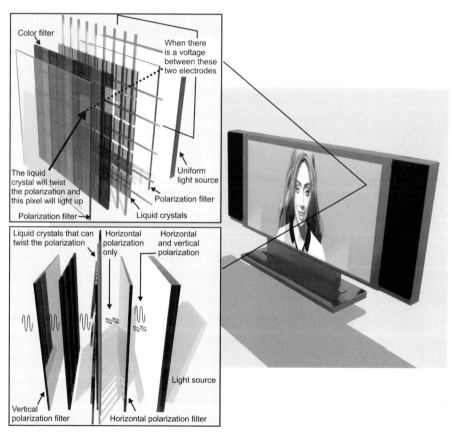

FIGURE   The technology behind an LCD display. (See color plate.)

11.4

The plasma screen is based on each pixel emitting its own light while the LCD display is based on each pixel being able to block out light. Today it is more expensive to produce large LCD displays than plasma displays. On the other hand, there are limitations to making small plasma displays—it is hard to make tiny pixels that emit light. For that reason, the market from 107 cm (42 inches) and up is dominated by plasma displays and the market for smaller flat-panel TV sets is ruled by the LCDs. But LCDs have started to compete efficiently, even in the larger sizes, and the 102-cm (40-inch) LCD panel will probably be one of the most common display systems during the next few years.

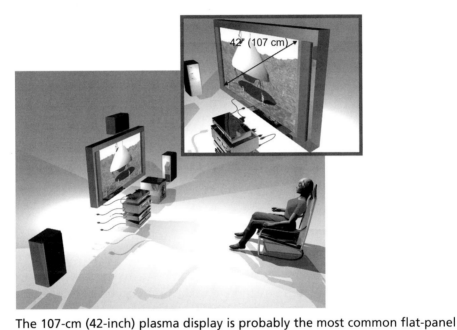

FIGURE 11.5 The 107-cm (42-inch) plasma display is probably the most common flat-panel TV, but the 102-cm (40-inch) LCD is a strong competitor.

Projectors

The most cinema-like pictures are obtained from projectors, because they can generate the largest pictures. Like flat-panel displays, there are two alternatives. The most common alternative is an LCD that works with each pixel blocking or revealing the light depending on its polarizing characteristics, as in Figure 11.6. In many cases, there is an LCD matrix for each color: red, green and blue. There are two basic problems in using LCD. The first is that the contrast ratio is limited and the second is that since the strong light of the lamp must pass through the LCD, it can overheat and be ruined.

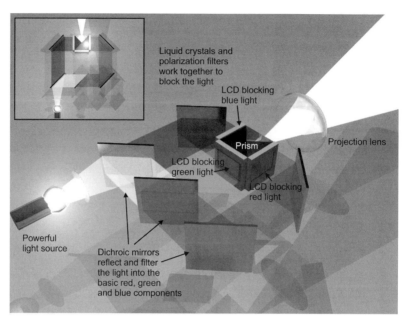

Liquid crystals and polarization filters work together to block the light

LCD blocking blue light

Prism

Projection lens

LCD blocking green light

LCD blocking red light

Powerful light source

Dichroic mirrors reflect and filter the light into the basic red, green and blue components

FIGURE

11.6

In LCD projectors, there are often three separate LCDs for each color. (See color plate.)

The competing technology is DLP, digital light processing and consists of a matrix with hundreds of thousands small mirrors whose orientation can be affected by electrical signals in the same way as the pixels in plasmas or LCDs. The micro-mirror chip is generally called DMD, for digital micro-mirror device. By pointing the mirrors in the right direction, the light from that pixel will be exposed on the projection screen. It is very similar to when you are traveling by car and suddenly get a reflection of the sun in a window that happens to be in the right angle to reflect the light straight towards you. The advantage in the DLP technology is that the contrast ratio in the picture will be much better than for LCD. The risk for the device to be over-heated by the light source is also much lower than in LCDs, since the light is reflected. This also makes it possible to use very bright light sources. In most cases only one DLP is used to produce all three colors. The three basic color pictures are produced in sequence by letting the light pass a rotating wheel with filters corresponding to the three basic colors (see Figure 11.7).

An alternative to a projector is a back-projection TV set. These devices are based on the same principles as all other projectors, but the sets become quite large. Therefore this technology has had big problems competing, especially with plasma displays.

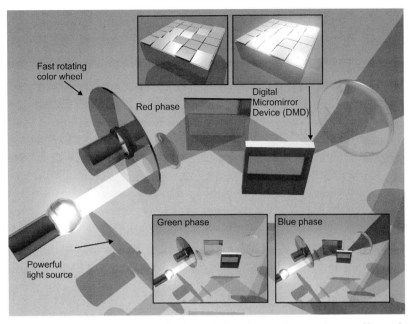

Fast rotating color wheel

Digital Micromirror Device (DMD)

Red phase

Green phase

Blue phase

Powerful light source

FIGURE

11.7

The DLP is based on a small chip with micro-mirrors. Controlling the angle of the mirrors determines whether a certain pixel will be bright or not. (See color plate.)

One of the largest drawbacks of projectors is the expensive replacement lamps and noisy fans.

Super-Slim CRTs and OLED Displays

However, there is a chance that the CRT technology may survive against all flat-panels and projectors. New super-slim CRTs are under development and manufacturers say they will be able to produce very cheap and slim CRTs that have better performance than the competing plasma and LCD technologies. Another strong competitor to the plasma and LCD displays might be OLED (Organic Light-Emitting Diode) displays that will provide much thinner displays than ever before.

A problem affecting plasma screens, LCD displays and projectors is the compatibility with high definition transmissions. In Europe, it has been decided that TV sets and monitors that can reproduce the 720p and 1080i formats are said to be "HD Ready." 720p means 720 lines with progressive scan and 1080i is 1080 visible lines with interlaced scan. There will be more on HDTV in the next chapter.

ASPECT RATIOS

The most difficult problem when watching movies using conventional TV sets is that the picture format is too wide. The relationship between the width and the height of the picture is called the aspect ratio.

As early as the 1950s, the wider movie formats were introduced. Today movies presented in the cinema use the aspect ratio of 2.35:1 (i.e., that the picture is 2.35 times wider than the height of the picture). Most television sets have an aspect ratio of 4:3 (equivalent to 1.33:1), which means that the movies are too wide to fit on the television screen. When movies that are filmed in wider formats are to be presented on TV screens, something has to be done to accommodate the difference in aspect ratio.

The most common way to handle this used to be pan and scan. In this system, an operator would manually selects the most interesting part of the picture for display on the 4:3 TV screen. Using just the center part of the picture does not work very well. This means that the left or right edge (or a little of both) is trimmed off for TV viewing (see Figure 11.8).

Aspect ratio 1:2.35   Aspect 1:1.33 (4:3)

FIGURE

11.8

Pan and scan means that the presently most important part of the cinemascope screen (2.35:1) is selected to be presented within the 4:3 (1.33:1) window.

The alternate solution is letting the viewer watch the whole scene. This means the whole image is reduced to fit the full width of the image, and black bars are added to the top and bottom of the screen, as in Figure 11.9. This format is called "letterbox" format. The advantage is the viewer will see everything, but the drawback is that a large portion of the screen is left just black and a large number of lines in the signal are not used. This is a waste of capacity in the transmission system, really, and it results in worse resolution in the picture.

Aspect ratio 1:2.35   Aspect 1:1.33 (4:3)

FIGURE

11.9
In the letterbox format, black bars are added to change the aspect ratio of the image.

The problem of having different aspect ratios is an old one, as old as Cinemascope and Panavision movies. Pan and scan and letterbox have been in use for decades, but letterboxing has been enjoying increased popularity recently.

Widescreen TV sets are becoming quite popular in Europe and North America. Widescreen TV sets have an aspect ratio of 16:9 (1.78:1) instead of 4:3 (1.33:1). The new widescreen television aspect ratio is still not as wide as the cinematic format (2.35:1) but it is a compromise between these two worlds. Since 16:9 is much closer to the cinematic format, the problems involving different aspect ratios are reduced.

However, as long as there are some TVs that are not widescreen sets, there will be problems. A program that is produced in the new 16:9 format has to be presented in the letterbox format on a conventional 4:3 format TV (see Figure 11.10). Even if the difference in aspect ratio is not as great as when a movie in the cinematic 2.35:1 format is to be shown, the picture will get smaller than if the program had been produced in the old 4:3 format.

 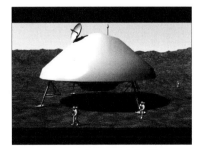

Produced in 1:1.78 (16:9)   Shown in 1:1.33 (4:3)
for widescreen TV   on a conventional 4:3 TV

FIGURE

11.10
A program that is produced in the 16:9 (1.78:1) format will be presented in letterbox format on a 4:3 (1.33:1) TV set.

The most common CRT widescreen TV has an 81-cm (32-inch) picture diagonal. This is the size that usually replaces an old 74-cm (29-inch) 4:3 format TV, which has a picture diagonal of 74 cm (29 inches). If a production in the 4:3 format is to be presented with the original aspect ratio, it has to be letterboxed on the side. For this reason, the 4:3 picture will get smaller in an 81-cm (32-inch) widescreen TV than if shown on a conventional 74-cm (29-inch) TV screen.

FIGURE

11.11

A conventional 4:3 format picture on a 74-cm (29-inch) 4:3 format TV set (left) will be larger than the same picture on a 81-cm (32-inch) widescreen TV (right) with the correct aspect ratio for the transmission. The pictures are to scale.

In a widescreen TV, there are possibilities to make automatic as well as manual change of aspect ratio. Most people that own a widescreen set choose to use the complete screen all the time without taking the transmitted aspect ratio into account. Strangely enough, the average viewer tends to get used to having the wrong aspect ratio when watching 4:3 transmissions. The picture will get stretched, as shown in Figure 11.12. However, there are some different tricks to reduce this problem. One of these methods is to avoid stretching the middle part of the picture where the viewer keep his sight most of the time.

FIGURE

11.12

The correctly letterboxed 4:3 format picture on a 16:9 widescreen TV (left). If the entire screen is to be filled when receiving a 4:3 format picture, the picture will get deformed when it is stretched horizontally (right).

The advantages of using a widescreen TV set are most evident when watching movies. A movie that is transmitted using the letterbox format will provide a larger picture in an 81-cm (32-inch) 16:9 set than on a 74-cm (29-inch) 4:3 set. However, since the movie is already wider than the 16:9 screen (2.35:1), there will still be black panels above and below the picture on the widescreen TV set.

Cinemascrope 1:2.35

 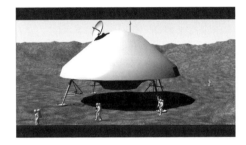

Reproduced on a 29-inch
4:3 TV set

Reproduced on a 32-inch 16:9
widescreen TV set

FIGURE

11.13

A cinemascope picture 2.35:1 is considerably larger on an 81-cm (32-inch) 16:9 TV set than on a conventional 74-cm (29-inch) 4:3 format TV set. The figure shows the correct proportions between the sizes of the screens.

In digital transmissions, the programs are normally transmitted in true widescreen format. True widescreen means that the picture is pressed together horizontally if watched on a 4:3 format screen. On the widescreen TV set, the picture is stretched into normal proportions again.

Figure 11.14 shows the picture in a true 16:9 transmission on a 16:9 format screen. At the bottom, you can see how the picture is presented on a 4:3 format screen without and with letterboxing. The problem is opposite the one we had when watching a 4:3 transmission on a 16:9 screen. In that case, the picture was horizontally stretched. In this case, when a 16:9 transmission is to be presented on a 4:3 format screen, the picture is horizontally compressed. The alternative is creating a 4:3 picture in the letterbox format.

"True" 16:9 transmission

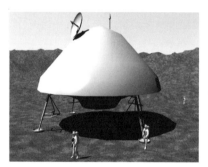

The 16:9 picture reproduced
on a 4:3 format screen

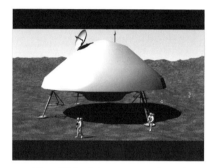

The 16:9 picture reproduced
using letterbox format on a
4:3 format screen

FIGURE

11.14

A true widescreen transmission will get pressed together horizontally if shown on a conventional 4:3 TV set.

How Program Companies Handle Compatibility Problems

It is obvious that the program companies want to produce as much of their content as is possible in the new 16:9 format. And of course they also want to have movies in their program schedules. They also want as many viewers as possible to enjoy their broadcasts, no matter what kind of TV sets the viewers use. The solution is to letterbox the programs produced in the 16:9 format into the 4:3 format when using analog distribution systems, such as analog terrestrial transmitters or in analog cable. This makes the proportions to look right on a conventional 4:3 TV set. And most viewers have learned to accept the letterbox format when they watch a movie. The drawback in doing this is that people who have 16:9 widescreen sets have to zoom in on the picture to get rid of the black panels on top and at bottom of the picture. The result is a lower-resolution picture.

In digital broadcasts, the 16:9 format is used instead. Then people with widescreen sets will make maximum use of the signal and all visible lines will be used to provide optimum resolution. In the video signal there is also a signal, the WSS (wide screen signaling) that tells widescreen TV sets whether the transmission is in widescreen format or not.

However, if the viewer has a 4:3 TV set, the conversion into letterbox adapted for the 4:3 format will take place in the digital receiver itself. And if you receive a digital signal, you have to have a digital receiver. The same thing applies to DVD players where you can also set the format of the output video signals to suit your TV set. If the picture is not converted into letterbox format, the picture will be compressed (having the wrong proportions) when presented on the 4:3 screen.

There are reasons for checking the settings in your DVD player and your digital receiver (see Figure 11.15). If you have a mix of 4:3 and 16:9 sets connected to the same digital receiver there might be a lot of switching in between the formats. Some digital receivers have a shortcut for this on the remote. Some of the latest 4:3 sets also have a built-in feature to produce letterbox from a widescreen format transmission. This might be another way of solving a part of the problem of having a mix of 4:3 and widescreen sets connected to the same digital receiver.

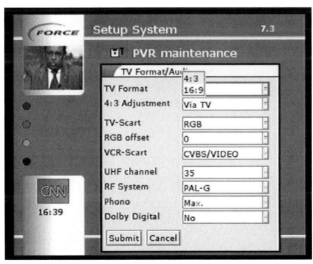

FIGURE

11.15

Many digital receivers and DVD players enable you to select the desired aspect ratio.

CONNECTING HOME CINEMA COMPONENTS

In a home cinema system, it is important to get the maximum picture quality. To get a sharp picture with pure colors, the digital receiver should be connected using the RGB interface rather than the composite video. Using the scart connector, you will get the RGB signals if you select it in the TV format menu, as shown in Figure 11.15.

The digital receiver is based on primarily providing the component RGB signals. These signals are then encoded into an ordinary PAL signal, which has lower quality but is more convenient for connecting to a VCR or to a RF modulator for additional connections through the aerial inputs of the TV sets.

In the scart connector of the digital receiver, you have access to the composite video and the component RGB signals which is shown in Figure 11.16. If you choose to use the RGB signals, the receiver will put a voltage on a separate pin to tell the TV set to feed the screen with these input signals. It is quite obvious that by using the RGB interface, the signal will pass the shortest route through the receiver, avoiding the PAL encoder of the digital receiver as well as the PAL decoder of the TV set (Refer back to Chapter 2, Figure 2.10). In addition, the screen is going to be fed by RGB signals anyway.

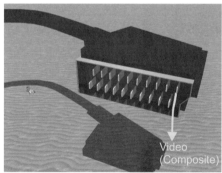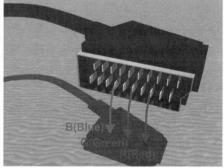

FIGURE

11.16

The composite and component RGB signals are available in the scart connector. The RGB signal provides the best picture quality. (See color plate.)

Note

The worst picture quality is achieved by using the built-in RF modulator in the digital receiver or the DVD device. The signals will not only have to pass through the PAL encoding and decoding circuits but also through the modulator as well as the tuner and demodulator circuits in the TV set.

More Advanced Ways to Connect Components

If you have a projector, a plasma or LCD TV you might have other alternatives—even better than RGB—to connect your display system.

Many DVD players have (Y,Pb,Pr) component connections. This way of connecting the display system requires three separate cables for the luminance and the two chrominance difference signals. Using the component connections, it also becomes possible to use progressive scanning (where the lines are drawn one after the other and not every second line as is the case for interlaced scanning). Progressive scanning provides a picture with less flickering.

The most advanced ways of connecting display systems are DVI and HDMI connections that provide digital interconnection. However these connections are only available in more expensive DVD devices, HDTV disc players and digital receivers for HDTV. The same applies for the analog component connections.

DVI and HDMI is the definitely the route for the future, at least when it comes to high quality connections in home cinema systems (more on HDTV in the next chapter).

HOME CINEMA SOUND

The next part of the home cinema is the sound system. A sound system for home cinema use is quite different from a conventional stereo system. The sound is multi-channel and there might be six to eight speakers, ensuring that the sound comes from different directions, just as in reality (see Figure 11.17).

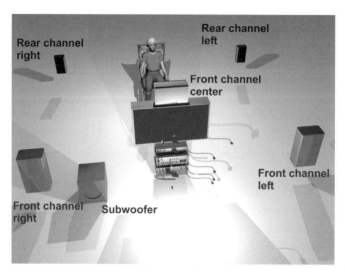

FIGURE

11.17

The home cinema sound system has six or more separate channels.

Multi-Channel Sound

The home cinema is not just a large quality picture; it is also a matter of high-quality sound reproduction. The difference between a home cinema sound system and a conventional two-channel stereo system is the number of audio channels. Any sound system that involves more than two sound channels is called multi-channel.

My first encounter with multi-channel sound was in the beginning of the 1970s when I discovered the button marked "Ambio phonic" on my stereo amplifier. Two additional speakers could be connected on the back of the device. According to the instruction manual, it was possible to get some kind of "spacious" sound if two extra speakers were connected. I became very curious and, after a while, purchased two additional speakers and soon a three-dimensional, spacious sound started to spread around the room.

The ambio phonic sound utilized phase differences in the audio signals of the right and left front channels to create both rear channels. My amplifier did not contain four separate amplifiers; it was a "cheat" four-channel system.

At about this time, the record companies started to introduce four-channel stereo. There were at least three different systems in the market. The simplest system, adopted by CBS, was called SQ and was based on the previously mentioned phase differences between the front channels. The rear channels were extracted from the basic two channels and used separate amplifiers. There was also a competing system called QS which worked in a similar way.

Finally there was a "real" four-channel system called CD-4. CD-4 had nothing to do with compact discs. Instead it was a system that put a sub-carrier above the audible spectrum containing both rear channels. Thirty years ago, it was quite hard to store more than two channels on a mechanical vinyl record.

The analog record player needle can only move in two directions: horizontally (left/right) and vertically (up/down). Using the combination of these two directions of movement, it is possible to encode two channels into the mechanical track of the record. This was the only way to separate the two channels, but there was always inevitable crosstalk between the channels. The CD-4 system was a real four channel system for long play records but never became widespread. To get the CD-4 system to work, you also needed a special pick-up needle ("the Shibata" needle) and a very expensive decoder to extract the rear channels. The only really efficient way to store multi-channel audio (more than two channels) in those days was on tape and multi-channel tape recorders were not used by ordinary consumers.

The four-channel stereo systems disappeared as the 70s passed by, perhaps because people were quite satisfied with their newly purchased two-channel stereo system. Another barrier was the extra trouble required to pull cables to the rear speakers. The only place where four speakers became popular was in the cars.

In the early 80s, compact discs (CDs) made an appearance, and they were recognized as a very good medium for multi-channel audio. The main problem in analog multi-channel audio storage is getting sufficient channel separation. In digital systems, it is easy to get a 100 percent separation between the channels. By multiplexing signals in time, as is done in the DVB transport stream, it is easy to keep the signals separated from each other.

However, the multi-channel sound didn't make its comeback until the end of the 1990s. However this was not primarily a come back for reproducing music—it was a comeback for movie sound reproduction. It was the efforts of the movie industry to introduce multi-channel sound in the cinemas that led to the use of multi-channel sound in DVD recordings and TV transmissions. The first multi-channel system to be used for movies was an analog system quite similar to the SQ system of the old days, the Dolby Surround system.

Dolby Surround

Dolby Surround is analog multi-channel sound that only requires two channels as carriers. From these two channels, a center channel is created that fits right between the two basic front channels. The center channel contains the audio that is in common for the two front channels. This means the mono part of the signals, such as the singer or the actor, is located right between the basic right and left front channels. Having a center channel ensures that this audio content really will originate at a point right between the two other front speakers. In an ordinary two-channel stereo system, this channel is simulated by the front speakers and the location of the singer or actor might be affected by your own position in the room. This is not acceptable if the center channel must always originate from the same location as the TV screen, in other words the center channel is there to ensure that the dialog really comes from the same location as where you see the picture.

The rear channels are also created using the differences between the front channels. In reality, these channels are the same even though separate amplifiers are used for each channel. In this way, the Dolby Surround system is quite similar to the more or less simulated SQ and QS systems of the 1970s. The only real difference is that the two basic channels are much more in control using digital carriers, such as DVDs and DVB or NICAM stereo transmission.

However, there is a new channel on top of all this, the sub-bass channels that are fed to the sixth speaker, the "subwoofer." The subwoofer channel is extracted from the two basic channels that are used as carriers. The subwoofer only reproduces the lowest frequencies of the audio spectrum and usually has its own built in amplifier. Some people say that this is the most important audio channel of them all. You can choose the volume and the frequency range to be reproduced by separate controls on the subwoofer itself.

Even though Dolby Surround is not a "real" multi-channel system, the movie industry has succeeding in using it in a believable way. By carefully encoding the differences representing the rear channels into the basic two channels, they are in control of the final output from the different speakers as the audio is presented in a cinema or in the viewer's home. Therefore movies and TV programs based on Dolby Surround give a much stronger impression than ordinary two-channel stereo sound.

The large advantage in using Dolby Surround is that any stereo storage or distribution system may be used. As a result, it is possible to record Dolby Surround on a conventional VHS Hi Fi recorder or to distribute Dolby

Surround using the A2 or the NICAM stereo distribution systems for analog TV. This has meant a lot to the VHS movie rental business.

Another nice feature of the Dolby Surround decoder is that it can be used quite efficiently to simulate spacious sound from sources that are not Dolby Surround encoded. You might say that Dolby Surround is a way to keep old two channel recordings alive.

A digital receiver will provide excellent two-channel stereo sound. These sound channels may be used as excellent carriers for the Dolby Surround sound and therefore most TV stations distribute the Dolby Surround versions of the movies if available.

A TV set uses several analog sound sources. In addition to the analog sound that is received by the TV set itself in A2 or NICAM stereo, there are scart connections from the VCR, the DVD recorder and the digital receiver. Undoubtedly, the simplest way to connect a home cinema amplifier to the TV set and always get audio that is coordinated with the video is to use the analog RCA connectors on the TV set (see Figures 11.18 and 19). Then you can be sure that whatever sound is associated with the program on screen will be played through your home cinema sound system as well. You will not have to change sound source on the home cinema amplifier when moving from one source of program to the next and you'll avoid a large number of cables.

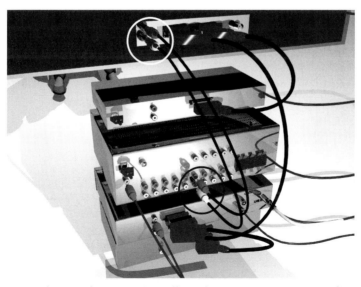

FIGURE

11.18

A good way of connecting all analog program sources of your TV set to the home cinema amplifier is to use the analog output RCA connectors on the TV set.

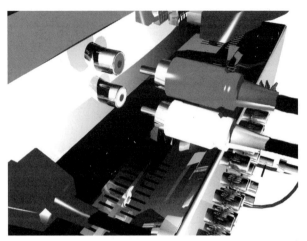

RCA connectors are the most common connectors for analog audio.

If there are no separate audio outputs on the TV set, separate analog audio cables have to be used between every device and the analog inputs of the home cinema amplifier. Many hours of soldering can be saved by buying ready-made cables with connectors.

Digital Multi-Channel Sound Systems

Using digital signals, it is easy to encode six or more separate audio channels into a DVD or into a digital TV (DVB) signal to create much more impressive sound than Dolby Surround. Therefore a digital receiver or a DVD device is an excellent program source for the home cinema.

Today there are two dominating digital multi-channel sound systems, Dolby Digital and DTS. Both systems have five separate audio channels and a sixth channel containing the information for the sub-bass channel. This is called a 5.1 system—the five refers to the audio channels and the 1 refers to the reduced audio channel that feeds the subwoofer.

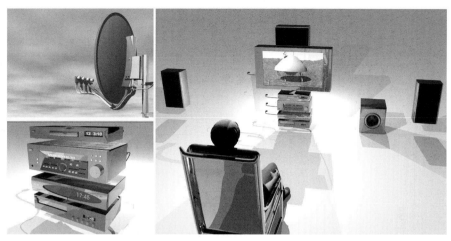

FIGURE

11.20

A digital receiver is an excellent program source in a home cinema system.

Dolby Digital

The Dolby Digital system is different from Dolby Surround in many ways. The six channels are now completely separated. The center and sub-bass channels are also completely separate channels, with no cross talk at all.

Dolby Digital is the most common digital multi-channel sound system. A bitrate of 384 kbit/s is quite common. This is not much, since an ordinary bitrate for the two-channel stereo sound in a DVB transport stream is at 256 kbit/s. Another name for Dolby Digital is AC-3 (Audio Code 3). There is a new version of Dolby Digital, Dolby Digital Plus that provides more efficient encoding. In this system the bitrate may be reduced to 256 kbit/s. This new system is an attempt to get more broadcasters to use Dolby Digital in their transmissions. Capacity costs money.

DTS (Digital Theatre System)

DTS Digital Surround is a lot of Dolby Digital. The largest difference is that DTS operate at higher bitrates. The fully feathered DTS signal is at 1,536 kbit/s but there are even less consuming versions at 768 and at 448 kbit/s.

Note

My own opinion is that DTS is better than Dolby Digital. Unfortunately DTS is not as common as Dolby Digital, which is more or less standard on any DVD. When it comes to multi-channel audio distribution via satellite, cable and terrestrial transmitters, there are a number of TV channels that have Dolby Digital transmissions for the movies and some other programs. There are some test transmissions using DTS, but is seems that Dolby Digital is more popular since it is more economical when it comes to bitrate.

Multi-Channel MPEG Audio

There is a European standard for multi-channel audio within the frameworks of MPEG. In practice, this standard has not been successful in competing with Dolby Digital and DTS.

Any digital signal that is stored on a DVD or is a part of a DVB transport stream distributed via satellite, cable or terrestrial transmitter can be used to carry a multi-channel audio multiplex. This sound multiplex may be encoded according to any of the multi-channel audio standards that have been mentioned here.

The digital sound multiplex has to be fed to a decoder extracting the six analog channels that may then be fed into the amplifiers. However, as can be seen in Figure 11.21, there will be six separate audio connections between the decoder and the amplifier. Amplifiers with analog inputs for an external decoder like the one in Figure 11.21 are not that usual.

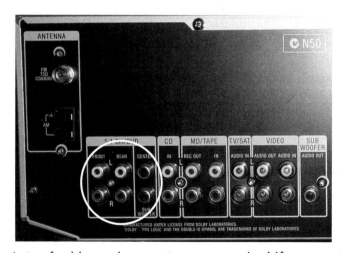

FIGURE

11.21

Lots of cables and connectors are required if a separate Dolby Digital or DTS decoder is to be connected to a home cinema amplifier using analog connections.

Instead, in most cases the decoders are built into the home cinema amplifier. Home cinema amplifiers have one or more digital inputs to take care of the complete digital multi-channel multiplex. There is a standard for this interface, called S/PDIF (Sony and Philips Digital Interconnect Format), that has become accepted everywhere. The S/PDIF connection can handle any kind of digital audio, even two-channel PCM linear encoded audio. The home cinema amplifier identifies which kind of digital audio format is available at the S/PDIF input. The kind of format identified is often presented on a display on the amplifier.

The S/PDIF connection exists in two versions, electrical and optical. The electrical version uses RCA connectors and a shielded cable (see Figure 11.22). Even a coaxial cable will do. The optical version is based on an optical fiber connection (see Figure 11.23). DVD players usually have an optical connection while electrical connections are quite common on digital receivers. It is even possible to buy opto/electrical converters if you do not have the right connection available.

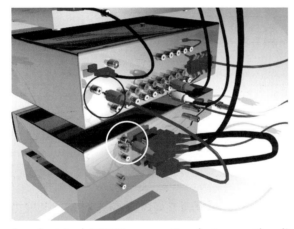

FIGURE

11.22

An electrical S/PDIF connection between the digital receiver and the home cinema amplifier.

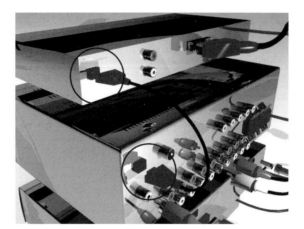

FIGURE

11.23

Optical fiber is used for the optical S/PDIF interconnection between the digital receiver and the home cinema amplifier.

Using the digital input of the amplifier means that the D/A (digital to analog) conversion takes place in the amplifier rather than the DVD player or the digital receiver. In most cases, the quality of the D/A converters are much better in the home cinema amplifiers than in the other devices, which means you will probably get better performance using the integrated D/A converters of the amplifier. This is also applicable for the two-channel PCM audio, so always use the S/PDIF interface whenever possible. The quality improves and the number of cables decreases.

The optical S/PDIF connector is one of the few applications for optical fibers in consumer use. Nowadays it is easy to connect optical fibers. The light does not come from a laser but from a LED emitting conventional red, visible light. Use the optical cables with care. There is a small cap for protection of the connector that has to be removed before connecting the fiber. The connectors are called Toslink connectors (see Figure 11.24) and exist in different versions depending on what kind of devices are to be connected. It is essential to note that the optical cables can not be bent in the same way as electrical cables. There has to be a certain radius at each bend and you must treat the cables carefully.

FIGURE Toslink cable for interconnection of optical S/PDIF interfaces.

11.24

Eventually, you might need a number of digital connections if you have a number of devices with S/PDIF outputs. Some home cinema amplifiers do not have an ample number of connections. Manual optical switches can be used to solve this problem. Of course, a manual electrical switch could also be used if you have electrical S/PDIF interfaces.

Digital Reception of Dolby Digital (AC-3)

Dolby Digital is well established on DVDs. However, some TV stations also have Dolby Digital multi-channel audio as a part of their service. In these transmissions, the AC-3 audio is encoded into a separate bit stream having its own PID in the DVB transport stream. The receiver must be able to detect that the digital multi-channel bit stream is available. Then this stream of bits has to be extracted and re-encapsulated according to the S/PDIF standard. The digital receiver has a menu where the viewer can select between using the ordinary stereo audio channels or the multi-channel audio (see Figure 11.25). The digital audio is then fed to the S/PDIF interface of the home cinema amplifier. The amplifier detects the signal and sends it to the appropriate decoder. Most of today's amplifiers have Dolby Digital and DTS decoders. From the decoders, the appropriate linear coded digital audio channels are sent to the D/A converters and then on to the appropriate amplifiers for the different channels that are connected to the speaker system.

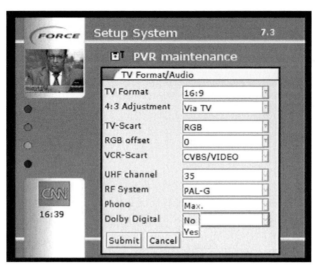

FIGURE

11.25

Choosing two-channel stereo sound or the Dolby Digital multi-channel audio.

The DVB standard supports Dolby Digital transmissions. However, you must be sure that the receiver has both an S/PDIF interface and the firmware to handle Dolby Digital. If the receiver is not ready for Dolby Digital because of the firmware, a software upgrade may solve the problem. Today there are lots of European satellite channels that use Dolby Digital. One of the first European stations to use Dolby Digital was the German channel Pro 7. There are also a number of pay movie service providers that have adopted Dolby Digital multi-channel sound in their broadcasts.

An important thing to remember is that when using a separate amplifier for the audio, the sound and the video go separate ways. In the digital world of flat-panel displays, there are delays caused by image processing in the display systems. This can cause lip sync problems which can be solved by delaying the audio deliberately. This is covered in more detail in Chapter 12, "HDTV and the Future of Television."

Even More Sound Channels

Most people would be satisfied with 5.1 audio. However, there are even higher versions of the multi-channel sound standards. In the 6.1 systems, there is an additional channel for it's a speaker located between the rear speakers and preferably a bit further back. The home cinema amplifier must have an additional output channel.

However, there might be problems finding a place for this rear center channel. The room for a system like this must be large enough to put the viewer more or less in the middle. Most people with a 5.1 system probably have their rear speakers located in the rear corners of the room and they sit where the rear center speaker should have been.

There are even 7.1 systems where there are two more rear channels and speakers.

The home cinema has awoken a new interest for sound reproduction at home. Not since the 1970s—when the stereo systems were introduced—have people been this interested in amplifiers and speakers.

PROGRAM SOURCES

As been discussed, there are several program sources that may be used for the home cinema. The most popular program source is undoubtedly the DVD player. But as soon as you have discovered the advantages in digital video, you also want the TV channels to be digital and you will probably buy a digital receiver and so on. Using large screen means you want less noise in the picture and therefore you will have to go digital.

If you can stand the noise, you can also continue to use you analog signal sources. NICAM stereo and Dolby Surround are capable of handling a lot just like your Hi Fi VCR, which may stick around for yet some years to come. And don't forget of your existing VHS cassettes.

But the home cinema is more than that. It is just as important to have a room with the right furniture and possibilities to make dark as it is to have the right equipment and programming. But it is still worth it, because it is the new gathering place for the family—the new bonfire where the stories of today are told. And that place is important.

12 | HDTV and the Future of Television

The Home Cinema is the latest contribution on the road towards an improved way of storytelling. Having a cinema with multi-channel sound and a large screen at home provides a very strong television experience.

TV media has evolved in two directions since its inception. The first is an increased number of channels, provided by satellites and other improved distribution media. Both the quantity of content and the geographical coverage of the channels have increased considerably. In recent years, television development has focused on quality. The change has been toward providing a larger and stronger presence and experience to the viewer.

FIGURE 12.1 Since the dawn of television the goal has always been to be able to provide a larger and more detailed picture.

HIGH DEFINITION TV (HDTV)

The ideas about increasing the resolution of the TV pictures have been around for a long time. The intention of HDTV was from the beginning to increase the resolution by a factor of four. In principle, this would give the viewer the possibility to sit at half the distance from the screen and then double the picture size in the field of vision.

Figure 12.2 shows some of the most common screen sizes. Standard TV in Europe has 576 horizontal lines, each consisting of 720 pixels (In North America, it is 486 lines also consisting of 720 pixels each). Most LCD and larger plasma screens are capable of displaying 1,366 x 768 pixels, which does not correspond with the resolution in the transmitted signals. Computer screens are really high resolution displays. A 48-cm (19-inch) computer screen usually has a resolution of 1,280 x 1,024 pixels.

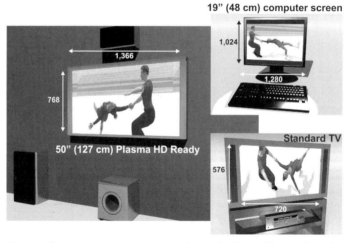

FIGURE 12.2   Comparing common screens and resolutions. (See color plate.)

By the 1980s, an analog HDTV system was introduced in Japan. This system was based on 1,125 lines, of which 1,035 lines are active in vertical resolution. It used an analog compression system called MUSE to make it possible to distribute the high resolution signal by means of the technology available at the time.

In Europe in the early 1990s, a HDTV standard based on 1,250 lines (including 1,080 active lines) was proposed. This would facilitate conversion to/from the European 625 line SDTV (Standard Definition Television) system since it was simply a matter of doubling the number of lines.

In 1992, when the Olympic Games were held in Barcelona, a final desperate attempt was made to introduce HDTV based on the analog MAC system. However, this also failed and HDTV was dead in Europe for many years to come.

New advances in the picture processing technology have made it quite easy to convert between any numbers of lines. Therefore a wide range of new system standards has evolved and HDTV has recently become quite successful in the United States and Japan. Some of these new systems are really more or less improvement of the existing SDTV system. One such example is the 480 line system with progressive scanning. The number of active lines in the North American 525 line system is 488. However the most commonly used HDTV system in the United States is the 1080i system based on a frame rate close to 60 Hz. As we will see, the most common systems in Europe will be the already existing 1080i system with 50 Hz frame rate and the coming 720p/50Hz system.

Interlaced and Progressive Scanning

Before we dig deeper into the various HDTV systems available today, we need to look closer at the principles of scanning a TV picture. As discussed in Chapter 1, conventional TV is based on interlaced scanning—the picture is split up in two frames, each containing every other line of the picture.

This concept is good as long as the picture does not contain too much movement. However, as seen in Figure 12.3, there will be "weaving" destroying the sharpness of vertical contours, if the objects in the picture move too much in the horizontal direction between two frames.

In progressive scanning, the lines are drawn right after each other. In addition to providing more stable vertical contours, this is also much better from a compression point of view. Modern kinds of display systems, like plasma displays and video projectors, can also provide a more stable picture when operating in progressive mode. More advanced DVD players also produce progressive scan signals that are intended to feed these kinds of displays.

Horizontal weaving effects
caused by interlaced scanning

FIGURE

12.3
Fast horizontal movement in interlaced scanned images will cause weaving effects. (See color plate.)

Picture Resolution

An interesting point is that for several years, most plasma displays sold in Europe had 480 lines of vertical resolution. This is quite strange since the number of active lines in the European system is 576 lines. Thus a plasma screen with standard resolution will provide fewer lines than is the case in an ordinary European CRT TV set. However, because the plasma screens are all manufactured in the same factories in Asia and it is simple to convert the signals from one line standard to another, the industry prefers to have the same kind of screens in Europe as in North America. So, for the first time, Europeans had to accept American vertical resolution in their TV sets.

However a plasma screen of this kind has one advantage. The horizontal resolution is 852 pixels, which corresponds to horizontal resolution expected when the vertical resolution is 480 pixels and the aspect ratio is 16:9. The 852 pixels of horizontal resolution are better than the standard TV widescreen format which only has a horizontal resolution of 720 pixels (see Figure 12.4).

However 480 line progressive scan television is not really HDTV. Instead it is some kind of enhanced standard television.

Today nobody speaks about the old 1,250 line or the 1,125 line systems. Instead it is either 720 progressive lines (called 720p) or 1,080 lines with interlaced scanning (called 1,080i) that have become the two systems of choice that will become worldwide standards. However, since North American systems are based on 60 Hz and European are 50 Hz, there will still be a difference in the regions. The 1,080i/50 Hz system is already used by some satellite TV channels in Europe.

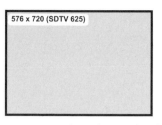

FIGURE

12.4

In conventional standard resolution widescreen TV sets, the pixels are "stretched" to form the widescreen 16:9 picture. Even the 4:3 picture has "stretched" pixels since a 4:3 aspect ratio picture would have needed 768 horizontal pixels to keep the same resolution horizontally as vertically.

It is interesting to have a look at Figure 12.5 before buying a display system. The majority of HD displays of today have 1,366 x 768 pixels in resolution. As a result, a 1,080i signal can not be displayed in full resolution.

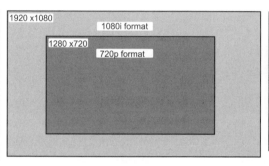

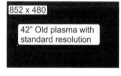

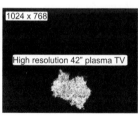

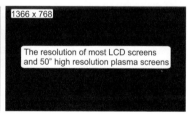

Combined transmission and display resolution

Transmission resolution for HDTV

Display resolution

FIGURE

12.5

In HDTV, the transmission systems do not have the same resolution as the display systems. The pictures always have to be scaled to the resolution of the screen.

This might also be one of the reasons why many program companies consider the 720p format since the advantages in using progressive scanning might be better than using 1,080 lines of resolution, which almost nobody can use anyhow. But progressive scanning is supported by all HD Ready sets.

Figure 12.6 compares the resolution in the picture observed at a detail level using the logo from C More HD from Canal Digital. It is obvious that the 852 x 480 plasma is quite limited when it comes to handling the 1,080i signal. The 1,366 x 768 pixel LCD takes care of this in a much better way. To the right, there is a letter "C" from a standard resolution picture from the same program provider on the same 1,366 x 768 pixel screen and in the same scale. It is obvious that the limitation now is the resolution of the incoming standard definition signal.

Plasma 852 x480   LCD 1,366 x 768 (HD Ready Flat-Panel)

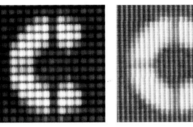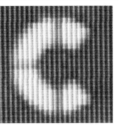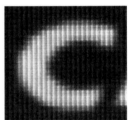

HDTV channel C More HD received in HD-format. The video signal is converted from 1.920 x 1,080 to 852 x 480 pixels by the plasma display system.

C More HD received in HD-format, The video is converted from 1,920 x 1,080 to 1,366 x 768 pixels by the LCD display system.

SDTV channel Canal + received in standard format 720 x 576 pixels and converted to 1,366 x 768 pixels by the LCD display system. (SDTV = Standard Definition TV)

FIGURE 12.6   Comparisons at pixel level between different screen resolutions and different signal resolutions (detail screenshots from Scandinavian pay TV operator Canal Digital channels C More HD and Canal+). (See color plate.)

The "HD Ready" Standard

In preparation for HDTV, all TV sets and display systems sold in Europe that meet the standards for HDTV have an HD Ready logo on their packaging. The requirements for a display to be regarded as "HD Ready" have been set by EICTA, The European Information & Communications Technology Industry Association.

A display system that is HD Ready must provide at least 720 lines of vertical resolution. It must be able to receive signals that are 720p as well as 1080i. There must be analog component inputs, Y, Pb, Pr, and either a DVI or HDMI connector for digital video.

Finally the set must be ready for high definition copy protection (HDCP).

PRACTICAL ASPECTS OF RECEIVING HDTV

Several of the pictures in this chapter are screen captures from promotional HDTV channels in Europe. These signals have been received using a computer-based satellite receiver from the Austrian company Digital-Everywhere. This unit belongs to the first generation of HDTV satellite receivers and can also receive conventional MPEG-2, DVB-S signals.

This is the same kind of satellite signals that is used for standard definition digital TV channels. As a result, the bitrate will increase by a factor of four compared to the standard definition signals. This also requires quite a lot of processing power. A 3.2 GHz Intel processor will have to work hard to cope with the 16 Mbit/s MPEG-2 bitstream that is provided by the FireDTV set-top box. This also means that the processing power of an HDTV receiver is much larger than in a conventional standard definition receiver.

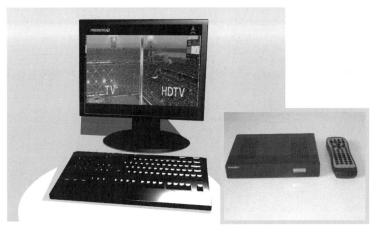

FIGURE

12.7

The computer is a good way of receiving HDTV because its screen is highly resolved and quite suitable for HDTV

HDTV CONNECTORS

HDTV means new interfaces. The scart connectors that have been in use in Europe for 25 years only work for standard definition signals. Therefore some new connectors are introduced when starting to use high definition TV receivers. However all HDTV receivers also down-convert the high definition signals to interface with standard definition TV sets, video recorders and DVD recorders. For this reason the scart outputs will hang around for many years to come.

There are 3 standard ways of bringing high definition signals to the display system: analog, digital and a new technology, high definition multimedia interface.

The analog way uses the component outputs of the HDTV receiver. This is the same kind of outputs, fitted with RCA connectors, that have been used to connect DVD players to enable progressive scan in the standard definition format.

However it is far better to use a digital connection between the receiver and the display system. In the first generation of HDTV receivers (see Figures 12.8 and 12.9), the digital video interface (DVI) connector is quite common in more advanced computer graphics cards.

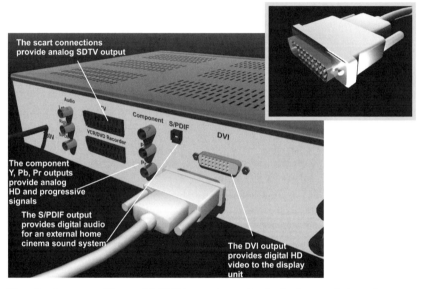

FIGURE 12.8

The first generation of HDTV receivers included a variety of connection options to interface with different kinds of display devices.

Scaling the video between different resolutions takes time in flat-panel display processors. If the receiver is connected to an external home cinema amplifier, this delay can cause lip sync problems. Delaying the S/PDIF audio output signal from the receiver compensates for this. In the menu system in Figure 12.10 there is a setting between 0-200 milliseconds. As an alternative there are home cinema amplifiers that have similar built-in audio delay features.

If you just use the internal audio system of the flat-panel display, you will not have any lip sync problems since the flat-panel takes the delay into account when processing the audio.

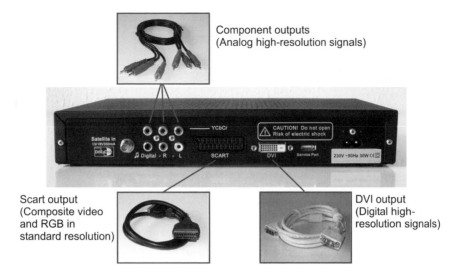

Component outputs
(Analog high-resolution signals)

Scart output
(Composite video
and RGB in
standard resolution)

DVI output
(Digital high-
resolution signals)

FIGURE

12.9

The Force 505SHD-SD MPEG-2 DVB-S receiver (OEM product from Emitor) is an example of the first generation European HDTV receivers. It has a DVI interface as well as component outputs and a common interface slot for CA modules.

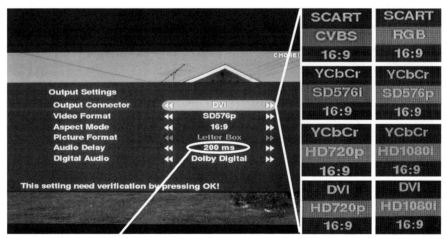

Audio delay to compensate for image
processing time in flat-panel display systems

Various video output settings

FIGURE

12.10

The HDTV receiver menu offers a number of video output alternatives. There is also an audio delay feature. (Screenshot from C More HD, Canal Digital combined with the menu system from Force 505SHD-SD).

THE HIGH DEFINITION MULTIMEDIA INTERFACE, HDMI

In the long run, there is a new interface which soon will be as common as the scart connector. It is the high definition multimedia interface (HDMI) connector. It is a slim device that can handle the high definition digital video signals and also the digital multi-channel audio that is an important ingredient in any home cinema system. Of course, the use of HDMI for audio as well requires some kind of integrated multi-channel audio system. The separate S/PDIF connection for digital multi-channel audio will be with us for many more years to come and will still make connection to an external sound system possible.

DVI and HDMI are compatible. By using a conversion cable you can connect HDMI interfaces to plasma TVs or other display systems with a DVI interface. Even in the future there will probably also be analog RCA connections for component video (Y, Pb, Pr) that carry high resolution video.

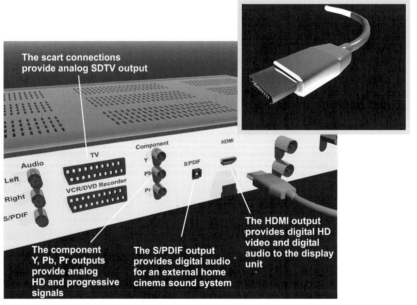

The scart connections provide analog SDTV output

The component Y, Pb, Pr outputs provide analog HD and progressive signals

The S/PDIF output provides digital audio for an external home cinema sound system

The HDMI output provides digital HD video and digital audio to the display unit

FIGURE 12.11   HDTV receivers now include a new connection for the video—either a DVI connector or an HDMI.

FIRST GENERATION HDTV TRANSMISSIONS IN EUROPE

The pioneer in HDTV in Europe was Euro 1080, later was renamed HD-1 and a second channel HD-2 was added along with a promotional channel HD-5. The station used MPEG-2 DVB-S signals to feed their 1,080i transmissions throughout Europe. Today this is a pay TV service, and it is possible to subscribe to the channel through 2010 with a one-time payment. The channel uses the Irdeto CA system and a receiver with Irdeto integrated may be used. Otherwise, an HDTV receiver with a common interface and an Irdeto CA module may be used. The previously mentioned FireDTV has a common interface, which is quite rare in computer-based digital TV reception systems (see Figure 12.12).

FIGURE
12.12

The Austrian FireDTV HDTV MPEG-2 DVB-S receiver for computers can be fitted with a CA module for HD-1 and the other channels from the same program company.

Another pioneer in the Scandinavian countries, Canal Digital, introduced the C More HD which was one of the first HDTV premium movie channels in Europe.

FIGURE 12.13   Euro1080, the pioneer in HDTV in Europe, now known as HD-1 (Screenshot from Euro1080, made before the channel name changed to HD 1; today there are also channels HD 2 and HD 5).

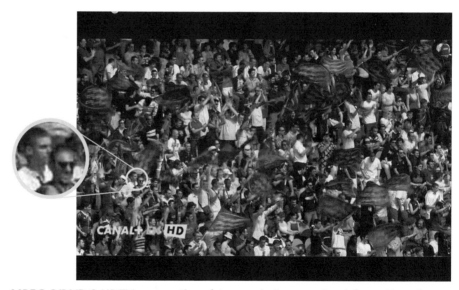

FIGURE 12.14   MPEG-2/DVB-S HDTV promotional transmission received from French pay TV operator Canal Plus. Sports events with audience pictures become more believable than ever before. Check the resolution in the enlarged part of the received picture from Canal Plus (Screenshot from Canal Plus, France). (See color plate.)

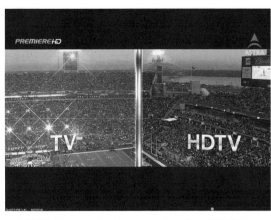

FIGURE

12.15

In Europe the first HDTV transmissions started in the MPEG-2/DVB-S format. (Screenshot from promotional MPEG-2 HDTV transmission from SES-Astra).

Second Generation HDTV Transmissions and Receivers in Europe

HDTV started up on satellite in Europe as 1,080i MPEG-2 transmissions using the same DVB-S standard as for the standard definition channels. The problem in using these systems is the high bitrate needed. Instead of four or five Mbit/s, as for a standard resolution channel, the bitrate end up at 16 Mbit/s, which means that only two HDTV channels can be housed in one transponder with a total capacity of 38 Mbit/s.

Therefore first-generation HDTV digital receivers are already being replaced by MPEG-4 boxes. The goal of using MPEG-4 (H.264/AVC, Advanced Video Coding) is to reduce the bandwidth consumption to about half of what is required for MPEG-2.

However the new MPEG-4 standard has proved quite hard to implement, especially real-time encoding needed for live transmissions. However in the long run, MPEG-4 is a necessity to handle the balance between providing improved picture quality and maintaining reasonable cost for transmission. It should also be remembered that the program providers will have to use dual transmission formats for many years before the standard definition transmissions may be closed. Dual transmission costs lots of money.

In addition to the improvements that can be achieved using MPEG-4, the new DVB-S2 standard, with improved error correction, will increase the bitrate that can be handled in one transponder from about 38 Mbit/s to close to 50 Mbit/s. The sum of these improvements will probably make it possible to put four or maybe five HDTV channels in each transponder. But it will take some years before this is a reality.

The German pay TV operator Premiere and the German commercial channels Sat 1 and ProSieben already use the combination of MPEG-4 and DVB-S2. Although it has been hard getting components for the production of the second-generation set-top boxes, it is for sure that these German channels have shown the way for the continued introduction of HDTV in Europe.

FIGURE

12.16

German pay TV operator Premiere was among the first to start DVB-S2 MPEG-4 based transmissions in Europe as the commercial German channels Sat 1 and ProSieben. (These screenshots are from promotional HDTV transmissions from SES-Astra, including Sat 1 HD, ProSieben HD and Premiere HD Sport).

At the time I write this book (summer, 2006) BSkyB (British Sky Broadcasting) also has HDTV transmissions that meet the MPEG-4 DVB-S2 standard. The BBC also has an MPEG-4 DVB promo satellite channel on air. However, due to lack of components, it's been hard so far for the Europeans to get hold of MPEG-4 receivers.

Today the need for HDTV is increasing in Europe, as in the rest of the world where large, flat-panel displays are getting popular. Really the bitrates used in standard television digital MPEG-2 based systems are based on the fact that the viewer uses a traditional maximum 32" cathode ray tube TV set. When the flat-panel TV sets were introduced it became obvious that there was a demand for better signal quality. HDTV is the route to go for the program companies to handle this new generation of larger and more demanding TV sets.

HDTV RECORDING

But there is a big complexity in moving to HDTV. People have several TV sets and very new standard resolution boxes in their homes. Even though it may seem very simple to record HDTV files on the hard disc a computer using devices like the FireDTV, it is not as easy to replace the conventional video recorder or DVD recorder. Of course, I can record the files on conventional recordable DVDs but the result is only about 30 minutes of recording on one disc when recording an MPEG-2 transmission at a bitrate of 16 Mbit/s.

You will need to have new recording devices that can handle the HDTV signals. Of course the easiest way to store HDTV is on a hard disc integrated in the digital HDTV receiver, in the same way as in a conventional standard resolution receiver. However permanent storage using removable discs is more difficult. It is here where the new Blu-Ray and HD-DVD formats for high resolution recording come in.

TELEVISION OF THE FUTURE

Regardless of the challenges and new technology required, HDTV will certainly be the big thing in the coming years, for home cinemas. How long it will take before all TV sets are changed into HDTV systems is hard to say, and maybe it will never happen. There might just be a market for different quality levels of television. But no doubt HDTV will be important.

What will happen after that?

The next natural next step is probably three-dimensional television. If what has been discussed in this book so far is the natural development of the TV media, 3D TV will be the ultimate challenge. It is also the technology that provides the most extensive possibilities as soon as its technical and commercial challenges have been conquered.

The human way of experiencing three dimensions is based on binocular viewing, which enables us to judge distances to objects. For this reason we have two eyes, but our eyes do not see exactly the same view. Objects that are far away are rendered quite alike by both eyes while closer objects seem to be at different locations in relation to the background. This can be seen in the Figure12.17, which shows a stereo pair of pictures.

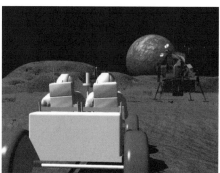

FIGURE

12.17

The stereo pair of picture on top can be experienced as a three dimensional picture if you focus at a distant and then quickly look down in the book without defocusing. (See color plate.)

The brain has the ability to provide an illusion of depth from these two pictures. The larger the differences, the closer the objects. We do not experience an exact picture of reality but rather an illusion created by our brains based on the signals we get through our eyes. And in reality, television and movies are based on a series of illusions. It is a matter of cheating the brain to make believe that we see what we see. We have seen several examples of this earlier in this book.

In order to experience a stereo pair of pictures as a 3D picture without any special glasses and devices, try to focus on a distant object. Then look straight into the book at the stereo pair in Figure 12.17. Each eye will then focus on one of the pictures respectively and a third picture will occur in between the others as is shown in Figure 12.18. This picture is a three-dimensional picture created in the brain from the two original pictures. Some training will help you to experience the other stereo pair of pictures that are shown in this chapter.

If you have problems experiencing the 3D effect, try using a piece of paper between your eyes to force them to look at one picture each.

It is quite clear that it is not easy to create a commercial product from 3D pictures. In the 1950s, the first attempts at 3D movies were made and it has been tried several times since. This is not a new invention. The most successful 3D product ever is probably the View Master, in Figure 12.19. The View Master is a modernization of the nineteenth century 3D viewing devices for still pictures.

FIGURE

12.18

The 3D image will appear directly between the two original images that represent the left and the right image channels.

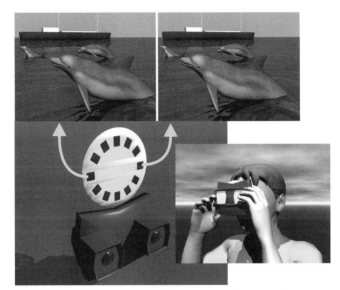

FIGURE

12.19

The View Master is one of few 3D products with commercial success.

3D Movies

During the 1950s, 3D movies where shown in the cinemas. In those days colored filters were used to separate the right and left picture channels. Red and green pictures were projected on the screen and the audience wore glasses with a red filter on one eye and a green filter on the other (see Figure 12.20). This has also been tested on television using color TV to carry the green and red picture channels. In the early 1980s, old movies from the 1950s were shown in Sweden in 3D in this way. The red and green glasses were sold everywhere.

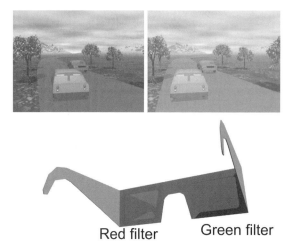

Red filter   Green filter

FIGURE

12.20

The first 3D movies used color filters on the projector's cinema audiences. (See color plate.)

3D Color Movies

One reason 3D movies were not a big hit in the 1950s was probably that the audience preferred 2D color movies instead of the red-green 3D movies experienced through those colored glasses.

By the 1970s, it was time for the next try. By projecting the picture channels of the movie through polarization filters and letting the audience wear glasses with polarized filters instead of red and green filters, 3D color movies became a reality. One of the picture channels was projected using a vertical filter and the other picture was projected using a horizontal filter (see Figure 12.21). This made the illusion almost complete. The only remaining problem was that people thought that is was uncomfortable to wear glasses to fool the brain to believe the illusion was true. This technique is still used today in Omnimax theaters and at other kinds of attractions where 3D movies are of interest.

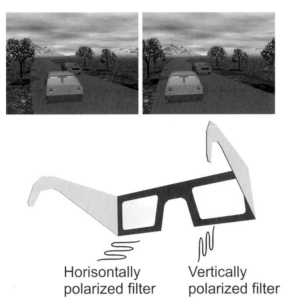

Horisontally
polarized filter

Vertically
polarized filter

FIGURE

12.21

The next generation of 3D movies was based on polarization rather than color. (See color plate.)

3D TELEVISION IN COLOR

By using color TV it is possible, as already been discussed, to broadcast color encoded 3D pictures. However3D television is more complicated.

During a 1987 visit in Japan, I experienced 3DTV through a cathode ray tube. At the Panasonic research labs, they had developed a system based on including every other picture in both of the picture channels. The secret lay in the glasses, which used an electronic way of turning the polarization field in one of two polarization filters to open and close the path of light to each eye very rapidly. These glasses were synchronized to the program so the viewer's left eye only saw the left image and vice versa.

The illusion worked very well. The advantage in this system was that conventional TV transmitters and TV receivers could be used to support the system. One of the memorable moments was a clown throwing a ball straight into my face, which I have recreated in Figure 12.22.

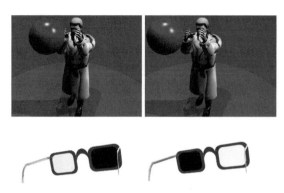

Every other
picture left

Every other
picture right

FIGURE

12.22

The concept behind 3D television on an ordinary CRT.

Today this system would have worked very badly, since the compression systems used for digital TV do not allow for big differences in picture content between two adjacent frames as we have discussed in Chapter 2, "What Is Digital TV?". 3D video techniques of today are in most cases based on synchronized video projectors equipped with polarization filters and letting the viewers wear glasses with polarization filters.

HOLOGRAPHIC TELEVISION

Another way of producing 3D pictures is using holograms often seen in science fiction movies such as the "Star Wars" series. If this ever becomes technically possible, there will be a number of practical consequences.

Since a hologram is an exact model of reality, it will be hard to create the background effects. Figure 12.23 shows the probable result of holographic television. The three men are sitting around a table watching a boxing match in a miniature, holographic format. For this application, this works quite well but they can not see the backgrounds for crowd reaction shots, for example. Instead they are the audience themselves. Even a soccer match would work quite well this way. An interesting aspect is that television like this would not require as much TV production effort or personnel as 2D coverage does. The viewer himself has all viewing angles possible and simply moves around the hologram to choose the desired viewing positions and angles himself.

FIGURE

2.23

A moving holographic presentation of an event at another place is a completely new and different concept of television.

The most probable development of 3DTV is that someone tries to develop a large flat-panel TV capable of showing 3D movies without glasses needed for the viewers. Similar technologies already exist today and are based on making each eye view only vertical stripes with picture content belonging to each picture channel. The illusion works very well but requires special, and expensive, CRTs. An additional problem is that there are restrictions concerning the distance of viewing. And, as with most other 3D systems, they do not work if the viewer is tilting his head too much. But in the long run, these problems will surely be solved and we will see the first large and cheap 3DTV.

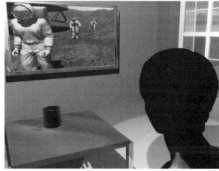

FIGURE

12.24

The future of 3DTV depends on the development of an inexpensive display system that does not require glasses for viewing. (See color plate.)

Virtual Reality

A completely different way of creating a three dimensional experience is through virtual reality (VR). VR is about 3D graphics. Using special glasses containing one display for each picture channel, it is possible to experience a very large picture (see Figure 12.25). The same principles may also be used for 3D movies. The most interesting thing is the possibility to generate a giant picture that fills your entire field of vision. However this would require highly resolved pictures, which might be a reality with future computers and bitrates. Maybe the VR glasses that have already been developed might be a short cut to 3DTV at an affordable price.

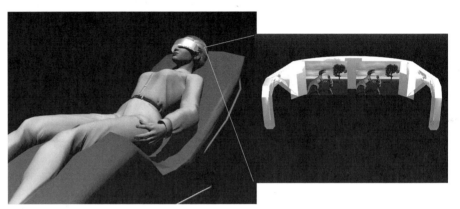

FIGURE

12.25
In VR, both picture channels are projected on the inside of the glasses.

But there is yet one vision beyond 3D movies that are reproduced in a pair of VR glasses.

Perhaps eventually, the movie companies will make virtual movies containing virtual environments and props as well as virtual actors. The future DVD recorder or receiver would contain an extremely powerful computer capable of animating and rendering a 3D movie in real time. The story in the movie is decided in advance but you would decide for yourself from what viewing angle the movie shall be rendered. As an example, you could watch the complete movie through the eyes of one of the principal characters.

This is also interesting because there are already today virtual movies that are produced in this way. As soon as the processing power is there, a consumer product may be developed. What will the future bring during the decades to come?

Augmented Reality

An even more realistic way of virtual reality is mixing virtual reality with real reality, to create augmented reality (AR) or "improved" reality. Perhaps this does not have a consumer application, but it could be very impressive in museums and at historical places, etc.

By letting the visitor wear VR glasses connected to a precision GPS navigator and an attitude-recognizing system, a central computer knows where a person is and in what direction he is looking. When that person moves around in a historical building, he would encounter virtual models of historical persons and experience historical events right on location (see Figure 12.26). Or why not meeting almost real ghosts?

FIGURE

12.26

The future audio and video technologies may give us completely new experiences such as augmented reality. (See color plate.)

A | Digital Television in North America

APPENDIX

FIGURE

A.1

North and South America have different technical standards than Europe, but the differences are not that large.

This book is full of European examples, and DVB was started up in Europe. However, most of the book's content is applicable everywhere in the world and DVB is now in use all over the world. For example, in the U.S., Dish Network is based on the DVB standard.

When it comes to broadcasting, North America is very often considered as very different from Europe, or Europe as very different from North America. However the differences are really quite small as I shall try to explain in this appendix.

It is a well-known fact that U.S. reception equipment cannot be used in Europe and vice versa. However, the compatibility has increased in the last decade. Today you find TV sets in Europe that handle NTSC recordings on DVDs without any problems at all. And the TV sets, which very often originate from the same factories in Asia, work with both European and North American signals. The manufacturers try to establish some kind of industrial world standard for all equipment. Of course this is the most economical solution for everyone.

COMMERCIAL TELEVISION SYSTEMS

North America has a long history in television, especially when it comes to commercializing the media, and this is the most significant difference.

In the U.S., a 525 line analog system has been used for a long time. System M has 486 active lines with interlaced scanning of 243 lines in 60 frames per second giving 30 pictures per second. This is to be compared to the European 625 line system with 576 active lines with interlaced scanning of 288 active lines in 50 frames per second, resulting in 25 pictures per second.

The choice of frame rate—60 Hz in North America and 50 Hz in Europe— is due to the AC power frequency. In the early days of television, it was easier to get rid of disturbances from power supplies and power lines using the same frame rate as the AC power frequency. In today's TV sets, there are other means to avoid these problems, so you can easily watch 60 Hz TV in Europe and 50 Hz signals in the U.S.

North America was early with color TV and established the NTSC system, developed in the 1950s and 60s, which were based on the black-and-white picture transmitted at near-full resolution.

A black-and-white picture on the American analog standard requires approximately 4 MHz bandwidth and in Europe about 5 MHz bandwidth. Of this, one MHz was removed in the upper frequency range of the video spectrum so the signal occupies the spectrum between 0 to 3 and 0 to 4 MHz respectively. In the spectral area between 3 and 4 (NTSC) or 4 and 5 MHz (PAL), a phase modulated subcarrier is put around the frequency 3.58 MHz (NTSC) and 4.43 MHz (PAL) respectively. The phases of the carrier indicate the color tone and the amplitude symbolizes the saturation of the color.

NTSC is really very similar to PAL (Phase Alternating Line), as seen in Figure A.2. The only real difference is in the meaning of phase alternating line—the phase reference (the burst) and the phase of the color signal on the line are alternated plus or minus 90 degrees for each consecutive line. This makes the PAL signal less sensitive to color tone problems because the radio waves are reflected at buildings, mountains and aircraft. Other than that, both systems are quite similar.

Analog television was based on a frequency modulated subcarrier for the audio. In the North American system the sound subcarrier is located at 4.5 MHz, while in Europe it is mostly at 5.5 MHz or 6.0 MHz (United Kingdom and Ireland). Eastern Europe has other versions of the 625 line system.

Many South American countries use NTSC just as in the U.S. and Canada but in some countries as in Brazil the unusual combination of PAL and the 525 line system has been used.

NTSC is also to be found in many Asian countries as in Japan and South Korea.

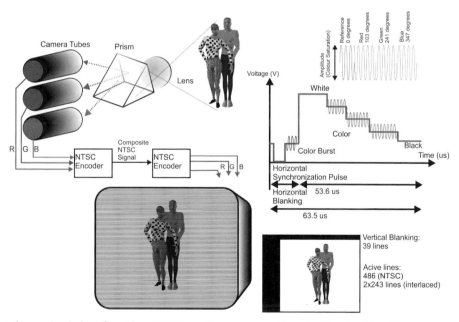

FIGURE

A.2

The principles for the NTSC system are quite similar to the European PAL system.

STEREO SOUND

Late in the 1980s, it became evident that people wanted stereo sound with the TV transmissions. One simple way to do this is adding a second frequency modulated subcarrier.

In the United States the MTS system (Multi-Channel Television Sound) was introduced. This works in a way that is very similar to ordinary pilot tone FM stereo transmissions. At the same time, the German A2 systems and the digital NICAM systems were introduced in Europe.

FREQUENCY PLANNING AND THE TRANSFER TO DIGITAL TV IN NORTH AMERICA

Terrestrial and cable TV in North America is based on 6 MHz channels, which was a suitable bandwidth for the 525 line NTSC channels. And the same channel bandwidth is used in cable TV. A difference between Europe and the U.S. is that the same bandwidth is used in all frequency ranges. In Europe there are 7 MHz channels in the VHF bands while 8 MHz is used in the UHF bands.

Figure A.3 shows the channels plans for North America.

Note that the cable networks use almost all the frequencies that can be fitted into the cables. This means that the cables carry channels that are in frequency ranges that are reserved for other services in the radio spectrum, so the cables must be well-shielded. The most dramatic is the use of the FM band for TV channels, cable channels 95–99.

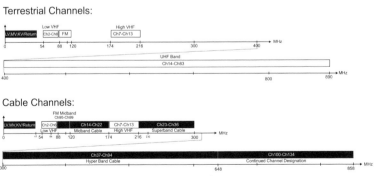

FIGURE

A.3

U.S. terrestrial and cable TV channel frequency ranges.

1n 1997, the Federal Communications Commission set the rules for the future of digital TV in the U.S. When digital TV was to be introduced, the broadcasters should also move to HDTV. The ATSC (Advanced Television Standards Committee) system has been adopted by the U.S., Canada, Mexico, Argentina, Mexico and South Korea. In the terrestrial portion of the ATSC system, just as in analog terrestrial television, amplitude modulation is used. Using 8-VSB means that the level of the carrier signal varies between eight different levels just as is shown in Figure A.4.

Instead of combined amplitude and phase angles, the symbols (each containing three bits) are defined by the amplitude of the carrier. In reality, the signal is a bit more complicated than this. A pilot signal is added to the baseband signal that is shown in Figure A.4

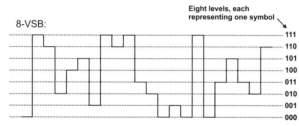

FIGURE

A.4

The baseband ATSC digital terrestrial signal is amplitude modulated with eight levels, each representing a set of three bits. A pilot is also added, giving the final signal a somewhat different structure.

The 8-VSB (vestigial side band) signal in a 6 MHz channel allows for a maximum useful bitrate of 19.39 Mbit/s which is enough to house an MPEG-2 compressed HDTV signal.

As in Europe the introduction of digital cable TV has been slower than satellite and terrestrial in the U.S. Though 8-VSB is used for terrestrial transmissions, cable operators may also use 16-VSB or 256-QAM, which provide significantly higher throughput in a 6 MHz channel. Due to the more stable conditions in cables than over the air, such methods are possible. Using 256-QAM puts us quite close to the DVB-C standard used for cable in other countries.

ATSC is, just like the DVB standard, based on the use of MPEG-2 and the standards have many other technical similarities. The largest difference between North America and Europe is the move directly from analog terrestrial TV to digital terrestrial HDTV. In Europe, digital terrestrial TV is adding more standard definition channels to the terrestrial networks.

The ATSC 8-VSB signal is less sensitive to noise than the DVB-T signal. The use of the bandwidth is also somewhat more efficient than the COFDM used in DVB-T. However, the DVB-T signal is better when it comes to reusing the same frequencies in single frequency networks, which may be one of the reasons DVB-T is used in Europe. Many countries are located close together and have to share the same spectrum, which is a scarce resource.

CONNECTORS AROUND THE WORLD

The most significant feature in European digital TV receivers is the use of scart cables. You do not find these scart connectors in other parts of the world. Scart connectors became mandatory in European TV sets in the 1980s. The major advantage of using scart connectors is that you can use component-encoded video signals. This was an important feature when the component encoded MAC system was introduced in some European markets. Another feature is that the scart also carries the analog stereo audio signals.

In American digital receivers, you find S-Video outputs instead of the scart outputs. This also gives you component signals, but not the RGB signals. Still, the use of S-video connection between the digital receiver and the TV set provides something that is better than the composite video signal. The audio has to be obtained separately from analog RCA or digital S/PDIF outputs.

In HDTV receivers, there are either DVI or HDMI connectors and the HDMI is surely the replacement for the scart in Europe. HDMI carries both digital audio and digital video. And the best thing of all is that it will be more or less world standard.

B

APPENDIX

North American Satellite Geography

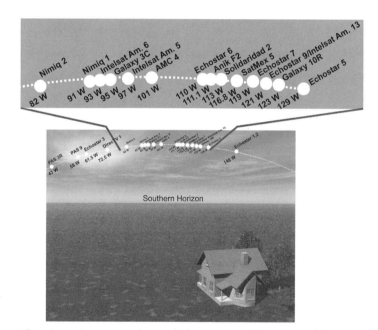

Southern Horizon

FIGURE

B.1

The American portion of the geostationary orbit extends from about 25 degrees west to 175 degrees west or more (depending on your longitudinal location).

The first digital network in the U.S. was the satellite-based DirecTV using digital to get more channels in the air. Analog direct to home satellite distribution really never got very popular in the U.S. but DirecTV broke the ice for DTH in America. Since DirecTV was introduced too early to be able to use any existing standard a proprietary non-DVB system, Digital Satellite Service (DSS), was

293

developed. DSS is based on similar principles as DVB, yet it is not compatible with DVB.

There are other non-DVB digital standards used for satellite distribution. DigiChiper was developed by General Instruments before the DVB standard was set. This proprietary system is used in several American satellites. Another example is the Japanese ISDB (Integrated Services Digital Broadcasting) system which also exists for terrestrial and cable applications.

The other major U.S. digital satellite TV operator, Dish Network, use the DVB standard. DVB can be used for both 525 and 625 line TV distribution. All systems, DVB, DSS and ISDB can of course also handle HDTV signals.

NORTH AMERICAN SATELLITE SYSTEMS

In North America there are a few domestic U.S. satellite systems, such as Echostar and Galaxy, which compete to carry the content providers. There are also more international systems as Intelsat and PanAmSat. In Canada there are the Anik and Nimiq systems and the Mexican market is dominated by Solidaridad and SatMex.

The downlink frequency bands used are C-Band 3.7–4.2 GHz and Ku-Band 11.7–12.75 GHz. In recent years, the Ka-Bands have also been brought into use: 17.0–20.0 GHz, 20.0–21.0 GHz and 31.8–32.8 GHz. The corresponding uplink frequency bands are 5.9–6.4 GHz, 14.0–14.5 GHz, 27.0–30.0 GHz, 30.0–31.0 GHz and 34.2–34.7 GHz.

The part of the geostationary orbit that is visible from North America is between approximately 25 degrees west and 175 degrees west, depending on where exactly you are (see Figure B.1). The maximum elevation angle is just under 60 degrees in the southernmost part of Texas when receiving from 101 degrees west. The maximum elevation angle in the northern part of the U.S. is at about 34 degrees. For comparison, Europe is much further to the north in relation to North America and the maximum elevation angle in the southernmost parts is at about 45 degrees and in the northernmost parts it is at about 10 degrees.

The American content providers Dish Network and DirecTV generally use CONUS coverage (see the example in Figure B.2). The receiving systems are generally 18- by 20-inch proprietary multi-focus antenna systems. The EIRP for the transponders used must be well above 48 dBW. Table B.1 includes some margins that make it possible to reduce the antenna diameter in dry areas.

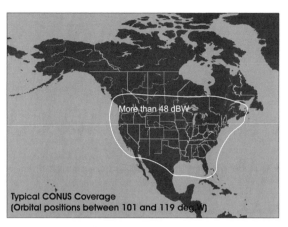

FIGURE

B.2

Typical CONUS (Continental U.S.) coverage.

SATELLITE RECEIVING SYSTEMS IN THE U.S.

American content providers have to use several orbital locations to reach their viewers. There are two obvious reasons for this. One reason is that the Ku-Band only has a bandwidth of 550 MHz in each orbital slot. Another reason is that there are several time zones within the U.S. continent, and it is appropriate to duplicate some of the channels to hit the various prime time windows.

In Europe it is quite different. There are separate content providers for each language area, all countries are in just one time zone, and there is a bandwidth of 2050 MHz in each orbital slot. For this reason each content provider normally resides in one slot.

In North America, many satellites operate within the frequency band 12.20 to 12.75 GHz. This is just 500 MHz and can be received by a single-band LNB as is shown in Figure B.3. To receive the signals in the frequency range, 12.20 to 12.75 GHz a local oscillator 11.25 GHz is used to convert the signal. This moves the input frequency band to the range 0.950–1.5 GHz. As a result all signals that may come out of the single-band LNB is in the range of 950–1500 MHz. Universal LNBs like those used in Europe are not required in North America.

Today there are also satellites that operate within the larger frequency range of 11.70 to 12.75 GHz, but still this can be handled by a single-band LNB having a local oscillator at 10.60 GHz (see Figure B.4).

It should also be noted that the North American Ku-Band satellites use linear, horizontal and vertical polarization just like the C-Band satellites do. There are also Ka systems used such as the WildBlue system for Internet distribution via satellite.

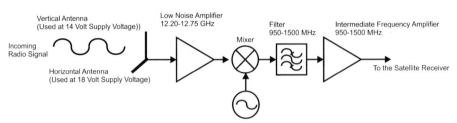

The local oscillator at 11.25 GHz makes the LNB to convert the incomming 12.20-12.75 GHz frequency band to 950-1500 MHz (this is just a portion of the L band covering 950-2150 MHz).

FIGURE

B.3

Since the American Ku-Band satellites operate within 550 MHz of bandwidth, single-band LNBs are sufficient in most cases.

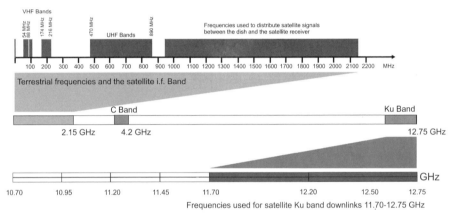

FIGURE

B.4

The part of the Ku-Band used in the U.S. is 11.70–12.75 GHz, which can be handled by a single-band LNB.

THE THREE LNB MULTI-FOCUS DISH

In the U.S., multi-focus antennas are used by the Dish Network and DirecTV to increase the number of channels for the subscribers. DirecTV, for example, has three orbital positions: 101, 110 and 119 degrees west. By using a three LNB multi-focus antenna, subscribers can receive all of them.

Dish network has even more orbital positions, but one example of using a multi focus dish is the combination of 110, 119 and 129 degrees west shown in Figure B.5.

In Europe, only DiSEqC-switches are used. DiSEqC switches are also used in North America but the content providers also have proprietary receiving systems were the switches are included. DiSEqC is an open standard for those that want to design their own reception systems. If using a DiSEqC-switch you will have to see to that you have a receiver with DiSEqC support.

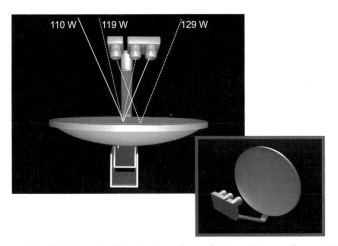

FIGURE

B.5

In the U.S., both Dish Network and DirecTV use three LNB multi-focus antennas to increase the number of channels for the viewers.

In Chapter 4, Table 4.2 shows that larger antennas were needed when using a secondary focus in a multi-focus dish. However since the antennas used by these content providers are shaped and the loss due to the use of the secondary focus will be quite small, we can still use Table B.1 to estimate the dish diameters required.

COVERAGE AND ANTENNA POINTING MAPS FOR NORTH AMERICA

Chapters 3 and 4 describe the European the North African and the Middle East satellite geography. To understand which satellites can be received, which antenna diameters are needed and how to find the satellites, you need information, just as in conventional geography where you need maps.

Figures B.6 to B.14 will help the North American reader can make full use of the information in Chapters 3 and 4.

The following tables give information about what antenna diameters can be recommended for reception at the different EIRP levels that are indicated in the coverage maps. These figures include some margins for rain attenuation (Ku-Band).

TABLE

B.1

Approximate antenna diameters at corresponding EIRP levels in Ku-Band

EIRP (dBW):	meters	feet
41	1.9	6.2
42	1.7	5.5
43	1.5	4.9
44	1.3	4.4
45	1.2	3.9
46	1.1	3.5
47	0.95	3.1
48	0.85	2.8
49	0.75	2.5
50	0.67	2.2
51	0.60	2.0
52	0.53	1.7
53	0.47	1.5

The antenna diameters required in the C-Band is smaller because the noise level (antenna temperature) in the atmosphere is less than Ku-Band and the noise figures of the LNBs are also somewhat better than Ku-Band. However, C-Band satellites are, in general, about 10 dB weaker than Ku-Band satellites.

TABLE

B.2

Approximate Antenna Diameters in C-Band.

EIRP (dBW):	meters	feet
28	5.8	18.9
29	5.1	16.9
30	4.6	15.0
31	4.1	13.4
32	3.6	11.9
33	3.2	10.7
34	2.9	9.5
35	2.6	8.4
36	2.3	7.5
37	2.1	6.7
38	1.8	6.0
39	1.6	5.3
40	1.4	4.8
41	1.3	4.2
42	1.15	3.8
43	1.12	3.7
44	0.91	3.0
45	0.81	2.7

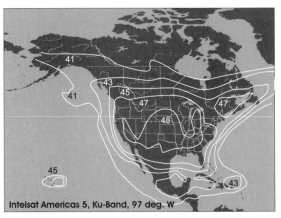

EIRP curves for Intelsat Americas 5, Ku-Band, at 97 degrees west.

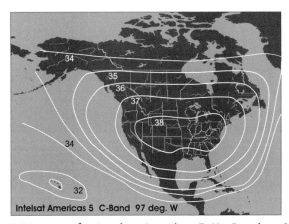

EIRP curves for Intelsat Americas 5, Ku-Band, at 97 degrees west.

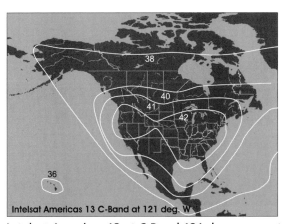

Intelsat Americas 13 at C-Band 121 degrees west.

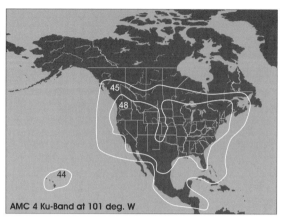

AMC 4 Ku-Band at 101 deg. W

FIGURE

B.9

AMC 4 Ku-Band at 101 degrees west.

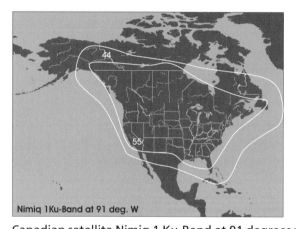

Nimiq 1Ku-Band at 91 deg. W

FIGURE

B.10

Canadian satellite Nimiq 1 Ku-Band at 91 degrees west Home of the Canadian content Provider Bell ExpressVu.

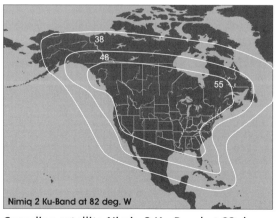

Nimiq 2 Ku-Band at 82 deg. W

FIGURE

B.11

Canadian satellite Nimiq 2 Ku-Band at 82 degrees west.

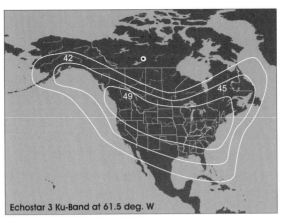

Echostar 3 Ku-Band at 61.5 degrees west. One of Dish Network's satellites.

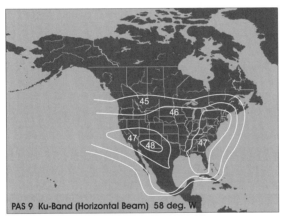

PAS 9 (PanAm Sat) Ku-Band at 58 degrees west.

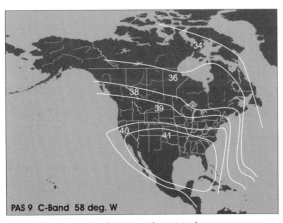

PAS 9 (PanAm Sat) C-Band at 58 degrees west.

FINDING THE SATELLITES AND ALIGNING THE ANTENNA

In Chapter 4, the elevation and azimuth angles were defined (Figures 4.3 and 4.5). Figures B.15 through B. include examples of elevation and azimuth maps for important American orbital slots.

Finally, in Figures B.29 and B.30, you find the North American polar mount adjustment angles for motorized antennas. These angles are defined in Figure 4.39.

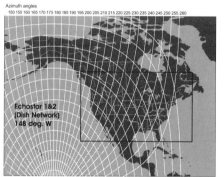
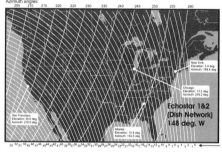

FIGURE

B.15

Elevation and azimuth curves for Echostar 1&2 at 148 deg. West (orbital slot of Dish Network).

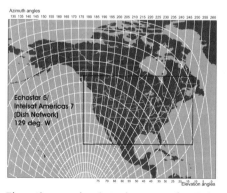
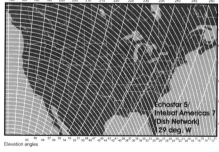

FIGURE

B.16

Elevation and azimuth curves for Echostar 5 & Intelsat Americas 7 at 129 deg. West (orbital slot of Dish Network).

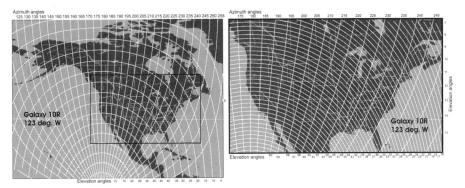

FIGURE
B.17

Elevation and azimuth curves for Galaxy 10R at 123 deg. West.

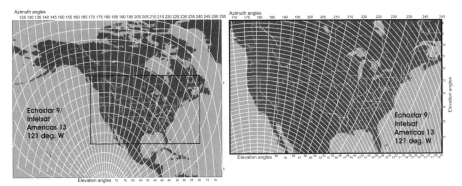

FIGURE
B.18

Elevation and azimuth curves for Echostar 9 at 121 deg. West.

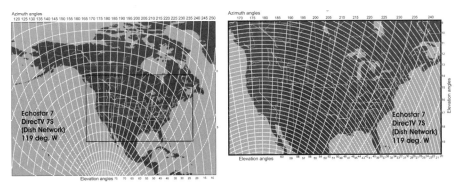

FIGURE
B.19

Elevation and azimuth curves for Echostar 7 & DirecTV 7S at 119 deg. West (orbital slot of Dish Network and DirecTV).

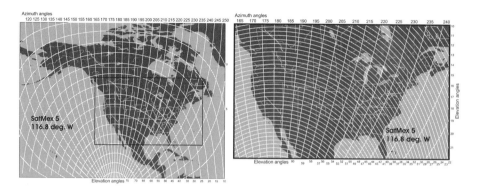

Elevation and azimuth curves for Satmex 5 at 116.8 deg. West.

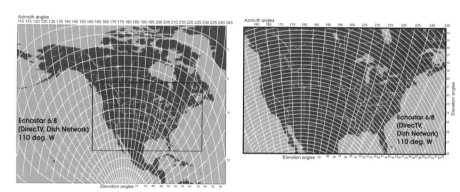

Elevation and azimuth curves for Echostar 6&8 at 110 deg. West (orbital slot of Dish Network and DirecTV).

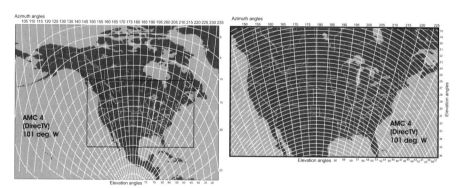

Elevation and azimuth curves for AMC 4 at 101 deg. West (orbital slot of DirecTV).

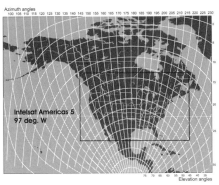
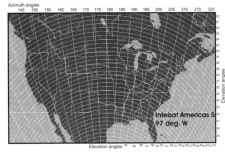

FIGURE
B.23

Elevation and azimuth curves for Intelsat Americas 5 at 97 deg. West.

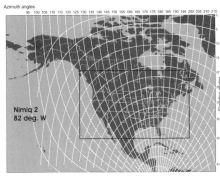
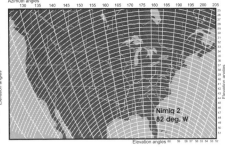

FIGURE
B.24

Elevation and azimuth curves for Nimiq 2 at 82 deg. West.

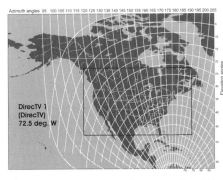
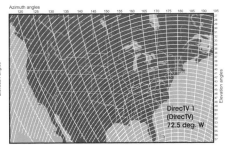

FIGURE
B.25

Elevation and azimuth curves for DirecTV 1 at 72.5 deg. West (orbital slot of DirecTV).

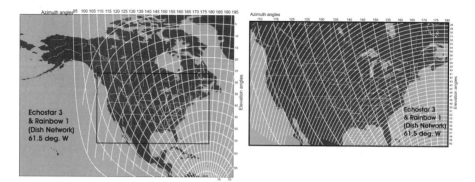

Elevation and azimuth curves for Echostar 3 at 61.5 deg. West (orbital slot of Dish Network).

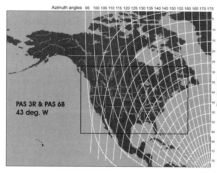
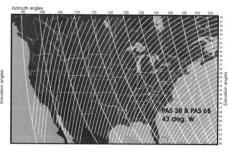

Elevation and azimuth curves for Echostar PAS 9 at 58 deg. West.

Elevation and azimuth curves for PAS 3R and PAS 6B at 43 deg. West.

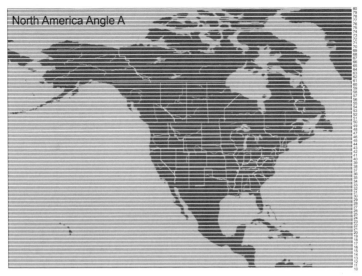

FIGURE

B.29

Angle A in a polar mount motorized antenna (See Figure 4.39 on page 105).

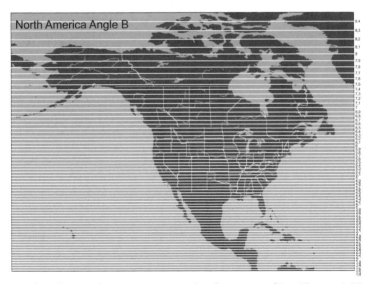

FIGURE

B.30

Angle B in a polar mount motorized antenna (See Figure 4.39 on page 105).

Index

SVCD, 232
Switch/Firewall, 220
Symbol, 86
Symbol Rate, 88
Synchronization, 7
Synchronization Word, 15, 30
Syncom 3, 44

T

Telephone and Computer Network, 218
Teletext, 7, 29,33
Teletext Handling, 33
Television, 1
Television, Electronic, 5
Television, Mechanical, 4
Televisor, 5
Terrestrial Channel Numbers (Europe), 139–140
Terrestrial Television, 137
Terrestrial Transmission Tower, 138
Tevebox STB, 156
Thor 3, East European Coverage Area, 64
Thor, 1 deg. W, Elevation and Azimuth Map, 77
Three LNB Multi-Focus Antenna, 297
Three-Axis Stabilized Satellites, 54
Time Shift, 223
TiscaliSat, 175
Torodial Antenna, 99
Torus Antenna, 99
Toslink Cable, 259
Transmission Towers, 40
Transmodulation QPSK to 64 QAM, 132
Transponder Bandwidth, 20
Transponder bandwidth, 57
Transponder Output Power, 20
Transport Stream, 29
Transport Stream Packet, 29
Triax, 218
Triple Play, 160
Triple Play ADSL Modem, 160
Tuner, 32–33, 84, 133
Turksat, 42 E, Elevation and Azimuth Map, 77
TV Bahrain, 165
TV Format Menu, 247
TV Systems, 7
Twin Tuner Receiver, 231–233
Twin Universal LNB, 211

Two LNB Dish (Two-Focus Antenna), 93
TWT (Travelling Wave Tube), 56

U

UHF (Ultra High Frequencies), 139
UHF Coaxial Network, 126
UHF Yagi Antenna Gain Curve, 144
Universal LNB, 81
Uplink, 42–43, 57–58

V

VCD, 232
VCR (Video Cassette Recorder), 13, 222–223
VHF (Very High Frequencies), 139
VHS (Video Home System), 13, 222–223
VHS Hi Fi Recorder, 252, 261
Viaccess, 179
Video 2000, 13, 223
Video Signal, 4
View Master, 278
VOD (Video On Demand), 182
von Braun, Werner, 44
VR (Virtual Reality), 284
VR Glasses, 285

W

Water Level, 78
Weaving Effects, 265–266
Weighted String, 78
Widescreen TV, 243
WildBlue, 176, 295
Winamp, 173
Windows Media, 162
Windows Media 9, 232
Windows Media Player, 168–171
Wireless Keyboard, 164
Wireless Scart Connections, 205–206
WLAN (Wireless Local Area Network), 220

Y

Yagi Antenna, 140–141
Yagi Antenna Beamwidth , 145
YUV Signals, 12

Z

Zinc Sulfide, 7, 12